THE WOLF OF WOK STREET

This book is dedicated to Danny Kuan Kun Lim.

'Cook for a man, you feed him for a day. Teach him how to cook, you feed him for a lifetime.'

Thank you for never letting me go hungry, Dad.

THE WOLF OF WOK STREET

VINCENT LIM

RESTAURANT-QUALITY ASIAN FOOD IN 80 RECIPES

Hardie Grant
BOOKS

INTRODUCTION
6

HOW IT BEGAN—7
WHAT IS YUMYUM?—12
ALL ABOUT THE WOK—16
CHINESE KITCHEN ESSENTIALS—20
CHINESE PANTRY ESSENTIALS—24
BASICS—29

SMALL EATS
35

SOUP
61

NOODLES & RICE
75

SEAFOOD
101

POULTRY
133

MEAT
161

VEGETABLES
193

DESSERT
213

ABOUT THE AUTHOR — 234

INDEX — 236

INTRODUCTION

COOKING HAS ALWAYS BEEN A CENTRAL PART OF MY LIFE, NOT JUST AS A CHEF, BUT AS A WAY TO CONNECT WITH MY HERITAGE AND MY FAMILY. GROWING UP IN MY FATHER'S RESTAURANT, I WAS IMMERSED IN THE KITCHEN, BUT IT WASN'T JUST ABOUT PREPARING FOOD. IT WAS ABOUT CRAFTING SOMETHING SPECIAL WITH EACH DISH, A TRADITION THAT MY FATHER PASSED DOWN TO ME WITH CARE.

This book is my tribute to him. My father was a master of the wok, and watching him work his magic over the stove always felt like witnessing an art form. Wok cooking, with its fast-paced energy and bold flavours, has been the cornerstone of our restaurant's success. But beyond that, it's a practice that holds memories, lessons and a sense of home. I want to share those memories and lessons with you, in the hope that this dying art will continue to inspire new generations of cooks.

Wok cooking is more than just a method; it's a way of life in the kitchen. The speed, precision and technique it requires can transform the simplest ingredients into dishes that explode with flavour. Unfortunately, as more modern cooking methods take over, the skill of wok cooking is slowly fading away. My goal with this book is to offer an insight into this incredible technique, to show the beauty of wok cooking, and the endless possibilities it presents. These recipes are not only a reflection of my father's legacy but a celebration of rich culinary tradition.

HOW IT BEGAN

'To move with purpose, every movement should be for a reason. In a fast-paced environment every second matters.' – Danny Kuan Kun Lim

The story begins with the person who taught me how to cook: my father, Danny Kuan Kun Lim (林冠軍). Along with his two brothers, he owned one of the first Chinese restaurants in Temple, Texas: Emperors of China (皇上皇). In the 1990s, it became a well-known establishment where many of our family recipes were created.

Although I was born a couple of miles from the restaurant, I never knew any of this – or that my father could cook – till later in my life. After moving to Malaysia, I spent my early childhood in Cameron Highlands, where I always remember him in the nightclub/karaoke business, wearing a suit and tie, something so far from being a chef.

When I was about eight years old, my family decided to leave everything behind in Malaysia so my brother and I could get a better education. We arrived in Perth, Australia, and my dad moved away from his line of work and found a job at a Chinese takeaway joint called 'WokinaBox.'

I was in primary school at the time and I'd always ask him to get me a job. I wanted to help out with the bills but it wasn't until I was thirteen years old that the franchise owner finally agreed. I started from the bottom, as a dishwasher, and in every spare minute I asked my dad to teach me something new.

My dad always told me, 'Fried rice is the easiest dish to cook, but the hardest dish to master.' When it comes to frying rice, it's not about the seasonings, the real flavour comes from the wok cooking technique and mastery of ingredients. So when the shop was quiet I would practise using the wok.

By the time I was fifteen I was finally strong enough to handle the wok like my dad. And my dad thought I was good enough to be able to serve the customers. That same year my family bought the takeaway shop. The shop became part of the family's routine, and most days after school my brother and I would go straight to the shop to help out. And that's how I spent my childhood, as one of those kids in a Chinese takeaway shop.

By the time I was eighteen I had learnt every recipe from my dad's repertoire, every technique and every detail on how to run the restaurant from my dad. But not long after this, my dad had a stroke and his motivation to run the shop faded with his health. And as time passed, business slowed down. Soon we had to give up the restaurant.

I went to university while working full time as a barista in the airport my mum worked at. Eventually, I got my dad hired so we could work together again – even my brother worked there. It was one of the best jobs I've ever had – it was a little lighter, more carefree, because we didn't have to worry about the stress of owning a business. We had fun.

Thanks to everything I learnt at our little takeaway joint, cooking Western food came easily. Within a year I got promoted to a chef position and managed the food at twelve different locations. Eventually, I was offered a role to cook for a prestigious airline's first-class lounge. The role was harder and I had to face fussy clients and long hours, but the constant menu rotation meant I got to experience so much more and learn new cuisines incredibly quickly. For a while everything seemed to be falling into place.

But as you know, life isn't that straightforward. My mum got sick with cancer, and once again everything felt like it was falling apart. I couldn't keep up with my university workload, and I started to fail most of my classes. And with our family's debt growing due to the medical bills, we had debt collectors knocking on our door.

Those were the toughest years of my life. At the time when I wanted to be building my future and discovering my passion, I put my life on hold. Instead, I sacrificed my twenties to survive, a story I'm sure many of you can relate to. I was cooking Western and Middle-Eastern food that I had no passion for making and no memories of eating. Don't get me wrong, I was grateful I had a job, the best I've ever had actually, but it just wasn't me. It wasn't what I wanted to do, or where I wanted to be.

On 13 February 2017, the unimaginable happened. My dad passed away. At twenty-two years old, I lost my dad, my hero, my mentor. Life is tough. The world isn't fair sometimes, and bad things can happen simultaneously. Debt collectors were still knocking on my door. The world didn't stop moving even though mine had just stopped.

Two weeks later, I went back to work and university. There were still bills to pay, work to be done. But this time was different. Everything felt meaningless.

Life insurance paid us a sum of $70,000. I guess in this world everything and everyone has a price. For the next five months, I spent every single day thinking about how I could get my family out of the trenches. From all the condolence calls, I learnt that my grandfather (my mum's dad) owned a Chinese restaurant in the Blue Mountains. He was getting old and no one in the family wanted to take over this restaurant.

That same week, I dropped out of university, quit my job, left everything behind and moved to Sydney to take over what would become the most famous restaurant in the Blue Mountains, Lawson Chinese.

I didn't learn to cook because I wanted to be the best chef or because I loved cooking. I learnt to cook to support my family and serve the best food I could to our customers. Every dish I make has a purpose, rooted in memories and history. The recipes in this book are not just about taste – they're part of my journey. They are dishes I've served thousands of times to my customers, friends and family.

This book is for anyone learning how to cook, anyone wanting to understand Asian food, anyone wanting to open a restaurant or anyone like me, who needed to put food on the table.

INTRODUCTION

A LITTLE BIT OF YUMYUM

WHAT IS YUMYUM?

A WORLD OF UMAMI, A CULINARY SECRET WEAPON, AN INGREDIENT THAT AMPLIFIES THE NATURAL FLAVOURS OF FOOD WITHOUT OVERPOWERING THEM AND THE FIFTH TASTE SENSATION THAT ADDS DEPTH, RICHNESS AND SAVOURY DELICIOUSNESS TO EVERY BITE. YUMYUM IS MY VERY OWN ALL-ROUNDER, SEASONING MADE WITH THREE CORE INGREDIENTS: MSG, WOK-ROASTED SALT AND WHITE PEPPER.

WHY MSG IS ESSENTIAL TO CHINESE COOKING

MSG, or monosodium glutamate, plays a crucial role in Chinese cooking, serving as a powerful enhancer of umami – the deep, savoury taste that defines much of the cuisine. Umami, which translates to 'deliciousness' in Japanese, is the fifth basic taste, alongside sweet, salty, sour and bitter. It's that complex, mouthwatering flavour found in broths, meats and fermented foods, and MSG helps intensify this savoury depth.

In Chinese cooking, achieving a balance of flavours is key. Dishes often combine salty, sweet, sour, bitter and umami elements, and MSG is used to elevate and round out these flavours. By boosting umami, MSG deepens the richness of soups, stir-fries and braises without overpowering the natural taste of the ingredients. Its ability to enhance flavours without significantly altering them makes it an essential ingredient in Chinese kitchens.

Traditionally, Chinese cuisine relies on ingredients naturally rich in glutamate, such as soy sauce, fermented black beans, mushrooms and dried seafood. MSG amplifies these natural flavours, bringing out the best in each component. Whether it's adding complexity to a simple stir-fry, enriching a broth, or perfecting a marinade, MSG helps unlock the full potential of a dish's ingredients.

In essence, MSG is a flavour enhancer that captures the essence of umami, ensuring every bite of a dish is layered, satisfying and rich. Its ability to boost flavour without excess salt or fat makes it indispensable in Chinese cooking, allowing for full-bodied, balanced meals that hit all the right notes.

DEBUNKING THE MYTHS AROUND MSG

Monosodium glutamate, commonly known as MSG, has long been a controversial ingredient, often falsely blamed for causing headaches, allergic reactions and various health issues. Despite this bad reputation, MSG is a natural and safe flavour enhancer that has been used for over a century. Scientific research has thoroughly debunked the common myths surrounding MSG, showing that it poses no greater risk than regular table salt. The fear and misinformation surrounding MSG are largely based on outdated assumptions rather than evidence.

The controversy began in 1968, when a letter published in the *New England Journal of Medicine* speculated that eating Chinese food – particularly dishes containing MSG – caused symptoms such as headaches, palpitations and nausea, a phenomenon labelled 'Chinese Restaurant Syndrome'. Though the claim was based solely on anecdotal evidence, it sparked widespread concern, leading many to believe that MSG was harmful. As a result, restaurants and food manufacturers began labelling products as 'No MSG' to alleviate customer fears. However, numerous studies have since shown that MSG is not responsible for these symptoms.

Scientific organisations, including the U.S. Food and Drug Administration (FDA), the World Health Organization (WHO) and the European Food Safety Authority (EFSA), have all concluded that MSG is safe for consumption. The FDA even classifies MSG as 'Generally Recognized as Safe' (GRAS), the same designation given to salt, sugar and vinegar. Controlled studies have found no consistent link between MSG and adverse reactions in the general population. In the rare cases where individuals report sensitivity to MSG, symptoms are often due to other factors, such as the overall high sodium or fat content in the food.

MSG is simply the sodium salt of glutamate, an amino acid that occurs naturally in many foods, such as tomatoes, Parmesan cheese and mushrooms. It enhances the umami flavour – the fifth basic taste – without adding a distinct flavour of its own. The body processes glutamate from MSG in exactly the same way as it processes natural glutamate found in foods, with no difference between the two sources.

In addition to being safe, MSG can also help reduce overall sodium intake. It contains only about one-third the sodium of table salt, making it a great way to boost flavour while cutting down on excess sodium. By adding MSG to a dish, you can enhance its savoury depth without relying on as much salt, making it a valuable tool for reducing sodium consumption while maintaining flavour.

Extensive research has debunked the myths surrounding its health risks, and scientific consensus confirms that MSG can be enjoyed without worry. Whether you're preparing stir-fries, soups or marinades, MSG can elevate the taste of your dishes by adding a rich umami flavour – no harm, just great taste.

HOW I DEVELOPED YUMYUM

YumYum was born out of necessity in my restaurant kitchen back in 2017. I was teaching my chefs how to season dishes with pure MSG, but we encountered a challenge. Since MSG itself doesn't have a strong, distinct taste, it was difficult for the team to gauge how much to use in each dish. Too little, and the effect was barely noticeable. Too much, and it could overwhelm the dish. I knew there had to be a simpler, more consistent way to achieve the desired balance, so I set out to create it.

After some trial and error, my brother (Marcus Lim) and I found the perfect blend: a golden ratio of MSG to wok-roasted salt and white pepper. The result is YumYum – a versatile, all-purpose seasoning that makes it easy to enhance the flavour of any dish without overthinking the measurements. The blend offers a subtle saltiness from the roasted salt, a gentle heat from the white pepper, and that coveted umami boost from the MSG. The beauty of YumYum lies in its balance – it doesn't overpower or alter the flavours of a dish but rather amplifies what's already there, bringing out the richness and depth of every ingredient.

HOW TO USE YUMYUM

YumYum is a go-to seasoning that can be used in almost any dish in need of a flavour boost – whether you're looking to enhance a classic recipe or add more flavour to a new creation. It's particularly useful in stir-fries, fried rice, soups, and even marinades, where it enhances the natural flavours of vegetables, meats and sauces. Because it has such a mild and neutral base, you can sprinkle it into your dish as you cook or use it as a finishing touch just before serving.

For example, a simple vegetable stir-fry transforms with a sprinkle of YumYum – what may have been an everyday dish suddenly has depth, complexity and that perfect umami finish. You can also use it in fried rice, adding a pinch as you stir in your ingredients to give the dish a savoury kick without needing to adjust the soy sauce or other seasonings.

YumYum is also excellent for quick, flavourful marinades. Mix it with soy sauce, garlic and a little sesame oil for an easy marinade that brings out the best in chicken, pork or tofu. Or, for a quicker boost, simply rub it directly onto meats or sprinkle over roasted vegetables right before serving.

ALL ABOUT THE WOK

THE WOK IS THE HEART OF CHINESE COOKING — A VERSATILE AND INDISPENSABLE TOOL THAT HAS BEEN USED FOR CENTURIES. ITS UNIQUE SHAPE AND DESIGN ALLOW YOU TO COOK FOOD QUICKLY AND EVENLY, MAKING IT ESSENTIAL FOR STIR-FRYING, DEEP-FRYING, STEAMING, BRAISING AND EVEN SMOKING. A GOOD WOK IS MORE THAN JUST A COOKING VESSEL — IT'S THE KEY TO CREATING THE AUTHENTIC FLAVOURS AND TEXTURES THAT DEFINE CHINESE CUISINE. WHETHER YOU'RE A BEGINNER OR A SEASONED COOK, MASTERING THE WOK IS THE FIRST STEP TO MASTERING CHINESE COOKING.

WHY USING A WOK IS IMPORTANT

The wok's design is simple, yet genius. Its rounded bottom allows for high-heat cooking, ensuring that food cooks evenly and quickly. The sloped sides make it easy to toss and turn ingredients, preventing them from sticking and allowing flavours to meld together. This versatility means you can cook a wide range of dishes, from stir-fries and noodles to soups and stews, all in one pan.

The wok's ability to handle intense heat makes it a powerful tool for locking in flavours while maintaining the texture and integrity of the ingredients. Unlike flat pans, the wok gives you control over the heat zones – ingredients can be seared at the bottom and then pushed up the sides to keep warm while you continue cooking. This multi-zonal cooking is one of the reasons the wok is so essential in Chinese kitchens.

WHAT IS WOK HEI (鑊氣)?

One of the key characteristics of Chinese cuisine is 'wok hei', or the 'breath of the wok'. It's the elusive, smoky flavour that comes from cooking food at very high temperatures, allowing oils, sugars and proteins to caramelise and infuse the dish with a unique aroma and taste. Wok hei can only be achieved through the high-heat cooking that the wok is designed for.

Wok hei adds depth and complexity to dishes, making them taste slightly charred yet flavourful without being burnt. It's the difference between a good stir-fry and a great one, and it's the reason you'll often see flames leaping around a wok in professional Chinese kitchens. To achieve wok hei at home, you'll need a high heat source (a wok burner is ideal) and the confidence to cook your ingredients quickly and with minimal stirring. The magic happens in seconds, and the result is a deeply flavourful dish that's packed with that signature smokiness.

CHOOSING A WOK

Not all woks are created equal, and choosing the right one for your kitchen is crucial to getting the most out of it. The most traditional and widely recommended option is a carbon steel wok. Carbon steel woks are lightweight, heat up quickly and develop a natural non-stick surface over time. They are also durable and relatively inexpensive.

When selecting a wok, it's important to match the size of the wok to your heat source. The smaller your burner or fire, the smaller your wok should be. A large wok on a small burner won't heat evenly, making it difficult to achieve that essential wok hei. If you have a powerful burner, a larger wok will allow you to cook bigger portions and take full advantage of the heat. For most home cooks, a wok between 30–35 centimetres (12–14 in) in diameter is ideal, but again, the size should complement the heat output of your stove.

Another important feature to look for is the handle connection. A good wok should have a strong, secure handle, preferably riveted or welded firmly to the wok. This ensures safe handling, especially when tossing or stir-frying at high heat. The handle should feel solid and comfortable in your hand, making it easier to manoeuvre the wok as you cook.

SEASONING A WOK

Seasoning a wok is a crucial step before using it for the first time, especially if it's made of carbon steel or cast iron. Seasoning creates a protective, non-stick surface that improves the flavour of your dishes and helps the wok develop wok hei. It also prevents rusting, extending the life of your wok.

To season a new wok, start by washing it thoroughly with soap to remove the protective factory coating. Then, dry it completely and place it over medium heat. Once the wok is hot, rub a thin layer of oil (like peanut or vegetable oil) all over the inside surface using a paper towel or cloth. Let the oil heat until it begins to smoke, then turn off the heat and let the wok cool down. Wipe off any excess oil, and repeat this process a few times until the wok develops a smooth, slightly shiny surface. Over time, with continued use, your wok will darken and develop a natural patina that enhances flavour and improves its non-stick qualities.

STORING A WOK

Storing your wok properly is essential to maintaining its quality. After each use, it's important to clean the wok correctly – simply rinse it with warm water and use a soft brush to remove any stuck-on food. Avoid using soap or abrasive sponges, as these can strip the seasoning from your wok.

Once your wok is clean, dry it thoroughly to prevent rust. You can place it on the stove over low heat for a few minutes to ensure all moisture is gone. After drying, apply a very thin layer of oil to the surface to protect it between uses. Store your wok in a dry place, either hung on a hook or in a cupboard, to avoid moisture exposure.

Proper care and storage will keep your wok in excellent condition, allowing it to last for many years. Over time, your wok will become an indispensable part of your kitchen, growing more seasoned and more flavourful with each dish you create.

INTRODUCTION

CHINESE KITCHEN ESSENTIALS

YOU DON'T NEED A VAST ARRAY OF TOOLS TO GET STARTED WITH CHINESE COOKING – JUST A FEW ESSENTIAL ITEMS THAT WILL CARRY YOU THROUGH COUNTLESS DISHES. EACH PIECE IS DESIGNED TO SERVE MULTIPLE PURPOSES, MAKING YOUR KITCHEN MORE EFFICIENT AND LESS CLUTTERED. A WOK CAN ACT AS A FRYING PAN, A DEEP FRYER, A STEAMER – AND, ONCE YOU GET COMFORTABLE, EVEN A PASTA POT. SIMILARLY, A WOK LADLE IS NOT JUST FOR STIRRING BUT CAN ALSO BE USED FOR SCOOPING, MIXING AND MEASURING. THEY'RE THE SAME TOOLS USED DAY-IN, DAY-OUT BY THE MOST SEASONED MASTERS OF CHINESE CUISINE.

WOK BURNER

The key to achieving the signature smoky flavour in Chinese cooking – known as 'wok hei'(see page 18) – is high heat, and a wok burner is the most effective way to reach those temperatures.

Heat is fundamental to Chinese cooking. It adds layers of flavour, sears the outside of food to lock in juices, and creates the perfect texture in stir-fries and other dishes. A wok burner provides the intense heat needed for quick cooking, helping you achieve that coveted wok hei with ease. There are many types of wok burners on the market, from built-in induction cooktops to portable outdoor stations. The important thing is finding one that fits your kitchen and cooking style.

That said, you don't absolutely need a wok burner to cook the recipes in this book. On a standard home cooktop, you can still get great results by cooking in smaller batches and avoiding overcrowding the wok. However, if you're serious about your Chinese cooking, a wok burner will deepen the flavour of your food and cut down cooking time, allowing you to spend less time at the stove and more time enjoying your meals.

OIL POT

Oil is a central element in Chinese cooking, whether you're stir-frying, deep-frying or flash-frying. An oil pot is an essential tool for managing your cooking oil efficiently. It allows you to strain, store and reuse oil, which is important when oil is used so frequently in Chinese dishes.

An oil pot, equipped with a fine mesh strainer, helps remove food particles after frying, ensuring your oil stays clean for future use. This not only saves money but also maintains the quality of your dishes. You can find oil pots at most Asian grocery stores, but a sturdy, heatproof metal bowl or container works just as well. Proper oil management keeps your kitchen tidy and makes frying easier.

STRAINER

A strainer works in tandem with your oil pot, allowing you to quickly drain excess oil after frying or blanching food. When you're flash-frying meats or vegetables, simply pour the contents of your wok into the strainer, which sits on top of the oil pot. The strainer lets oil drain away while you continue cooking. This is especially useful for recipes that require fried ingredients to be added back into a dish later, ensuring they stay crisp without being overly oily.

Additionally, a strainer's rounded shape makes it perfect for scooping deep-fried or blanched items from the wok with precision. Whether you're removing dumplings, fried chicken or vegetables from hot oil, the strainer is an essential tool for both safety and efficiency.

WOK LADLE AND SPATULA

In Chinese cooking, the wok ladle and spatula are extensions of your arm. These tools are essential for managing the quick, high-heat cooking of a wok. A wok ladle is incredibly versatile – it's used for stirring, breaking up rice or noodles, scooping ingredients and serving the final dish. Its rounded shape makes it ideal for following the curve of the wok, allowing you to mix and toss ingredients evenly.

The wok spatula, on the other hand, is perfect for tasks that require precision. The flat edge is great for sliding under food like eggs or delicate fish and it excels at separating and flipping noodles or stir-fried ingredients. If you're new to wok cooking, using both a ladle and a spatula can make it easier to stir and combine ingredients without having to toss the wok itself. Over time, as your confidence grows, you can learn the one-handed wok-tossing technique while using the other hand to assist with the ladle or spatula.

STEAMING STAND

Steaming is a fundamental cooking method in Chinese cuisine, and a steaming stand transforms your wok into a steamer. Simply place the stand in the centre of the wok, add water to the bottom, and rest a plate or bowl of food on top. This set-up is perfect for steaming everything from fish and dumplings to vegetables and buns. The stand keeps your plate elevated above the water while allowing steam to circulate and cook your food evenly.

Steaming is a healthy and gentle way to cook, and the versatility of using your wok as a steamer makes it even more valuable in the kitchen.

WOK LID

A wok lid turns your wok into an ideal vessel for braising and steaming. Just as you would use a lid on a regular pot or pan, the wok lid helps trap heat and moisture, allowing for even cooking. It's especially useful for dishes that need to simmer or for steaming items placed on a stand. The wok lid also helps intensify flavours during braising, ensuring that your food stays juicy and tender while cooking through.

INTRODUCTION

CHINESE PANTRY ESSENTIALS

BUILDING A SOLID COLLECTION OF PANTRY ESSENTIALS IS THE FOUNDATION FOR MASTERING ANY CUISINE, AND CHINESE COOKING IS NO EXCEPTION. THE HEART OF CHINESE CUISINE LIES IN A CORE SET OF SEASONINGS AND INGREDIENTS, EACH BRINGING ITS OWN UNIQUE FLAVOUR AND CHARACTER TO THE DISH. WITH JUST A HANDFUL OF THESE STAPLES IN YOUR PANTRY, YOU'LL BE WELL-EQUIPPED TO COOK A WIDE VARIETY OF CHINESE DISHES, FROM QUICK STIR-FRIES TO RICH BRAISES.

Every dish in Chinese cuisine is a harmonious blend of these essential ingredients. The more you familiarise yourself with each one, the more versatile your cooking will become. For instance, combine sesame oil with chicken bouillon powder to make a fragrant sesame chicken, or mix five-spice powder with YumYum to craft a delicious five-spice mix (see page 33) for dishes like salt and pepper calamari or pork ribs. The possibilities are endless – the key is understanding how each ingredient works with the others.

Learning Chinese cooking is like mastering kung fu. Just as the best martial artists are grounded in the basics before attempting fancy moves, the best cooks master fundamental seasonings before venturing into complex recipes. It's important to become familiar with each pantry essential, understanding how to use it in multiple ways rather than just for one dish. This allows you to truly 'own' your kitchen, adapting recipes and creating flavourful dishes with what you have on hand.

In this book, I want to teach you how to create something remarkable from what may seem like nothing, starting with this collection of Chinese pantry essentials.

YUMYUM

This is my personal blend of MSG, white pepper, and salt, a go-to seasoning that enhances the flavour of almost any dish. It's the secret weapon in my kitchen and brings out the umami notes in a subtle but significant way. If you don't have YumYum on hand, MSG is the best alternative. This blend can be sprinkled on everything from stir-fried vegetables to fried rice, giving dishes an extra layer of depth and savouriness.

CHICKEN BOUILLON POWDER

Chicken bouillon powder is a staple in Chinese kitchens for boosting the flavour of soups, stir-fries and marinades. It provides a savoury base, much like a concentrated chicken stock, and enhances the richness of any dish. It's commonly used in recipes where a quick flavour boost is needed, such as fried rice, braised meats or simple soups. The beauty of chicken bouillon powder is this versatility – it can instantly add umami and depth to even the simplest dishes.

SHAOXING WINE

Shaoxing wine (Chinese cooking wine) is a type of Chinese rice wine that adds complexity to both marinades and cooked dishes. It helps tenderise meats while adding a subtle sweetness and aroma that elevates the overall flavour profile. Often used in braises, stir-fries and sauces, this wine is a crucial ingredient for achieving the authentic taste found in Chinese restaurants.

SESAME OIL

Known for its deep, nutty flavour and rich aroma, sesame oil is a finishing oil rather than a cooking oil. A little goes a long way, and it is typically drizzled over dishes right before serving to add a fragrant, toasty note. It's a must-have for cold dishes like salads or noodle bowls and enhances hot dishes like stir-fries and soups.

LIGHT SOY SAUCE

Light soy sauce is a cornerstone in Chinese cuisine. It's lighter in colour but saltier than dark soy sauce, making it ideal for seasoning during the cooking process. Light soy sauce adds a salty, umami-rich depth to stir-fries, marinades and soups. It's also great for dipping sauces. In Chinese cooking, it's frequently used as the main seasoning in dishes where you want to enhance flavours without darkening the appearance of the food.

DARK SOY SAUCE

Darker, thicker and slightly sweeter than light soy sauce, dark soy sauce is used primarily to add colour and a richer flavour to dishes. It's often used in braised dishes like red-cooked pork, where its deeper, molasses-like flavour can shine. While it still has a salty kick, dark soy sauce is more mellow and less sharp than light soy sauce. When used together, light and dark soy sauces create a perfect balance of flavour and colour.

WHITE PEPPER

White pepper is widely used in Chinese cuisine for its sharp, slightly fermented taste. It's milder but more complex than black pepper, making it perfect for soups, stir-fries and marinades. White pepper is often added towards the end of cooking to give dishes a subtle heat and fragrant finish. It's also frequently used in Chinese hot and sour soup and is the spice of choice for Cantonese dishes.

FIVE-SPICE POWDER

This aromatic blend typically includes star anise, cloves, Chinese cinnamon (cassia), Sichuan peppercorns and fennel seeds. Five-spice powder is used in both sweet and savoury dishes, providing a warm, fragrant kick. It's great for seasoning meats like pork, chicken and duck before roasting or stir-frying. You can also add it to braises for a deeper, more complex flavour. It's the perfect seasoning for dishes like five-spice ribs or to give simple stir-fries a unique twist.

POTATO STARCH

Potato starch is a popular thickening agent used in Chinese cooking to create a glossy sauce that clings beautifully to meats and vegetables. It's often used in place of corn starch because it offers a silkier texture. You'll find it in dishes like mapo tofu or any stir-fry where you want a smooth, velvety sauce.

CORNFLOUR

Like potato starch, cornflour (cornstarch) is a key ingredient for thickening sauces; however, I use it more often as a crisp coating on fried foods. It's a bit more common in home kitchens than potato starch and widely available. In addition to being used in batters and for thickening, it's often used as part of a marinade to tenderise or 'velvet' meat, making it softer and more succulent after cooking.

INTRODUCTION

BASICS

VELVETED BEEF

MAKES 250 G (9 OZ) VELVETED BEEF

VELVETING IS A SIMPLE TECHNIQUE GIVES MEAT THAT MELT-IN-YOUR-MOUTH TEXTURE FOUND IN YOUR FAVOURITE STIR-FRIES. THE MARINADE CREATES A PROTECTIVE COATING, SEALING IN MOISTURE DURING COOKING, WHILE THE CORNFLOUR BREAKS DOWN PROTEINS SLIGHTLY, RESULTING IN A TENDER TEXTURE.

BEEF

250 g (9 oz) topside, rump or tenderloin, sliced thinly against the grain
¼ teaspoon bicarbonate of soda (baking soda)
2 tablespoons water
3 tablespoons cornflour (cornstarch)

SEASONING

1 teaspoon chicken bouillon powder
½ teaspoon dark soy sauce
½ teaspoon salt
½ teaspoon sugar
¼ teaspoon YumYum or MSG
¼ teaspoon white pepper
1 tablespoon vegetable oil
1 teaspoon sesame oil
2 teaspoons Shaoxing wine (Chinese cooking wine)

Place the sliced beef in a large bowl and add the bicarbonate of soda along with the water. Stir the mixture until the beef is well coated and combined. Next, add the cornflour and continue stirring until the beef has completely absorbed all the liquid. This step ensures that the beef will remain tender during cooking.

Once the beef is well coated, season it by adding the chicken bouillon powder, dark soy sauce, salt, sugar, YumYum or MSG, vegetable oil, sesame oil and Shaoxing wine. Stir thoroughly to ensure the seasoning is evenly distributed throughout the beef.

Cover the bowl and allow the beef to rest. For the best flavour and texture, let it marinate overnight for use the next day or, if you're short on time, for at least 1 hour. If you'd like to prepare the beef in advance, you can freeze the seasoned beef for up to a month. For optimal results, freeze the beef first and then defrost it before cooking.

VELVETED CHICKEN

MAKES 300 G (10½ OZ) VELVETED CHICKEN

VELVETING CHICKEN WORKS THE SAME WAY AS VELVETING BEEF, ENSURING THE MEAT STAYS TENDER AND JUICY, EVEN AFTER STIR-FRYING AT HIGH HEAT. IT'S A GREAT TRICK FOR MAKING SURE YOUR CHICKEN TURNS OUT PERFECTLY SOFT AND FULL OF FLAVOUR.

CHICKEN

250 g (9 oz) chicken breast, sliced thinly against the grain
¼ teaspoon bicarbonate of soda (baking soda)
1 tablespoon water
2 tablespoons cornflour (cornstarch)

SEASONING

1 teaspoon chicken bouillon powder
½ teaspoon salt
½ teaspoon sugar
¼ teaspoon YumYum or MSG
¼ teaspoon white pepper
1 tablespooon vegetable oil
1 teaspoon sesame oil
2 teaspoons Shaoxing wine (Chinese cooking wine)

Place the sliced chicken in a large bowl and add the bicarbonate of soda along with the water. Stir the mixture until the chicken is well coated and combined. Next, add the cornflour and continue stirring until the chicken has completely absorbed all the liquid.

Once the chicken is thoroughly coated, season it by adding the chicken bouillon powder, salt, sugar, YumYum or MSG, white pepper, vegetable oil, sesame oil and Shaoxing wine. Stir until all the ingredients are evenly mixed and the seasoning is well distributed.

Cover the bowl and allow the chicken to rest. For the best flavour and texture, freeze the chicken overnight and defrost before cooking the next day. (You can also prep ahead – and leave it frozen for up to a month.) If you're pressed for time, marinating for at least 1 hour will still give you results.

VELVETED PRAWNS

MAKES 10 VELVETED PRAWNS

VELVETING PRAWNS (SHRIMP) HELPS THEM STAY PLUMP, TENDER AND JUICY THROUGHOUT THE COOKING PROCESS. IT ENSURES THE PRAWNS KEEP THEIR DELICATE TEXTURE WHILE LOCKING IN THAT SWEET FLAVOUR.

10 prawns (shrimp)
1 teaspoon chicken bouillon powder
1 tablespoon cornflour (cornstarch)
large pinch of bicarbonate of soda (baking soda)
½ teaspoon YumYum or MSG
1 teaspoon Shaoxing wine (Chinese cooking wine)
1 teaspoon sesame oil
large pinch of salt
2 tablespoons vegetable oil

Peel and devein the prawns, leaving the tails intact if preferred. Rinse the prawns under cold water, then pat them dry with paper towels, ensuring they are completely dry before proceeding. This step is important to ensure proper seasoning and cooking.

In a mixing bowl, combine the chicken bouillon powder, cornflour, bicarbonate of soda, YumYum or MSG, Shaoxing wine, sesame oil, salt and vegetable oil. Stir the mixture until everything is well combined. Add the prawns to the bowl and gently massage them into the marinade, ensuring the seasoning is evenly distributed and absorbed by the prawns.

For the best flavour and texture, let it marinate overnight for use the next day or, if you are short on time, for at least 1 hour.

SWEET AND SOUR SAUCE

MAKES 1 CUP

SWEET AND SOUR SAUCE IS A MUST HAVE IN ALL CHINESE RESTAURANTS. THE SAUCE CAN NOT ONLY BE USED IN DISHES LIKE RAINBOW BEEF AND SWEET AND SOUR PORK, IT CAN ALSO BE USED AS A DIPPING SAUCE FOR YOUR SPRING ROLLS AND FRIED DIM SIMS!

1 tablespoon vegetable oil
80 ml (2 ½ fl oz/⅓ cup) water
80 ml (2 ½ fl oz/⅓ cup) white vinegar
1 teaspoon Worcestershire sauce
60 ml (2 fl oz/¼ cup) tomato sauce (ketchup)
65 g (2¼ oz/⅓ cup) sugar
few drops of liquid red food colouring or a pinch of powdered
1½ teaspoons potato starch
80 ml (2½ fl oz/⅓ cup) water

In a wok or saucepan mix together the oil, water, white vinegar, Worcestershire sauce, tomato sauce, sugar and a few drops of red food colouring.

Stir well until the sugar is dissolved. Adjust the sweetness and sourness to your taste by adding more sugar or vinegar if needed. Turn the heat onto medium and cook until simmering.

Combine the potato starch and water until smooth and add it slowly to the sauce while stirring.

Continue to heat the sauce for another 1–2 minutes, stirring occasionally, until the sauce has thickened.

BASICS

PORK LARD

MAKES 375 ML (12½ FL OZ/1½ CUPS)

I LOVE TO KEEP HOMEMADE PORK LARD AT HAND FOR A KITCHEN STAPLE THAT ADDS A SUPER FRAGRANT AND SAVOURY FLAVOUR TO MY DISHES. IT'S PERFECT FOR STIR-FRIES, GIVING VEGGIES A RICH BOOST, OR FOR FRYING UP RICE AND NOODLES. PLUS, THE CRISPY PORK CRACKLINGS YOU GET AS A BONUS ARE A TASTY LITTLE SNACK!

500 g (17 oz) pork fat
2 slices of ginger
2 spring onions (scallions)
3 tablespoons Shaoxing wine (Chinese cooking wine)

Cut the pork fat into 2 cm (¾ in) cubes and set aside. In a wok, bring the water to boil. Once boiling, add the pork fat cubes along with the ginger slices, spring onions and Shaoxing wine. Blanch the pork fat for a few minutes, allowing it to soften slightly.

After blanching, strain the pork fat from the water, discarding the ginger and spring onions. Return the strained pork fat to the wok and add enough fresh water to just cover the cubes.

Cook the pork fat over low heat for about 15 minutes, or until all the water has evaporated. Once the water is gone, you'll be left with rendered pork lard and golden, crunchy pork cracklings.

Store for up to 1 week in an airtight container.

CHICKEN STOCK

MAKES 3 LITRES (101 FL OZ/12 CUPS)

MASTER CHICKEN STOCK IS THE FOUNDATION FOR COUNTLESS CHINESE RESTAURANT DISHES. ITS RICH, SAVOURY FLAVOUR ELEVATES SOUPS, SAUCES AND STIR-FRIES, ADDING DEPTH AND WARMTH. HAVING A HOMEMADE BATCH ON HAND ENSURES THAT EVERY MEAL IS PACKED WITH HEARTY, COMFORTING FLAVOUR!

2 chicken leg quarters
4 slices of ginger
1 medium carrot, sliced
1 onion, whole
1 teaspoon white peppercorns
3 litres (101 fl oz/12 cups) water
2 teaspoons YumYum or MSG
3 tablespoons chicken bouillon powder
1½ teaspoons sugar
1½ teaspoons salt

Place the chicken, ginger, carrot, onion and peppercorns in a large pot. Pour in the water (topping up if needed so it covers the ingredients) and bring the mixture to a boil. Once boiling, reduce the heat and let it simmer for 2 hours, skimming off any impurities that rise to the surface.

After 2 hours, stir in the YumYum or MSG, chicken bouillon powder, sugar and salt, allowing the flavours to meld together. Continue simmering for another 30 minutes. Once done, strain the stock, and it's ready to use in your recipes.

If you're not using the stock immediately, store it in the fridge for up to 4 days or in the freezer for up to 3 months.

GINGER SCALLION OIL

MAKES 375 ML (12½ FL OZ/1½ CUPS)

GINGER SCALLION OIL IS THE PERFECT PAIRING FOR HAINAN CHICKEN, ADDING A BURST OF FRESH, FRAGRANT FLAVOUR. ITS VERSATILITY DOESN'T STOP THERE — THIS SIMPLE YET FLAVOURFUL OIL CAN BE DRIZZLED OVER NOODLES, RICE, OR EVEN USED AS A DIPPING SAUCE FOR DUMPLINGS AND OTHER DISHES. IT'S A GO-TO CONDIMENT THAT BRINGS A PUNCH OF SAVOURY GOODNESS.

8 large spring onions (scallions)
10 g (½ oz) ginger
240 ml (8 fl oz/1 cup) vegetable oil
3 tablespoons sesame oil
3 teaspoons salt, to taste
1 teaspoon YumYum or MSG
1 teaspoon chicken bouillon powder

Thinly slice the spring onions including the white parts, and peel and finely chop the ginger. Place them into a heatproof bowl.

In a small saucepan, heat the vegetable oil over medium heat until it's hot but not smoking. Carefully pour the hot oil over the spring onions and ginger in the bowl. The hot oil will sizzle, cooking the ingredients and releasing their flavours.

Stir in the sesame oil, salt, YumYum or MSG and chicken bouillon powder. Allow the sauce to cool to room temperature before using, as the flavours will continue to develop as it sits.

Store the ginger scallion oil in an airtight container in the refrigerator for up to 1 week.

FIVE-SPICE SALT AND PEPPER

MAKES 1¼ CUPS

FIVE-SPICE MIX IS A GAME-CHANGER WHEN IT COMES TO SEASONING. IT'S THE KEY TO CREATING DISHES LIKE SALT AND PEPPER SQUID OR SALT AND PEPPER PORK RIBS, GIVING THEM THAT BOLD, AROMATIC FLAVOUR. THIS VERSATILE BLEND CAN ALSO BE SPRINKLED ON STIR-FRIES, ROASTED MEATS, OR EVEN FRIED SNACKS TO BRING AN EXTRA KICK OF SPICE AND DEPTH.

2 teaspoons Chinese five-spice
2 tablespoons chicken bouillon powder
1 teaspoon white pepper
2 tablespoons salt
1 tablespoon YumYum or MSG
2 teaspoons sugar

In a small bowl, combine the Chinese five-spice, chicken bouillon powder, white pepper, salt, YumYum or MSG and sugar. Use a small whisk or spoon to thoroughly mix the ingredients until they are evenly distributed.

If you're not using the seasoning immediately, transfer the mix to an airtight container. It can be stored in a cool, dry place for up to 3 months.

BASICS

SMALL EATS

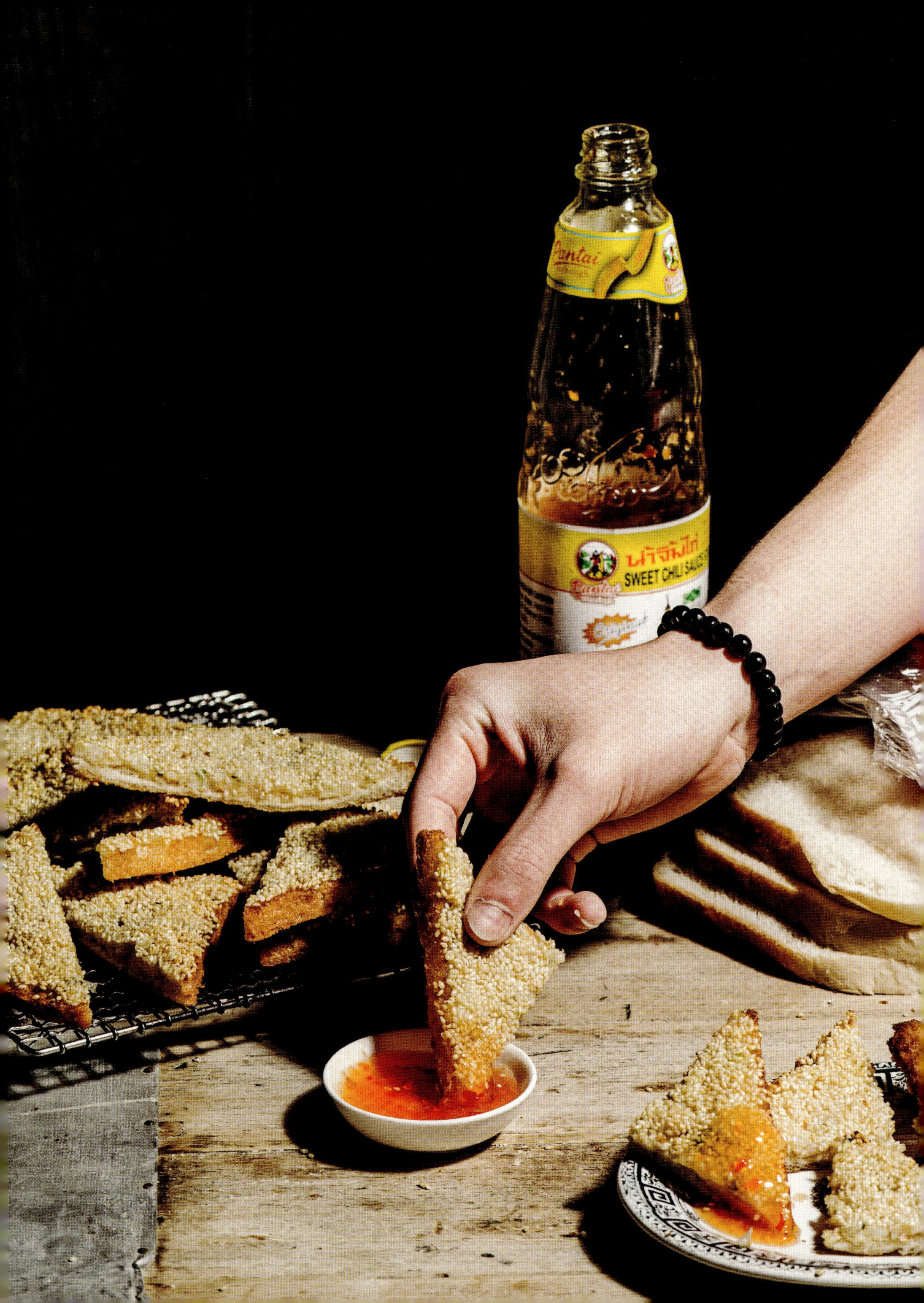
Pantai

SERVES 8

PRAWN TOASTS

PRAWN TOASTS ARE A CRISPY AND SAVOURY FAVOURITE, FEATURING A LAYER OF SEASONED PRAWN PASTE SPREAD OVER BREAD THAT'S COATED IN SESAME SEEDS AND DEEP-FRIED TO GOLDEN PERFECTION. THIS SIMPLE YET DELICIOUS DISH IS A POPULAR APPETISER AT CHINESE RESTAURANTS, PERFECT FOR DIPPING IN SWEET CHILLI SAUCE!

PRAWN PASTE

30 white prawns (shrimp), peeled and deveined

½ teaspoon minced ginger

1 tablespoon minced garlic

1 tablespoon finely chopped spring onions (scallions)

1 tablespoon finely chopped coriander (cilantro)

1 large egg (approx. 65 g/2¼ oz)

½ teaspoon white pepper

2 teaspoons chicken bouillon powder

2 tablespoons cornflour (cornstarch)

1 teaspoon sugar

½ teaspoon YumYum or MSG

½ teaspoon sesame oil

½ teaspoon Shaoxing wine (Chinese cooking wine)

ASSEMBLY

8 slices of white bread, crusts removed

150 g (5½ oz/1 cup) white sesame seeds

vegetable oil, for deep-frying

sweet chilli sauce, for dipping

Start by placing the prawns, ginger, garlic, spring onions and coriander on a chopping board. Using a knife, chop everything together until the mixture forms a rough paste, ensuring the prawns still have some larger chunks for texture.

In a large bowl, mix the prawn paste with the egg, white pepper, chicken bouillon powder, cornflour, sugar, YumYum or MSG, sesame oil and Shaoxing wine. Stir until well combined.

Spread about 3 tablespoons of the prawn paste evenly across each slice of bread.

Spread the sesame seeds on a plate. Press the prawn-coated side of each slice of bread into the sesame seeds to coat.

Fill a wok or large pot halfway full with vegetable oil and heat to 170°C (340°F) over medium–high heat. To test if the oil is hot enough, drop in a small piece of white bread; if it bubbles and turns golden, the oil is ready.

Fry 4–5 toasts at a time, ensuring that the wok isn't over crowded. Carefully place the toasts prawn-side down into the hot oil and fry for about 1 minute per side, or until golden brown. Once cooked, remove the prawn toasts from the oil and drain on a wire rack or paper towels. Continue with the remaining toasts.

Cut the toasts into triangles and serve hot with sweet chilli sauce for dipping.

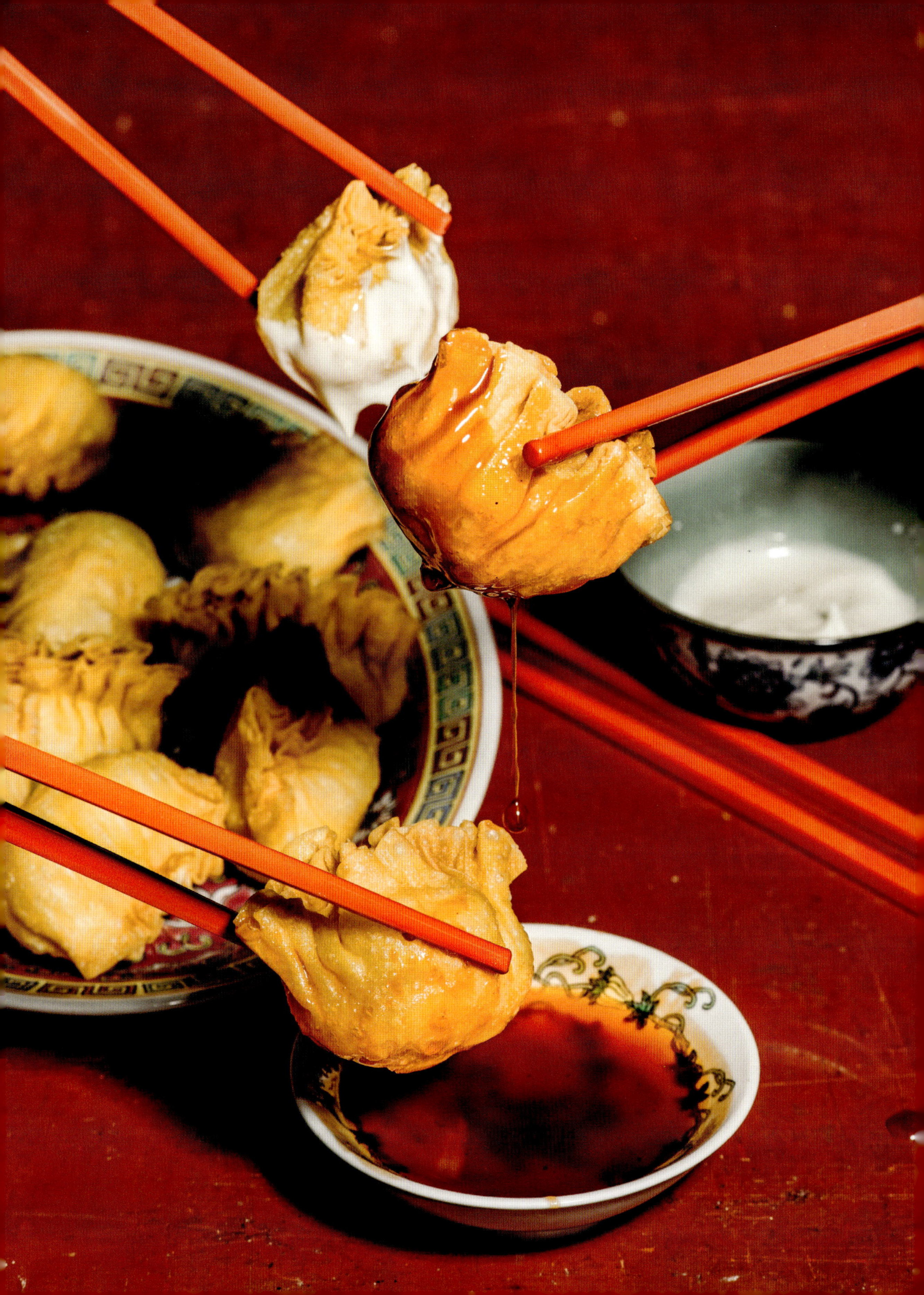

MAKES 16

PRAWN WONTONS

DEEP-FRIED PRAWN WONTONS ARE A CRISPY, GOLDEN DELIGHT, WITH JUICY PRAWN FILLING ENCASED IN A CRUNCHY WRAPPER. PERFECT FOR DIPPING IN SWEET CHILLI OR MAYO, THESE BITE-SIZED TREATS ARE A POPULAR SNACK OR APPETISER THAT ADDS A DELICIOUS CRUNCH TO ANY SPREAD.

300 g (10½ oz) large prawns (shrimp), peeled, deveined and roughly chopped

½ teaspoon grated ginger

1 teaspoon sesame oil

1 teaspoon Shaoxing wine

1 teaspoon chicken bouillon powder

1 tablespoon cornflour (cornstarch)

½ teaspoon YumYum or MSG

¼ teaspoon salt

16 wonton wrappers

vegetable oil, for deep-frying

In a mixing bowl, combine the prawns, grated ginger, sesame oil, Shaoxing wine, chicken bouillon powder, cornflour, YumYum or MSG, and salt. Mix the filling in one direction until it is well combined and streaks begin to form along the edge of the bowl – a sign you've reached the desired paste-like texture. For added springiness, using the traditional 'Da Xian' technique, pick up the mixture and firmly throw it back into the bowl a few times.

Cut the corners off the wonton wrappers, leaving you with a shape closer to a circle. Use a rolling pin to gently roll the wrappers out so they are 1 cm (½ inch) larger in diameter. Place a small spoonful of the prawn filling onto the centre of each wrapper, then fold the wrapper over the filling and pinch the edges together to form a 'bunch' at the top to, sealing the filling inside.

Fill a wok or large pot halfway full with vegetable oil and heat over medium–high heat until it reaches 180°C (350°F). To test if the oil is hot enough, drop in a small piece of wonton wrapper; if it bubbles and turns golden, the oil is ready.

Fry the wontons in small batches, cooking each batch for 2–3 minutes until they are golden brown and crispy.

Once fried, use a slotted spoon to remove the wontons from the oil and drain them on a wire rack or paper towels. Serve the prawn wontons hot with your favourite dipping sauce and enjoy!

MAKES 40 WONTONS

PORK AND PRAWN WONTONS

PORK AND PRAWN WONTONS ARE A CLASSIC CHINESE DISH, COMBINING JUICY PORK AND SUCCULENT PRAWNS WRAPPED IN DELICATE WONTON SKINS. WHETHER SERVED IN SOUP OR FRIED UNTIL CRISPY, THESE FLAVOURFUL BITES ARE A COMFORTING FAVOURITE.

300 g (10½ oz) prawns, peeled and deveined, roughly chopped

300 g (10½ oz) regular pork mince (not lean)

3 spring onions (scallions), thinly sliced

1 tablespoon grated ginger

1 teaspoon salt

½ teaspoon YumYum or MSG

¼ teaspoon white pepper

1 teaspoon sugar

1 teaspoon chicken bouillon powder

1 tablespoon sesame oil

1½ teaspoons cornflour (cornstarch)

1 tablespoon Shaoxing wine (Chinese cooking wine)

1 pack Cantonese wonton egg wrappers

In a large bowl, combine the prawns, pork mince, spring onions, grated ginger, salt, YumYum or MSG, white pepper, sugar, chicken bouillon powder, sesame oil, cornflour and Shaoxing wine. Mix the filling in one direction until it is well combined and streaks begin to form along the edge of the bowl, a sign you've got the desired cohesive texture. To further enhance the springiness and texture of the filling, pick up the mixture and firmly throw it back into the bowl a few times, using the traditional dumpling technique known as 'Da Xian'.

Place a small spoonful of the filling onto the centre of each wonton wrapper. Fold the wrapper over the filling and pinch the edges into the centre to form a 'bunch' at the top of the wrapper.

Repeat this process with the remaining wrappers and filling.

Your wontons are now ready to be boiled, steamed, fried or added to soup.

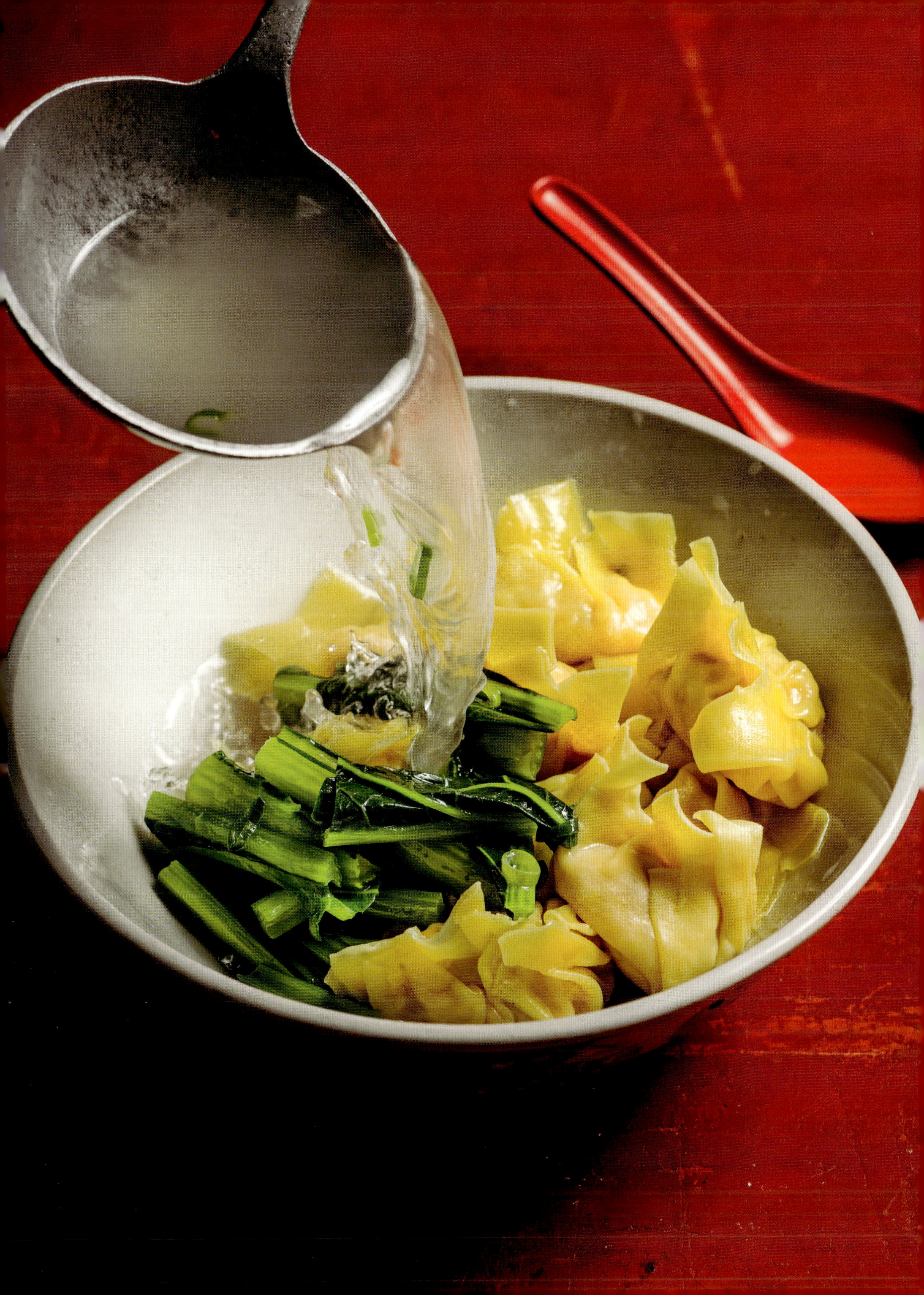

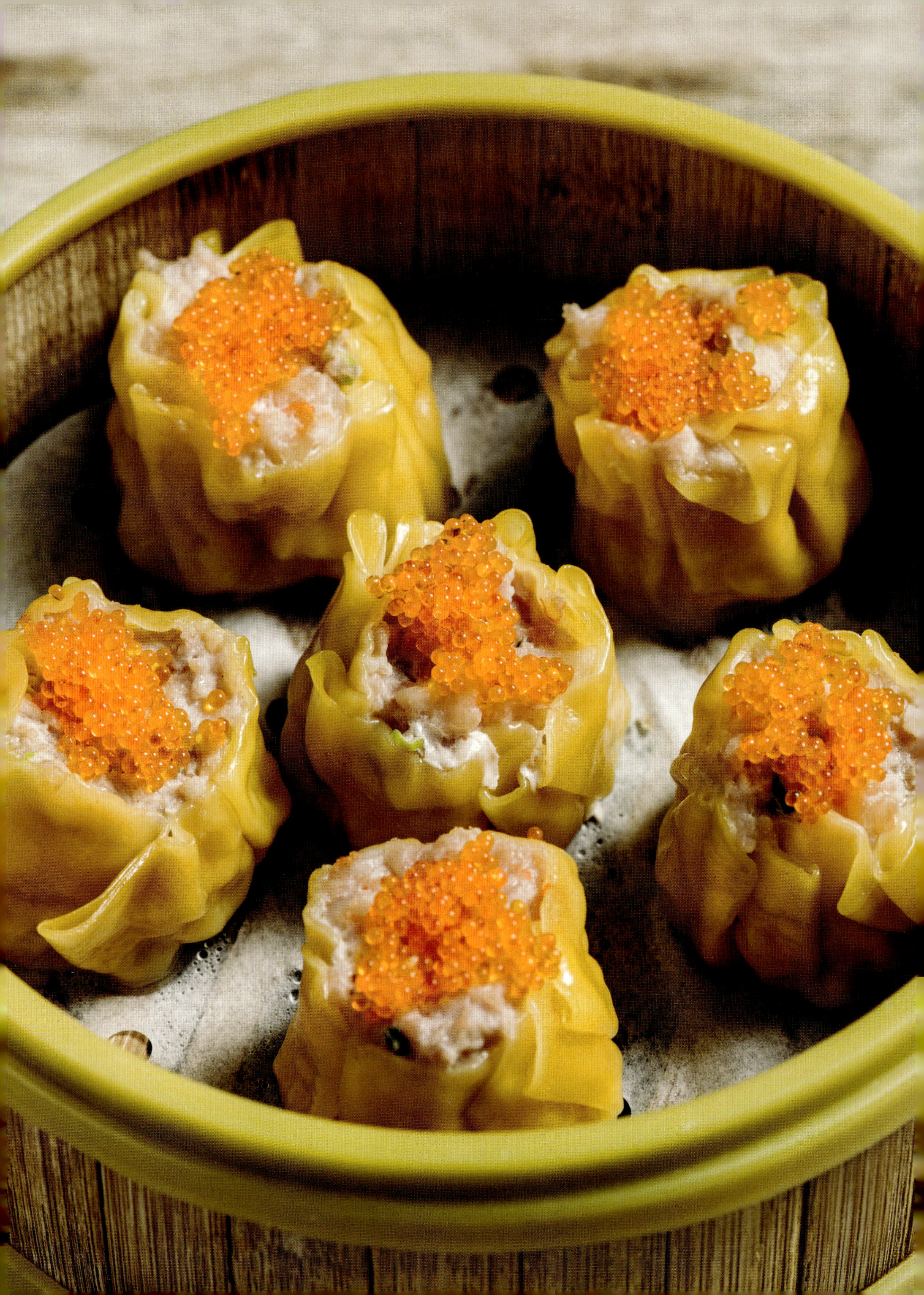

MAKES 20

PORK AND PRAWN SIU MAI

PORK AND PRAWN SIU MAI ARE A DIM SUM CLASSIC THAT BRINGS TOGETHER THE PERFECT BALANCE OF SAVOURY PORK AND SWEET, SUCCULENT PRAWNS (SHRIMP) WRAPPED IN A DELICATE WONTON SKIN. WHETHER YOU'RE SERVING IT AS AN APPETISER OR MAKING IT THE STAR OF YOUR MEAL, THIS RECIPE IS DESIGNED TO HELP YOU ACHIEVE THAT TENDER, JUICY FILLING WITH JUST THE RIGHT BURST OF FLAVOUR.

500 g (1 lb 2 oz) pork shoulder, finely diced

1 teaspoon salt

½ teaspoon sugar

150 g (5½ oz) prawns (shrimp), peeled, deveined and roughly chopped

100 g (3½ oz) pork lard

1 tablespoon potato starch

½ teaspoon white pepper

½ teaspoon YumYum or MSG

½ teaspoon chicken bouillon powder

1 tablespoon Shaoxing wine

2 teaspoons sesame oil

4 dried shiitake mushrooms, soaked until soft and finely chopped

8 small dried scallops, soaked until soft and shredded

20 wonton wrappers

4 tablespoons tobiko (flying fish roe)

In a large bowl, combine the diced pork shoulder, salt and sugar. Knead the mixture with your hands for about 7 minutes until the meat becomes sticky, or use a food processor or electric mixer for faster results. Add the prawns to the bowl and continue kneading for an additional 4 minutes until the mixture becomes sticky enough to form a ball. For added springiness, use the traditional 'Da Xian' dumpling technique: pick up the mixture and firmly throw it back into the bowl a few times.

Next, add the pork lard and potato starch, kneading until fully combined. Incorporate the white pepper, YumYum or MSG, chicken bouillon powder, Shaoxing wine, sesame oil, chopped mushrooms and shredded scallops into the mixture. Knead for another 3 minutes to ensure everything is evenly mixed. Cover the filling mixture with plastic wrap and refrigerate overnight to allow the flavours to develop.

When you're ready to assemble the siu mai, remove the chilled filling from the fridge. Use a rolling pin to flatten out the wonton wrappers a little, then trim them into octagon shapes. Place 1 tablespoon of filling in the centre of each wrapper. Form an 'O' shape with your thumb and first finger, placing the filled wrapper in the centre, and use a fork to gently press the filling into the hollow you've created, allowing the wrapper to fold upwards naturally to form the classic siu mai shape. Flatten the top of each siu mai with a butter knife and place them on a tray lined with baking paper.

Repeat the process with the remaining filling and wrappers to make about 20 siu mai. Line a steamer with baking paper, cutting holes in it to prevent condensation and sticking. Heat a large pot or wok with water until it begins to steam. Place the siu mai in the steamer, ensuring they aren't touching each other, and steam for 10–12 minutes until fully cooked. Serve the siu mai hot, garnished with tobiko. Any leftover cooked siu mai can be frozen in an airtight container for up to 2 weeks.

MAKES 30—40 DUMPLINGS

TRUFFLED CHICKEN AND ABALONE XIAO LONG BAO

THIS IS A LUXURIOUS TWIST ON THE CLASSIC SOUP DUMPLING. WITH TENDER CHICKEN, FLAVOURFUL ABALONE, AND A HINT OF AROMATIC TRUFFLE, EACH BITE OFFERS A DELICATE BALANCE OF SAVOURY AND INDULGENT FLAVOURS. THE CHICKEN STOCK CONTAINS CORDYCEPS AND MILK VETCH (ASTRAGALUS), TRADITIONALLY USED IN CHINESE MEDICINE TO BOOST IMMUNITY AND HEALTH. IT'S BELIEVED THAT THESE INGREDIENTS, SLOWLY SIMMERED, HELP NOURISH THE BODY. YOU CAN FIND THESE AT ANY CHINESE GROCER.

SMALL EATS

CHICKEN STOCK

4 chicken drumsticks, skin removed and reserved

4 chicken feet

4 litres water

15 goji berries

15 cordyceps

1 milk vetch root (astragalus)

2 slices of ginger

½ × 425 g (14 oz) tin abalone and juices

CHICKEN GEL

500 ml (17 fl oz/2 cups) Chicken stock (above)

2 teaspoons chicken bouillon powder

½ teaspoon YumYum or MSG

2 teaspoons agar-agar powder

CHICKEN FILLING

reserved chicken skin (above)

500 g (1 lb 2 oz) chicken mince

1 tablespoon sesame oil

2 tablespoons Shaoxing wine (Chinese cooking wine)

1 tablespoon truffle oil (optional)

1 teaspoon chicken bouillon powder

1 teaspoon YumYum or MSG

6 tablespoons Chicken stock (above)

¼ teaspoon salt

XIAO LONG BAO WRAPPERS

250 g (9 oz/2 cups) dumpling flour, or regular flour

pinch of salt (optional)

160 ml (5½ fl oz/⅔ cup) warm water (around 40–45°C/ 105–115°F)

In a pressure cooker, add the chicken drumsticks, chicken feet, and water. Cook on high pressure for 2 hours. Once the pressure releases, add the goji berries, cordyceps, milk vetch root, ginger slices, and abalone and juice. Simmer for an additional 30 minutes. Strain the stock, reserving the liquid. Set aside 500 ml (17 fl oz/2 cups) of stock for the chicken gel and use the remaining stock for the filling.

For the chicken gel, combine the reserved chicken stock with the chicken bouillon powder, YumYum or MSG and agar-agar powder in a pot. Whisk and bring the mixture to a high heat to boil. Remove from heat, pour into a tray, and refrigerate until set. Once firm, chop the gel finely for use in the filling.

For the chicken filling, render the chicken skin until crispy. Start by drying the skin thoroughly. Place a pan over medium–low heat and lay the skin flat in the cold pan. Cook slowly for 10–15 minutes, flipping occasionally, until the skin turns golden and crispy as the fat renders out. Remove the crispy skin and drain it on paper towels, then pour the rendered fat through a sieve into a small bowl. Once cooled, chop the crispy skin into small pieces and set aside.

In a large bowl, combine the chicken mince, rendered chicken fat, chopped chicken skin, sesame oil, Shaoxing wine, truffle oil (if using), chicken bouillon powder, YumYum or MSG, chicken stock and salt. Mix in one direction until the mixture becomes sticky and stringy in texture. Weigh the chicken mince mixture, then fold in an equal amount of the finely chopped chicken gel, mixing gently to combine.

To make the wrappers, combine the dumpling flour and salt (if using) in a large bowl. Gradually add warm water while stirring until a dough forms. Transfer to a floured surface and knead for 8–10 minutes until smooth and elastic. Cover with a damp cloth and let it rest for at least 30 minutes.

Once it has rested, divide the dough into two logs, each 2.5 cm (1 in) in diameter, and cut into small 10 g (¼ oz) pieces. Roll each piece into a thin, round wrapper, about 7–8 cm (3 in) in diameter, with the edges thinner than the centre. This ensures the centre is sturdy enough to hold the filling and the edges can be formed into delicate pleats – you can do this by using your rolling pin around the edges rather than rolling across the whole surface and stretching out the middle.

To assemble the xiao long bao, place a spoonful of chicken filling in the centre of each wrapper. Pleat the edges up over the filling and seal the dumplings in the classic xiao long bao shape, leaving a small hole in the centre (this allows steam to escape from the dumpling as it steams, preventing it from bursting). Line a steamer with baking paper or cabbage leaves, cutting holes in it to prevent condensation and sticking, and place the xiao long bao inside, ensuring they are not touching. Steam over boiling water for 8–10 minutes until cooked through. Serve hot with your favourite dipping sauces and enjoy!

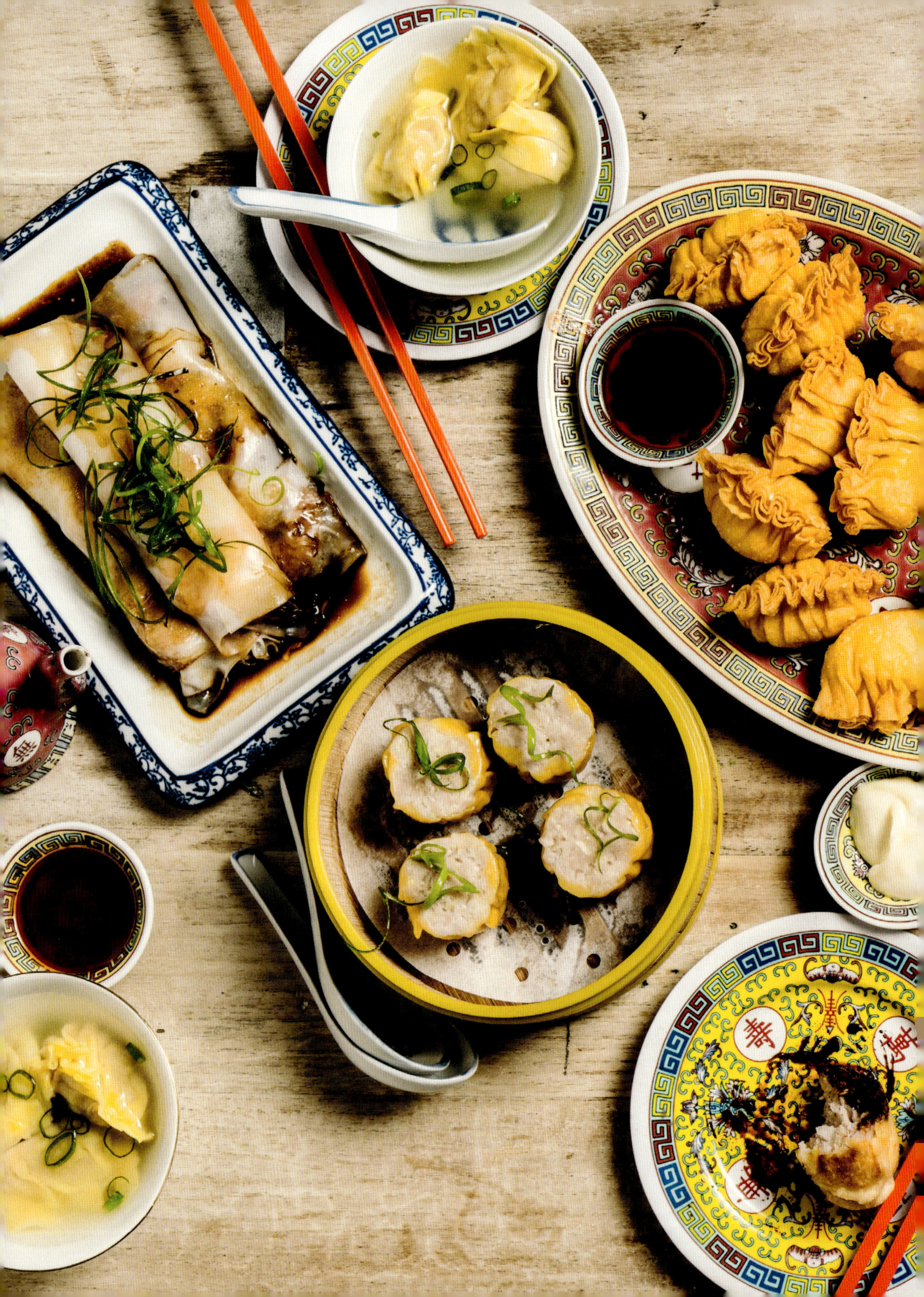

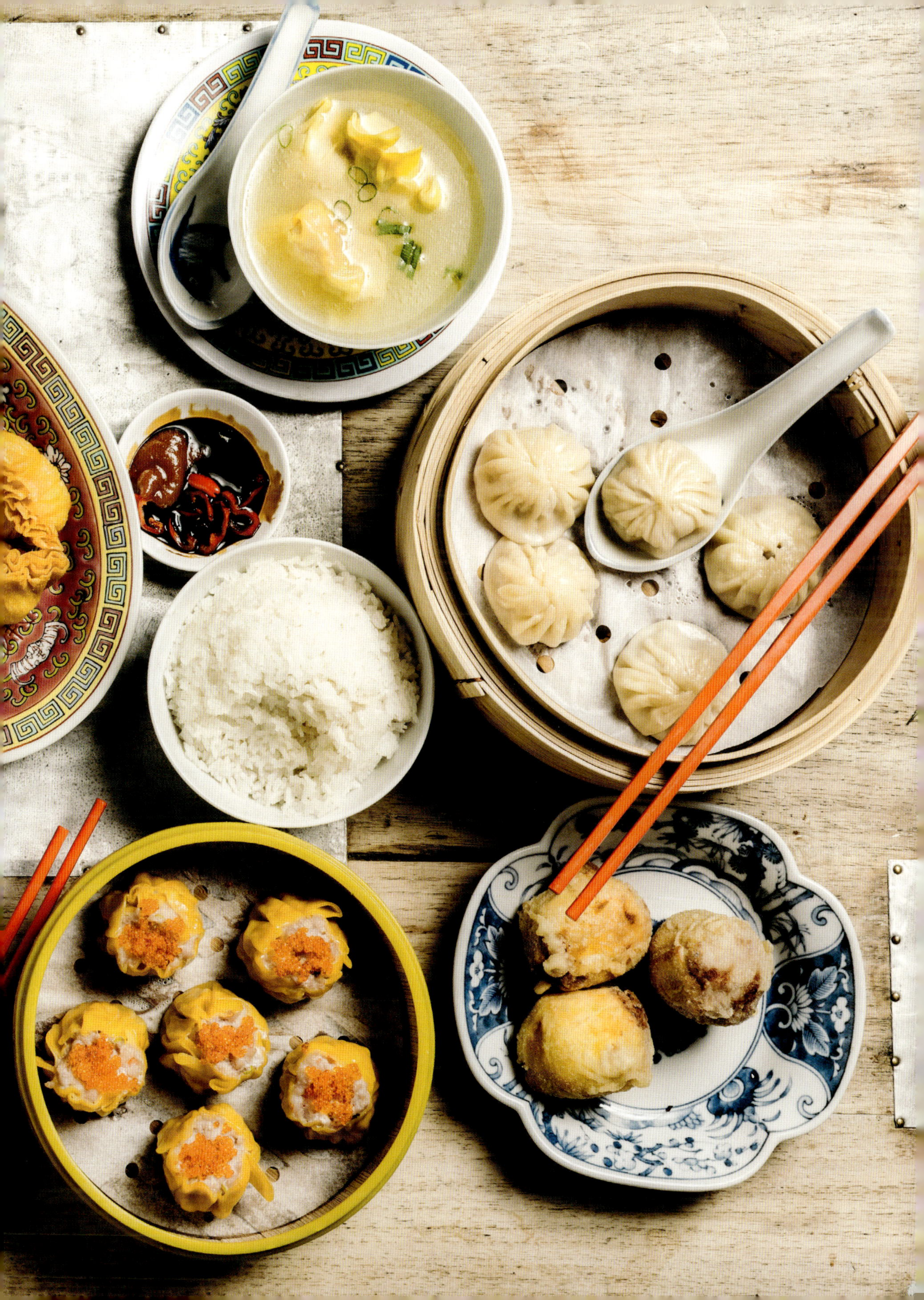

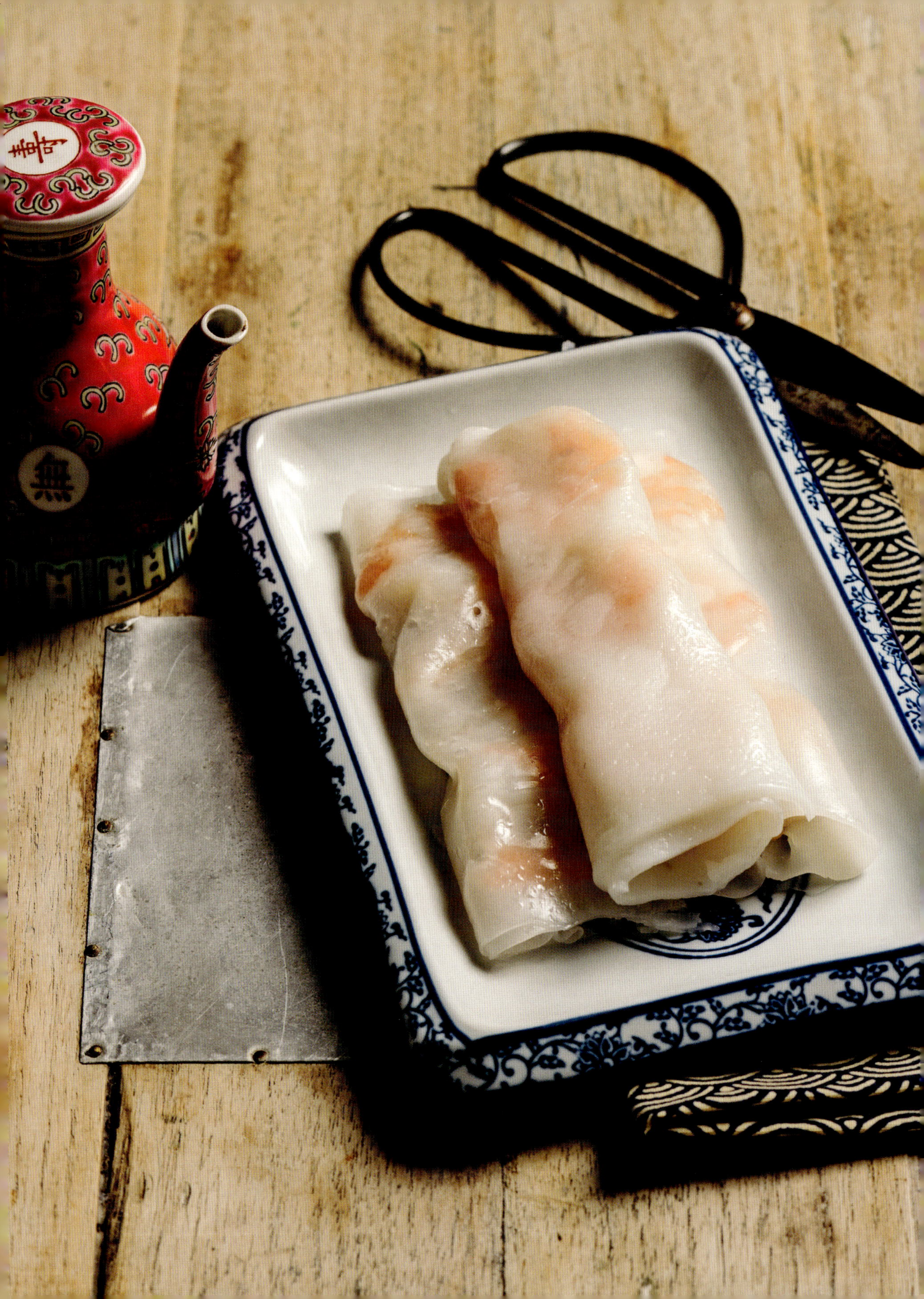
無

SERVES 4

PRAWN CHEUNG FUN

PRAWN CHEUNG FUN IS A DIM SUM STAPLE OF SILKY RICE NOODLES WRAPPED AROUND PLUMP, JUICY PRAWNS (SHRIMP). THIS RECIPE GIVES YOU THE CHEAT'S WAY TO MAKE THESE DELICIOUS ROLLS, PERFECT FOR RE-CREATING THAT AUTHENTIC DIM SUM EXPERIENCE AT HOME.

PRAWNS

16 prawns (shrimp), peeled and deveined

2 teaspoons cornflour (cornstarch)

½ teaspoon YumYum or MSG

pinch of salt

1 teaspoon sesame oil

RICE ROLLS

80 g (2¾ oz/½ cup) rice flour (regular, not glutinous)

50 g (1¾ oz/⅓ cup) cornflour (cornstarch)

1 tablespoon potato starch

pinch of salt

¼ teaspoon vegetable oil

340 ml (11½ fl oz/1⅓ cups) water

SAUCE

3 tablespoons light soy sauce

1 teaspoon YumYum or MSG

3 teaspoons sugar

1 teaspoon sesame oi

40 ml (1¼ fl oz) water

In a bowl, combine the prawns, cornflour, YumYum or MSG, salt and sesame oil. Mix until well combined, then set aside

For the rice rolls, in a large jug, whisk together the rice flour, cornflour, potato starch, salt, oil and water until the mixture is smooth and well combined.

Prepare a large wok, pot or steamer that fits a plate. Brush the plate with a thin layer of oil. Fill the wok, pot or steamer about a quarter full of water (approximately 4 cm/1½ in). Place the oiled plate on a small bowl inside the wok or steamer, ensuring the plate is level. Cover with a lid and heat until the water reaches a boil.

Once the water is boiling, uncover and pour enough rice roll batter onto the plate to cover the base in a thin layer. Tilt the plate to spread the batter evenly. Place 4 prawns in a row on one side of the rice roll. Cover with the lid and steam for 4 minutes, or until the prawns and rice roll are cooked through.

Uncover, then use a scraper or spatula to carefully roll up the rice noodle, starting from the prawn side. Lift the roll from the plate and transfer it to your serving plate. Repeat the process with the remaining batter and prawns.

For the sauce, combine the soy sauce, YumYum or MSG, sugar, sesame oil, and water in a small jug or bowl. Heat the sauce in the steamer for a few minutes, or microwave until warm. Pour the warm sauce over the prawn cheung fun before serving.

SMALL EATS

MAKES 20 DUMPLINGS

HAR GOW

PRAWN HAR GOW IS ANOTHER DIM SUM CLASSIC, KNOWN FOR ITS JUICY PRAWN (SHRIMP) FILLING WRAPPED IN A DELICATE SKIN. AFTER COUNTLESS TESTS, THIS RECIPE DELIVERS THE PERFECT CHEWY TEXTURE, PRODUCING DUMPLING WRAPPERS THAT STEAM UP BEAUTIFULLY TRANSLUCENT AND COMPLEMENT THE SUCCULENT PRAWNS INSIDE.

FILLING

200 g (7 oz) prawns (shrimp), peeled and deveined

1 teaspoon minced ginger

¼ teaspoon salt

½ teaspoon sugar

¼ teaspoon YumYum or MSG

2 teaspoons cornflour (cornstarch)

2 teaspoons pork lard or oil

1 teaspoon sesame oil

1 tablespoon Shaoxing wine (Chinese cooking wine)

WRAPPERS

50 g (1¾ oz/¼ cup) potato starch, plus 3 tablespoons extra

100 g (3½ oz/½ cup) wheat starch

2 teaspoons pork lard, room temperature

180 ml (6 fl oz/¾ cup) boiling water

Use the flat side of a cleaver or a food processor to mash the prawn meat until it's slightly chunky but not fully pureed. In a mixing bowl, combine the mashed prawns and ginger, stirring the mixture in one direction. Add the salt, sugar, YumYum or MSG and cornflour, continuing to stir in the same direction until well combined. Incorporate the lard, sesame oil and Shaoxing wine, stirring again until fully mixed. Cover the filling and refrigerate while preparing the wrapper dough.

For the wrapper dough, combine the 50 g potato starch, wheat starch and lard in a bowl. Pour the boiling hot water into the mixture, stirring quickly to combine. The dough will initially be sticky, but continue mixing until everything is well incorporated. Sprinkle the remaining 3 tablespoons potato starch onto a clean work surface and knead it into the hot dough until it is fully absorbed. Divide the dough in half, rolling each portion into a log about 2 cm (¾ in) in diameter. While working with one log, keep the other in a ziplock bag somewhere warm to prevent it drying out.

Slice each log into 10 equal pieces, each weighing about 10 g (¼ oz), for a total of 20 portions. Keep the dough portions covered with plastic wrap to prevent them drying out. Take one portion, roll it into a ball, then flatten it on a silicone mat. Use a rolling pin to roll the dough into a thin wrapper about 7 cm (2¾ in) in diameter. Place 15 g (½ oz) of filling in the centre of each wrapper.

Fold the dumpling in half to create a half-moon shape. Make pleats along the folded edge, pressing each pleat firmly with your fingers to seal the dumpling. Continue pleating until you've created 9–10 pleats or until the dumpling is fully sealed. Pinch the along the pleated edge to gently curve the edge to form the classic har gow shape. Repeat the process for the remaining dumplings, keeping them covered to prevent them drying out.

Prepare a steamer by placing an oiled sheet of baking paper inside. Wrap a tea (dish) towel around the lid to catch any condensation. Place the dumplings on the oiled baking paper, leaving about 1.5 cm (½ in) between each dumpling.

Steam the dumplings over boiling water for 8–10 minutes, or until the wrappers become translucent and the filling is fully cooked. Once steamed, remove the dumplings from the steamer and serve immediately with your favourite dipping sauces.

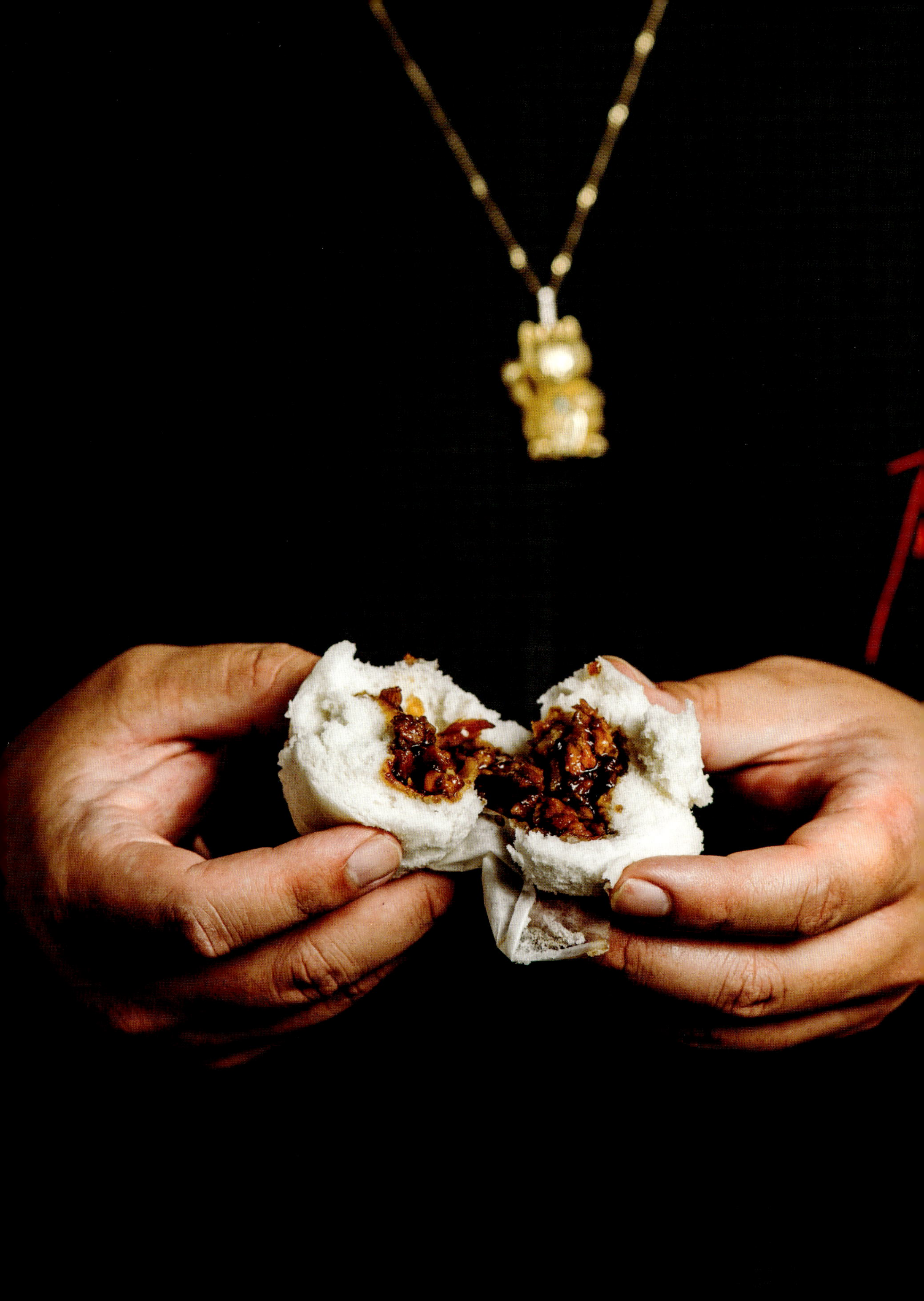

MAKES 20 BUNS

CHAR SIU BAO

CHAR SIU BAO, OR BBQ PORK BUNS, ARE A BELOVED DIM SUM DISH — TENDER, SWEET-SAVOURY CHAR SIU PORK WRAPPED IN A SOFT, FLUFFY STEAMED BUN. THESE DELICIOUS BUNS ARE PERFECT FOR BREAKFAST, AS A SNACK OR AS PART OF YOUR DIM SUM SPREAD.

BUN DOUGH

600 g (21 oz/5 cups) steamed bun flour
120 g (4½ oz) sugar
pinch of salt
300 ml (10 fl oz/1¼ cups) warm water
7 g (¼ oz/2½ teaspoons) instant yeast
1 teaspoon sugar
60 g (2 oz) shortening or pork lard, melted

FILLING

Easy char siu pork (page 179)
120 ml (4 fl oz/½ cup) water
1 heaped tablespoon cornflour (cornstarch)
1 tablespoon sugar
2 tablespoons oyster sauce

In a large bowl, combine the bun flour, sugar and salt. In a jug, mix the warm water, yeast and 1 teaspoon of sugar until the yeast dissolves. Add the wet ingredients to the dry mixture, stirring until a smooth dough forms. Once combined, incorporate the melted shortening or lard, kneading the dough until smooth and elastic.

Shape the dough into a ball, place it back in the mixing bowl, and cover with plastic wrap or a damp tea (dish) towel. Let it sit in a warm spot for 1–2 hours, or until it doubles in size. While the dough is rising, chop the char siu pork into small pieces.

Combine the water, cornflour, sugar and oyster sauce in a saucepan over medium heat. Add the chopped pork, stirring until the sauce thickens. Once done, remove the filling from the heat and refrigerate until completely cooled.

When the dough has doubled in size, punch out the air and knead it briefly. Divide the dough into 20 portions, each weighing about 50 g (1¾ oz). Line a baking tray with baking paper. Take each dough portion, flatten it into a circle, and place a tablespoon of the chilled filling in the centre. Gather the edges and pinch them at the top to seal the bun.

Place the filled buns on the lined tray. Cover the buns with plastic wrap or a damp tea (dish) towel and let them rest for 30 minutes. Line a steamer with baking paper, cutting holes in the paper to prevent condensation and sticking. Heat a large pot or wok with 4 cm (1½ in) of water in the bottom until it begins to steam. Working in batches, place the pork buns in the steamer, ensuring they aren't touching each other, and steam over high heat for 10 minutes until fully cooked and fluffy.

MAKES 6

SAN CHOY BAO

TRADITIONAL SAN CHOY BAO IS A CLASSIC IN CHINESE CUISINE, BELOVED FOR ITS REFRESHING CRUNCH AND SAVOURY FLAVOURS. IT'S TYPICALLY MADE WITH MINCED CHICKEN OR PORK, CRUNCHY WATER CHESTNUTS AND FRESH BEAN SPROUTS, ALL WRAPPED IN CRISP LETTUCE LEAVES – THE PERFECT PLAY OF TEXTURES AND FLAVOUR!

2 dried shiitake mushrooms
2 tablespoons vegetable oil
1 tablespoon minced ginger
1 garlic clove, minced
200 g (7 oz) chicken thigh, cut into 1 cm (½ in) cubes
1 king oyster mushroom, roughly chopped
45 g (1½ oz/½ cup) fresh bean sprouts
100 g (3½ oz) water chestnuts, finely diced
15 g (½ oz/¼ cup) finely sliced spring onions (scallions)
handful of coriander (cilantro) sprigs
6 small iceberg lettuce leaves

SAUCE

1 tablespoon light soy sauce
1 teaspoon white sugar
¼ teaspoon YumYum or MSG
2 tablespoons Shaoxing wine (Chinese cooking wine)
1 teaspoon oyster sauce
¼ teaspoon sesame oil

Soak the shiitake mushrooms in hot water for 30 minutes, then drain and chop them roughly. Heat the vegetable oil in a large wok or frying pan over medium–high heat. Add the minced ginger and garlic, stir-frying for about 30 seconds until fragrant.

Next, add the chicken to the wok, breaking it up with a spatula, and cook until it is browned and fully cooked. Stir in the sauce ingredients, mixing well to coat the chicken evenly with the sauce.

Add the soaked and chopped shiitake mushrooms, king oyster mushrooms, bean sprouts and water chestnuts to the wok. Stir-fry for an additional 2–3 minutes until the vegetables are tender and everything is heated through. Finally, stir in the finely sliced spring onions and coriander; cook for 1 minute more.

Remove the pan from the heat and spoon the mixture into the prepared lettuce leaves. Serve immediately.

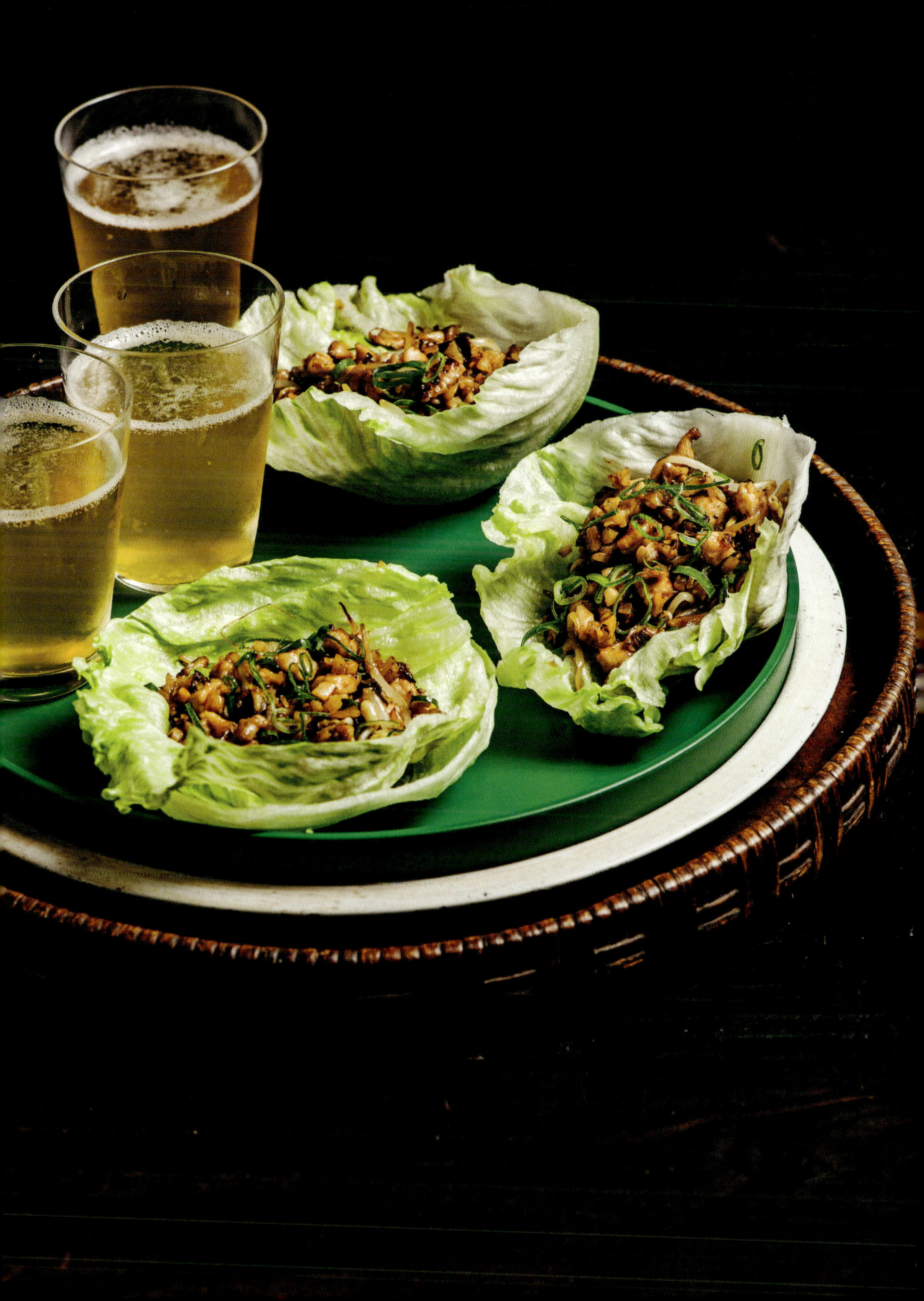

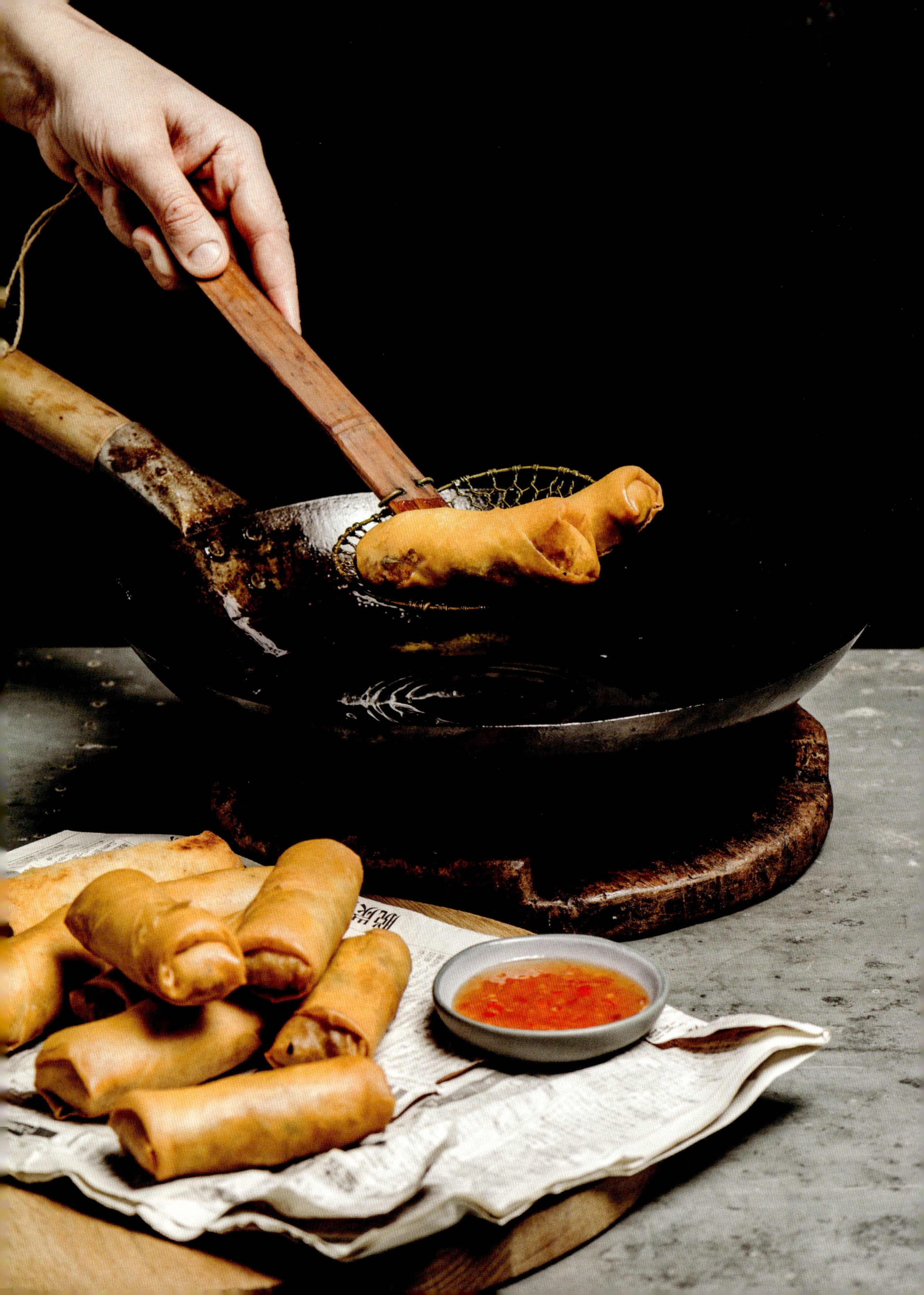

MAKES 16

PORK SPRING ROLLS

FILLED WITH A SAVOURY MIX OF PORK, VEGETABLES AND VERMICELLI, THESE CRISPY SPRING ROLLS ARE A DELIGHTFUL ADDITION TO ANY MEAL. SERVE THEM HOT WITH YOUR FAVOURITE DIPPING SAUCE FOR A SATISFYING CRUNCH AND A JUICY BURST OF FLAVOUR.

10 wood ear mushrooms
2 bundles mung bean vermicelli
500 g (1 lb 2 oz) pork mince
1 carrot, grated
8 garlic cloves, minced
1 spring onion (scallion), thinly sliced
1 tablespoon chicken bouillon powder
1 teaspoon YumYum or MSG
1 teaspoon sugar
½ teaspoon salt
¼ teaspoon black pepper
1 tablespoon Shaoxing wine (Chinese cooking wine)
1 tablespoon oyster sauce
1 tablespoon sesame oil
1 tablespoon potato starch
1 pack spring roll wrappers (approx. 275 g/9½ oz)
vegetable oil, for deep-frying

Soak the wood ear mushrooms and mung bean vermicelli in separate bowls of hot water for 15 minutes. Drain, then thinly slice the wood ear mushrooms and roughly chop the mung bean vermicelli. In a large bowl, combine the pork mince, grated carrot, soaked and sliced wood ear mushrooms, chopped mung bean vermicelli, minced garlic and thinly sliced spring onion. Add the chicken bouillon powder, YumYum or MSG, sugar, salt, black pepper, Shaoxing wine, oyster sauce, sesame oil and potato starch to the mixture. Mix everything thoroughly until the filling is well combined and slightly sticky.

Lay a spring roll wrapper flat on a clean surface, with one corner pointing towards you to form a diamond shape. Place a spoonful of the filling mixture near the bottom corner of the wrapper. Fold the bottom corner over the filling, then fold in the sides tightly. Roll the wrapper upwards, keeping it snug around the filling. Wet the top corner of the wrapper with a little water to seal the spring roll.

Repeat the process with the remaining wrappers and filling. Wrap any remaining spring roll wrappers in plastic wrap and reserve in the freezer for next time.

Fill a wok, deep fryer or large pot halfway full with vegetable oil and heat to 180°C (350°F) over medium–high heat. You can also test the oil with a wooden chopstick – if bubbles form around it when lowered in, the oil is hot enough. Fry the spring rolls in batches, making sure not to overcrowd the pot. Fry for 3–5 minutes, or until golden brown and crispy. Use a slotted spoon to remove the spring rolls from the oil, and drain them on paper towels. Serve hot with your favourite dipping sauce.

MAKES 40

DIM SIMS

DIM SIMS, A BELOVED STAPLE IN AUSTRALIAN-CHINESE CUISINE, COME IN TWO DELICIOUS VARIETIES: FRIED AND STEAMED. THESE DUMPLINGS ARE FILLED WITH A SAVOURY MIXTURE OF PORK AND CABBAGE, OFFERING A CRISPY CRUNCH WHEN FRIED OR A SOFT, JUICY BITE WHEN STEAMED. A MUST-HAVE AT ANY CLASSIC AUSSIE-CHINESE RESTAURANT.

2 cups (approx. 3–4 leaves) finely chopped green cabbage

½ onion, diced

500 g (1 lb 2 oz) pork mince

1 egg

1 teaspoon chicken bouillon powder

1 teaspoon YumYum or MSG

½ teaspoon sugar

1 teaspoon salt

½ teaspoon white pepper

1 teaspoon sesame oil

2 tablespoons cornflour (cornstarch)

40 wonton wrappers

vegetable oil, for deep-frying (optional)

In a large bowl, combine the finely chopped cabbage, onion and pork mince. Add the egg, chicken bouillon powder, YumYum or MSG, sugar, salt, white pepper, sesame oil and cornflour. Mix the filling in one direction until it is well combined and streaks begin to form along the edge of the bowl. For added springiness, use the traditional 'Da Xian' dumpling technique: pick up the mixture and firmly throw it back into the bowl a few times.

Using a rolling pin, slightly flatten the wonton wrappers to make them about 1 cm (½ in) larger, then trim the wrappers into an octagon shape with a knife. Place a tablespoon of the filling in the centre of each wonton wrapper. To shape the dim sims, form an 'O' shape with your thumb and first finger, placing the filled wrapper in the centre, and use a fork to gently press the filling into the hollow you've created, allowing the wrapper to fold upwards naturally to form the classic dim sim shape.

Flatten the top of each dim sim with a butter knife and place them on a tray lined with baking paper. Repeat this process with the remaining filling and wrappers until all the dim sims are formed.

To steam the dim sims, prepare a steamer and line it with baking paper to prevent sticking. Place the dim sims inside the steamer, ensuring there is some space between each one. Steam the dim sims over boiling water for 10–12 minutes, or until the pork is fully cooked and the wrappers are tender.

Alternatively, for fried dim sims, fill a deep fryer or large pot halfway full with vegetable oil and bring it to 180°C (350°F) over medium–high heat. You can also test the oil with a wooden chopstick – if bubbles form around it when lowered in, the oil is hot enough. Fry the dim sims in batches, being careful not to overcrowd the pot. Cook for 3–4 minutes, or until they are golden brown and crispy. Remove the dim sims with a slotted spoon and drain them on a wire rack or paper towels.

Serve the dim sims hot with your favourite dipping sauce.

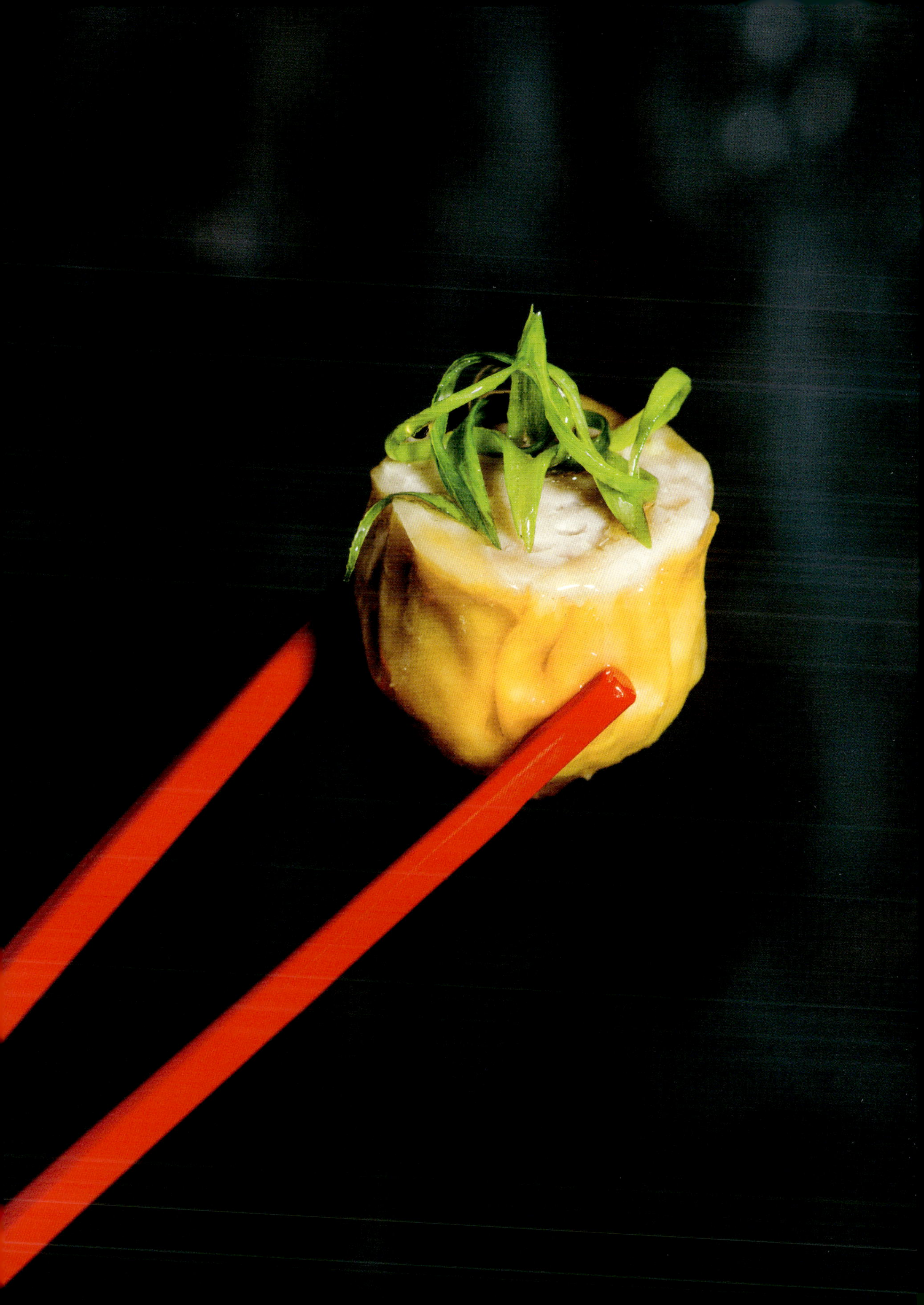

SOUP

SERVES 4

ABC SOUP

ABC SOUP IS A SIMPLE AND COMFORTING CHINESE SOUP MADE WITH BASIC INGREDIENTS LIKE POTATOES, CARROTS, TOMATOES, AND SOMETIMES CHICKEN OR PORK. IT'S A STAPLE IN MANY ASIAN HOUSEHOLDS, LOVED FOR ITS LIGHT YET FLAVOURFUL BROTH THAT'S PERFECT ANY TIME OF THE DAY.

300 g (10½ oz) pork ribs or chicken thighs

3 litres (101 fl oz/12 cups) water or chicken broth

3 large tomatoes, quartered

2 carrots, peeled and cut into 4 cm (1½ in) chunks

1 large potato, peeled and cut into 4 cm (1½ in) chunks

1 large onion, quartered

2 corn cobs, cut into thirds

2 teaspoons YumYum or MSG

3 tablespoons chicken bouillon powder

2 teaspoons sugar

2 teaspoons salt

Bring a pot of water to a boil and blanch the pork ribs or chicken thighs for 2–3 minutes to remove impurities. Once blanched, drain the water and set the meat aside.

Put the 3 litres of water or chicken broth in a large pot and bring it to a boil. Add the blanched pork ribs or chicken thighs, along with the tomatoes, carrots, potato, onion and corn.

Reduce the heat to low, cover the pot, and let the soup simmer for about 1.5 to 2 hours, until the vegetables are tender and the meat is fully cooked through.

Season the soup with YumYum or MSG, chicken bouillon powder, sugar and salt. Serve the ABC soup hot.

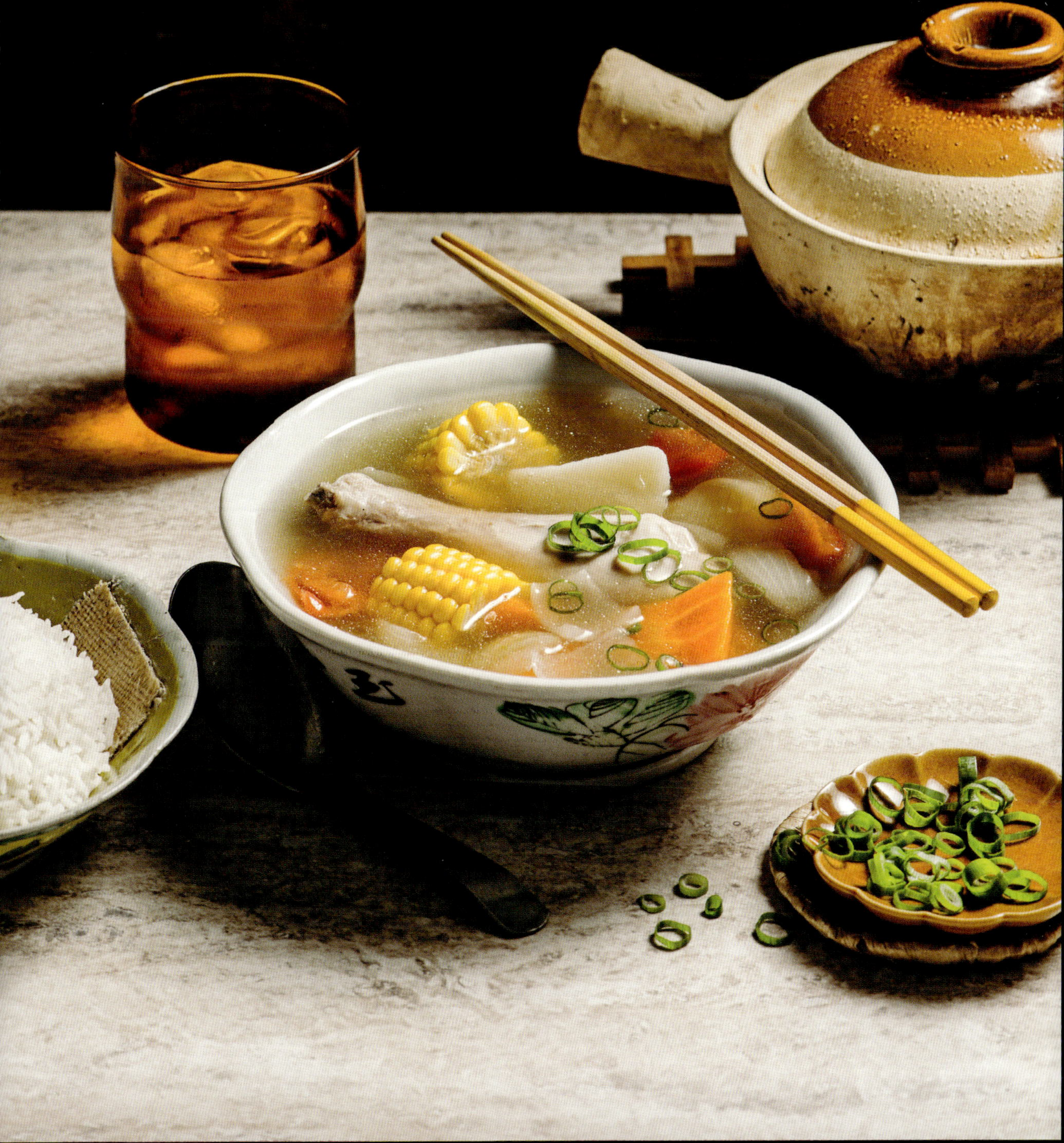

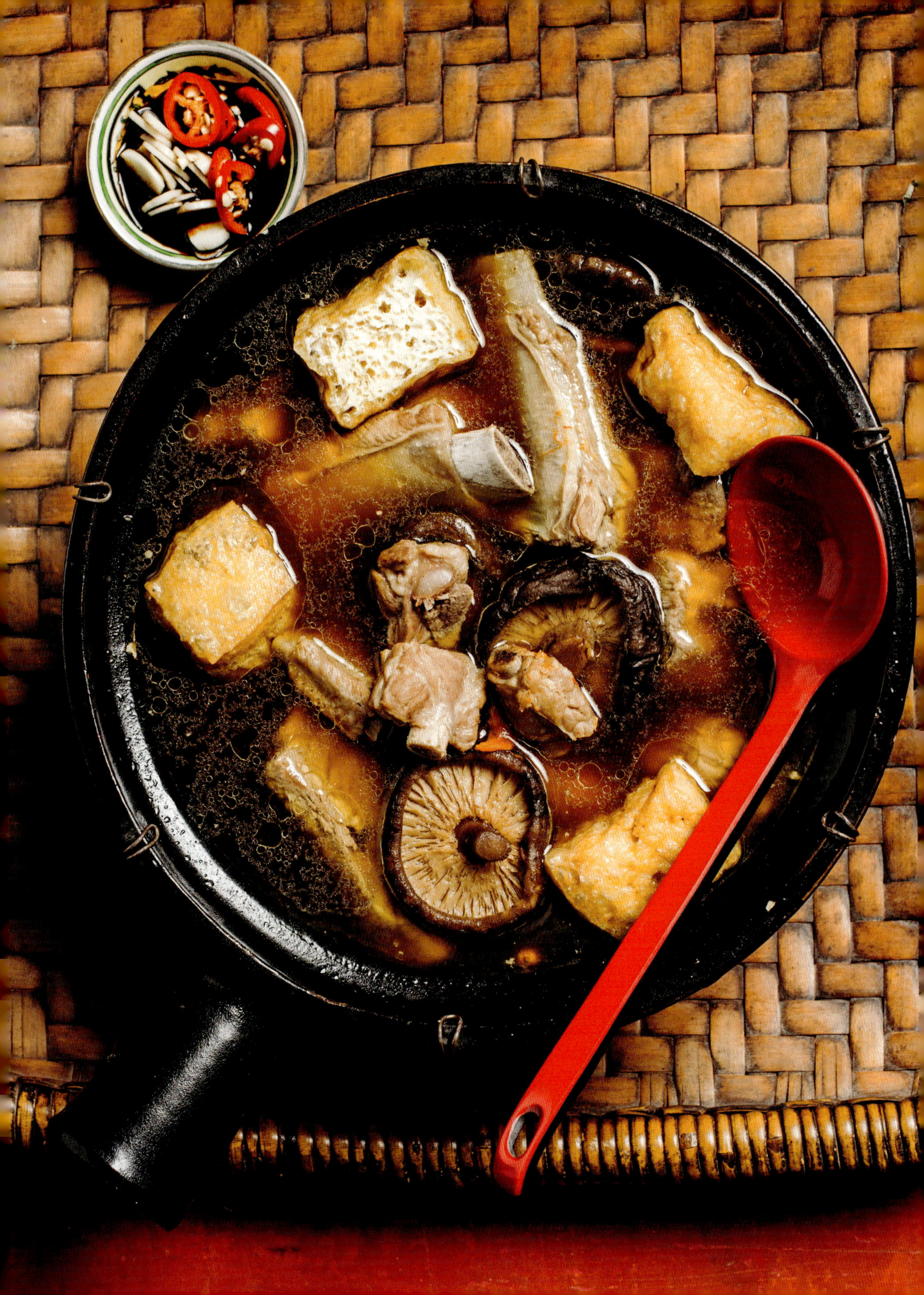

SERVES 4

BAK KUT TEH

BAK KUT TEH (PORK BONE TEA) IS A POPULAR CHINESE HERBAL SOUP MADE WITH TENDER PORK RIBS, SIMMERED IN A RICH BROTH INFUSED WITH AROMATIC HERBS AND SPICES. OFTEN ENJOYED AS A COMFORTING MEAL, IT'S KNOWN FOR ITS DEEP, EARTHY FLAVOURS AND IS A FAVOURITE IN MALAYSIA AND SINGAPORE. THE FOUNDATION OF BAK KUT TEH IS A HERBAL MIX MADE UP OF SOLOMON'S SEAL RHIZOME, STAR ANISE, CLOVES, FENNEL, PEPPERCORN, DATES, GOJI BERRIES, CODONOPSIS ROOT AND REHMANNIA – AND IS AVAILABLE AS A PREMIX AT ASIAN GROCERY STORES.

---

8 dried shiitake mushrooms

2 litres (68 fl oz/8 cups) water, plus extra for blanching

500 g (1 lb 2 oz) pork ribs, cut into small pieces

1 packet of herbal bak kut teh premix

1 packet tofu puffs (approx. 15 pieces), each puff torn in half

1 whole garlic clove

25 g (1 oz/¼ cup) goji berries

1 piece cane rock sugar (approx. 12 g/½ oz)

2 tablespoons dark soy sauce

2 tablespoons light soy sauce

½ teaspoon pepper

salt, to taste

Soak the shiitake mushrooms in hot water for 15 minutes. Fill a large pot with water and bring to a boil. Add the pork ribs and blanch them for 3–4 minutes until they are half-cooked. Once blanched, strain the pork ribs and rinse them under fresh water to remove any impurities.

Fill the pot with another 2 litres of water and bring it to a boil. Add the bak kut teh premix, blanched pork ribs, soaked shiitake mushrooms, tofu puffs, whole garlic clove and goji berries. Cover the pot, reduce the heat to low, and let the soup simmer for about 2 hours. This allows the flavours to meld together and the pork ribs to become tender.

After the soup has simmered for 2 hours, add the rock sugar, dark soy sauce, light soy sauce and pepper. Stir the soup well, adjusting the seasoning with salt to taste.

Let the soup simmer for an additional 5 minutes to fully incorporate the flavours. Serve the bak kut teh hot.

SERVES 2

CHICKEN SWEET CORN SOUP

CHICKEN SWEET CORN SOUP IS A COMFORTING AND CREAMY CHINESE FAVOURITE MADE WITH TENDER CHICKEN AND SWEET CORN. IT'S A SIMPLE YET FLAVOURFUL DISH THAT'S PERFECT AS A STARTER OR A WARMING MEAL ON A COOL DAY.

750 ml (25½ fl oz/3 cups) Chicken stock (page 32 or shop-bought)
240 ml (8 fl oz/1 cup) water
1 tin (400 g/14 oz) creamed corn
100 g (3½ oz) cooked shredded chicken breast
40 g (1½ oz) potato starch
60 ml (2 fl oz/¼ cup) water
1 egg, lightly beaten
1 teaspoon sesame oil
¼ teaspoon white pepper
salt, to taste
spring onion (scallion), finely chopped, to garnish

In a large pot, bring the chicken stock and water to a boil over medium heat. Once it reaches a rolling boil, stir in the creamed corn, allowing the soup to come back to a gentle simmer. This will help incorporate the sweetness from the corn into the broth.

Next, add the shredded cooked chicken breast to the pot and simmer for 2–3 minutes, just until the chicken is heated through.

In a separate small bowl, combine the potato starch and 60 ml water to create a slurry. Slowly drizzle the slurry into the soup while stirring constantly to help thicken it slightly and create a smooth texture.

Reduce the heat to low. While stirring the soup in a circular motion, gradually pour in the beaten egg to form delicate ribbons throughout the broth. This step adds richness and body to the soup.

Season the soup with sesame oil, white pepper and salt to taste, adjusting the seasoning as needed. Once everything is well combined, remove the soup from the heat.

Ladle the hot chicken sweet corn soup into bowls and garnish with finely chopped spring onion. Serve immediately.

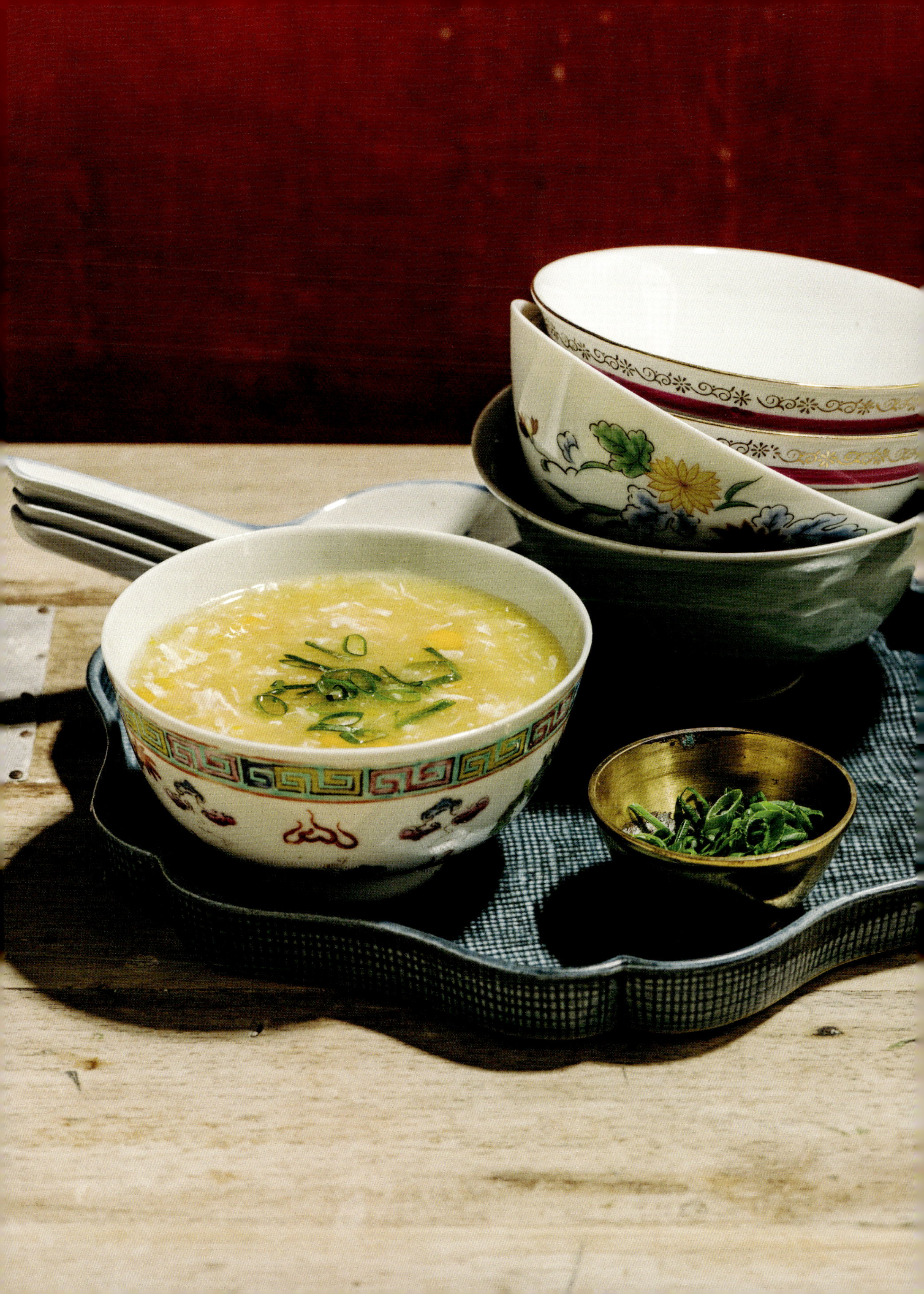

SERVES 4

HOT AND SOUR SOUP

HOT AND SOUR SOUP IS A BOLD, FLAVOURFUL DISH THAT HAS THE PERFECT BALANCE OF TANGY VINEGAR AND SPICY PEPPER. POPULAR IN CHINESE CUISINE, IT'S FILLED WITH INGREDIENTS LIKE TOFU, MUSHROOMS AND BAMBOO SHOOTS, MAKING IT A HEARTY AND SATISFYING SOUP.

PORK

100 g (3½ oz) pork shoulder, thinly sliced

1 tablespoon water

pinch of salt

2 teaspoons vegetable oil

1 teaspoon cornflour (cornstarch)

SOUP

3 dried lily flowers, halved lengthways

3 dried wood ear mushrooms

3 dried shiitake mushrooms

1 litre (34 fl oz/4 cups) Chicken stock (page 32 or shop-bought)

1 piece spiced dry tofu, thinly sliced into strips

2 bamboo shoots, thinly sliced

½ teaspoon chilli flakes (optional)

2 teaspoons sugar

½ teaspoon white pepper (or to taste)

1 tablespoon dark soy sauce

2 teaspoons light soy sauce

1 teaspoon sesame oil

1 tablespoon red vinegar

2 teaspoons Chinkiang vinegar (black vinegar)

1 tablespoon doubanjiang (spicy bean paste)

1 tablespoon potato starch

120 ml (4 fl oz/½ cup) water

50 g (1¾ oz) fresh firm tofu, thinly sliced into strips

1 large egg, lightly beaten

TO SERVE

spring onion (scallion), finely chopped, to garnish

coriander sprigs, to garnish

Soak the dried lily flowers, wood ear mushrooms and shiitake mushrooms in separate bowls of hot water for 15 minutes, then drain and finely slice.

In a small bowl, combine the thinly sliced pork shoulder with the water, salt, vegetable oil and cornflour. Mix well, ensuring the pork is evenly coated, and set it aside to marinate for 10–15 minutes.

In a large pot, bring the chicken stock to a boil over medium–high heat. Once boiling, add the rehydrated and sliced dried lily flowers, wood ear mushrooms and shiitake mushrooms, the spiced dry tofu, bamboo shoots, and chilli flakes (if using). Lower the heat to medium and let the soup simmer for 5 minutes, allowing the flavours to meld together.

After simmering, add the marinated pork slices to the pot and cook for another 2–3 minutes, or until the pork is just cooked through.

Season the soup with sugar, white pepper, dark soy sauce, light soy sauce, sesame oil, red vinegar, Chinkiang vinegar and doubanjiang. Stir the soup well to combine all the flavours.

In a separate small bowl, mix the potato starch with the water to make a slurry. Slowly pour the slurry into the soup, stirring constantly until the soup thickens to your desired consistency. Add the firm tofu to the soup.

Reduce the heat to low. Slowly drizzle the beaten egg into the soup while gently stirring in a circular motion to create delicate egg ribbons.

Once the egg is set, garnish the soup with finely chopped spring onion and coriander sprigs. Serve the hot and sour soup immediately for the best flavour.

SERVES 6

PORK RIB SOUP

CHINESE PORK RIB SOUP IS A COMFORTING AND FLAVOURFUL DISH, MADE BY SIMMERING TENDER PORK SOFT BONES. PORK SOFT BONES ARE A CUT OF PORK RIB THAT CONTAIN MORE CARTILAGE, PERFECT FOR BOILING DOWN IN SOUPS AS THEY BECOME SOFT AND ALMOST GELATINOUS. KNOWN FOR ITS NOURISHING QUALITIES, THIS LIGHT YET SAVOURY SOUP IS A STAPLE IN MANY ASIAN HOUSEHOLDS, OFTEN ENJOYED AS A SOOTHING MEAL THAT'S BOTH HEARTY AND HEALTHY.

water for blanching, plus 2½ litres (85 fl oz/10 cups) for the soup

750 g (25½ fl oz) pork soft bones

1 teaspoon whole black peppercorns

1 teaspoon whole white peppercorns

1 medium daikon radish, cut into chunks

25 g (1 oz/¼ cup) goji berries

6 large red dates

2 teaspoons YumYum or MSG

1 tablespoon pork bouillon powder

2 teaspoons sugar

2 teaspoons salt

In a large pot, bring about 3 litres (101 fl oz/12 cups) of water (or enough to generously cover the pork bones) to a boil over high heat. Once the water is boiling, add the pork soft bones and blanch them for 3–4 minutes to remove impurities. Drain the pork bones and rinse them under cold water to clean them thoroughly.

Refill the pot with the 2½ litres of water and bring it to a boil. Once boiling, add the blanched pork soft bones, whole black peppercorns, whole white peppercorns, daikon radish, goji berries and red dates.

Lower the heat to a gentle simmer, cover the pot, and let the soup cook for 2–3 hours. This slow cooking process will allow the flavours to develop and the pork bones to become tender.

When the soup has finished simmering, season it with YumYum or MSG, pork bouillon powder, sugar and salt. Stir well to combine then taste the soup, adjusting the seasoning as needed.

Serve the soup hot.

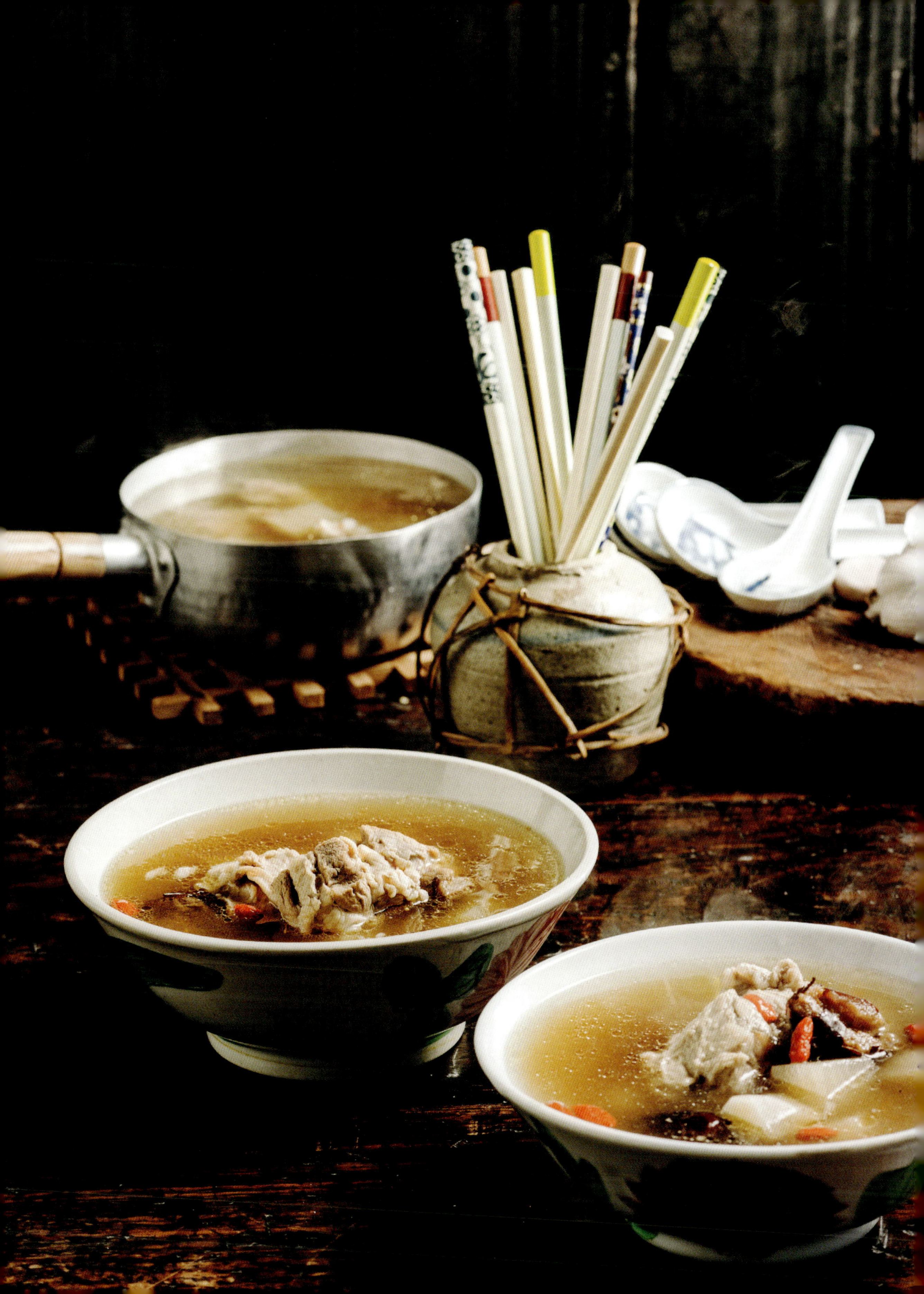

SERVES 4–5

BRAISED BEEF NOODLE SOUP

BRAISED BEEF NOODLE SOUP IS A HEARTY AND FLAVOURFUL DISH, FEATURING TENDER BEEF SLOW-COOKED IN A RICH BROTH INFUSED WITH SPICES AND SOY SAUCE. THIS COMFORTING BOWL OF NOODLES IS A SATISFYING MEAL, LOVED FOR ITS DEEP, SAVOURY FLAVOURS AND MELT-IN-YOUR-MOUTH BEEF.

72

SOUP

SOUP

1.5 kg (3 lb 5 oz) beef shin, cut into 5 cm (2 in) chunks

1 tablespoon red oil

1 × 5 cm (2 in) piece ginger, smashed

3 garlic cloves, smashed

2 spring onions (scallions), cut into 5 cm (2 in) segments

1 onion, cut into wedges

1 tomato, cut into wedges

2 dried chillies, torn in half

2 teaspoons tomato paste (concentrated puree)

1 tablespoon doubanjiang (spicy bean paste)

1 teaspoon sugar

60 ml (2 fl oz/¼ cup) light soy sauce

60 ml (2 fl oz/¼ cup) Shaoxing wine (Chinese cooking wine)

1 litre (34 fl oz/4 cups) water

1 lu bao (Chinese aromatic herb packet) or homemade spice sachet (see below)

TO SERVE

450 g (1 lb) fresh wheat noodles

3 heads of bok choy (pak choy)

coriander (cilantro), finely chopped

spring onions (scallions), finely chopped

pickled mustard greens, thinly sliced, to taste

HOMEMADE SPICE SACHET

(if not using shop-bought lu bao)

2 star anise

1 Chinese cinnamon stick (cassia)

2 bay leaves

2 teaspoons fennel seeds

2 teaspoons cumin seeds

2 teaspoons coriander seeds

1 tablespoon Sichuan peppercorns

¼ teaspoon Chinese five-spice

¼ teaspoon black pepper

Bring a large pot of water to a boil and add the beef shin chunks. Blanch them for 5 minutes to remove impurities, then drain and rinse the beef under cold water. Set aside.

In a large pot, heat the oil over medium heat. Add the smashed ginger, garlic, spring onions, onion, tomato and chillies, and stir-fry for 3–4 minutes until fragrant and the onions become translucent. Stir in the tomato paste, doubanjiang and sugar, cooking for an additional 2 minutes.

Return the blanched beef chunks to the pot and pour in the soy sauce, Shaoxing wine and water. Stir to combine. Add the lu bao or make a homemade spice sachet by wrapping the spices in a piece of cheesecloth and tying it up tightly. Bring the mixture to a boil, then reduce the heat to low, cover, and simmer for 2–3 hours until the beef is tender. Add more water if the water level reduces too much while simmering.

Once the beef is tender, remove it from the pot and slice it thinly. Set the sliced beef aside and cover with foil to keep warm.

About 10 minutes before serving, bring a large pot of water to a boil. Add the fresh wheat noodles and cook according to the package instructions. Drain and set them aside. In the same pot, blanch the bok choy for 1–2 minutes until just tender, then drain and set it aside.

To serve, divide the cooked noodles among serving bowls and ladle the hot broth over them. Top each bowl with the sliced beef and add a small handful of bok choy. Garnish with finely chopped coriander, spring onions and pickled mustard greens to taste.

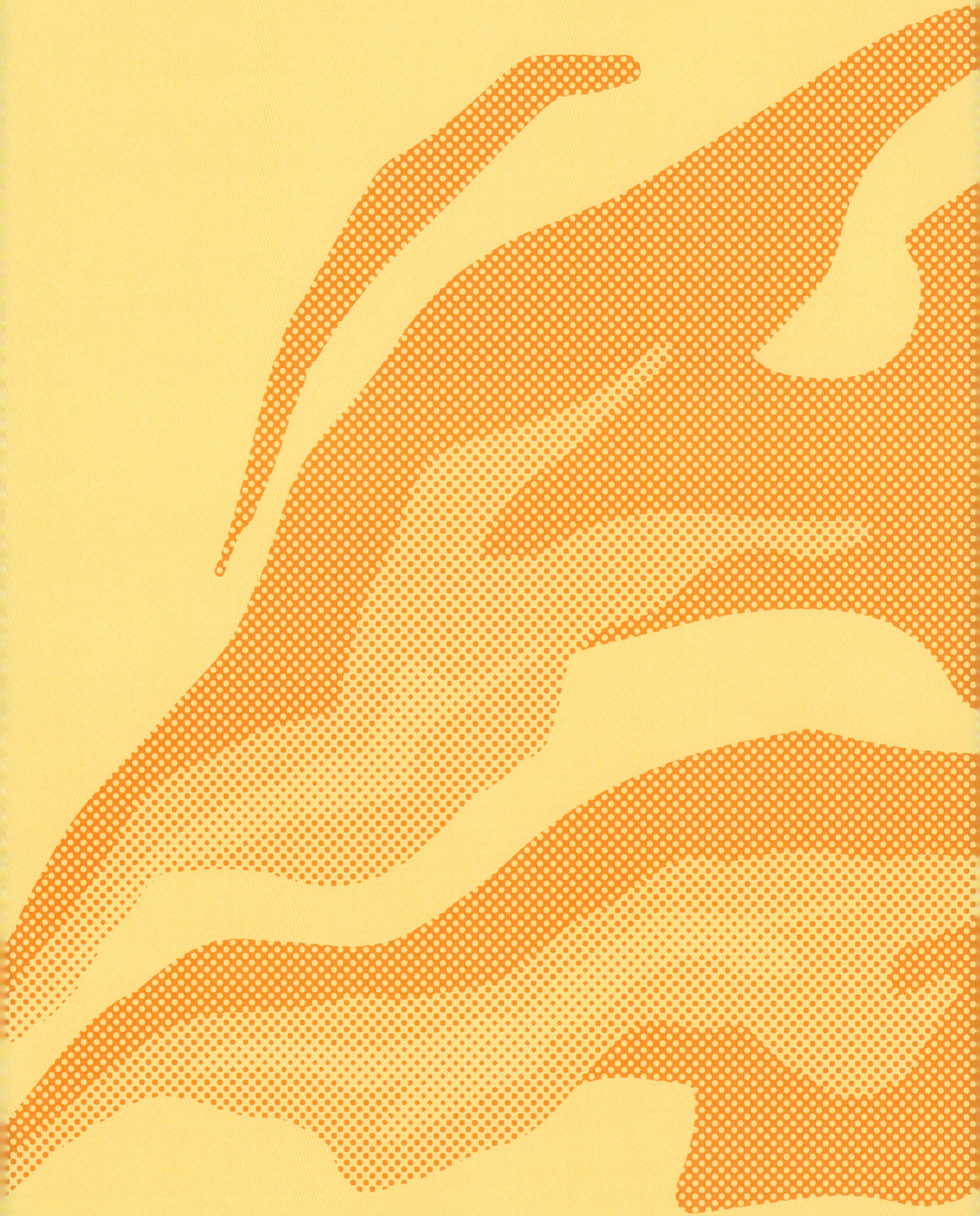

NOODLES & RICE

SERVES 3

CURRY WONTON NOODLE

THIS IS A FLAVOURFUL TWIST ON THE CLASSIC WONTON NOODLE DISH, THAT BRINGS TOGETHER TENDER WONTONS WITH SPRINGY NOODLES IN A RICH, AROMATIC CURRY BROTH. IT'S A COMFORTING AND SATISFYING MEAL THAT COMBINES THE BEST OF BOTH WORLDS – SAVOURY WONTONS AND BOLD CURRY FLAVOURS.

SOUP

2 tablespoons vegetable oil
1 onion, minced
3 garlic cloves, minced
1 tablespoon minced ginger
1 tablespoon minced lemongrass
1 tablespoon red curry paste
225 g (8 oz) boneless, skinless chicken thighs, thinly sliced
3 tablespoons curry powder
½ teaspoon turmeric
400 ml (13½ fl oz) coconut milk
950 ml (32 fl oz) Chicken stock (page 32 or shop-bought)
3 tablespoons fish sauce
1 teaspoon sugar
salt, to taste

NOODLES AND TOPPINGS

225 g (8 oz) fresh egg noodles
1 bunch choy sum
90 g (3 oz/1 cup) bean sprouts
12 Pork and prawn wontons (page 40)
vegetable oil, for deep-frying
spring onions (scallions), thinly sliced, to serve

Heat the vegetable oil in a large pot over medium heat. Add the minced onion, garlic, ginger and lemongrass, sautéing for 3–4 minutes until fragrant and the onion is softened. Stir in the red curry paste and cook for another 2 minutes, allowing the flavours to meld.

Next, add the thinly sliced chicken thigh to the pot and cook for about 5 minutes, until no longer pink. Sprinkle in the curry powder and turmeric, stirring to evenly coat the chicken, and cook for an additional 1–2 minutes.

Pour in the coconut milk and chicken stock, stirring to combine everything. Bring the mixture to a simmer and add the fish sauce, sugar, and salt to taste. Let the curry simmer for 15–20 minutes to develop the flavours.

While the curry is simmering, cook the egg noodles according to the package instructions. One minute before the noodles are finished, add the choy sum and bean sprouts to the pot. Cook for the remaining minute, then drain the noodles and vegetables together.

Fill a separate wok or large pot halfway full with oil and heat to 180°C (350°F) over medium–high heat (you can also test the oil with a wooden chopstick – if bubbles form around it, the oil is ready). Fry the wontons until they are golden brown and crispy, then remove them and drain on paper towels.

To serve, divide the cooked egg noodles, choy sum and bean sprouts between bowls. Ladle the curry broth with chicken over the noodles and vegetables, then top each bowl with crispy fried wontons. Garnish with thinly sliced spring onions.

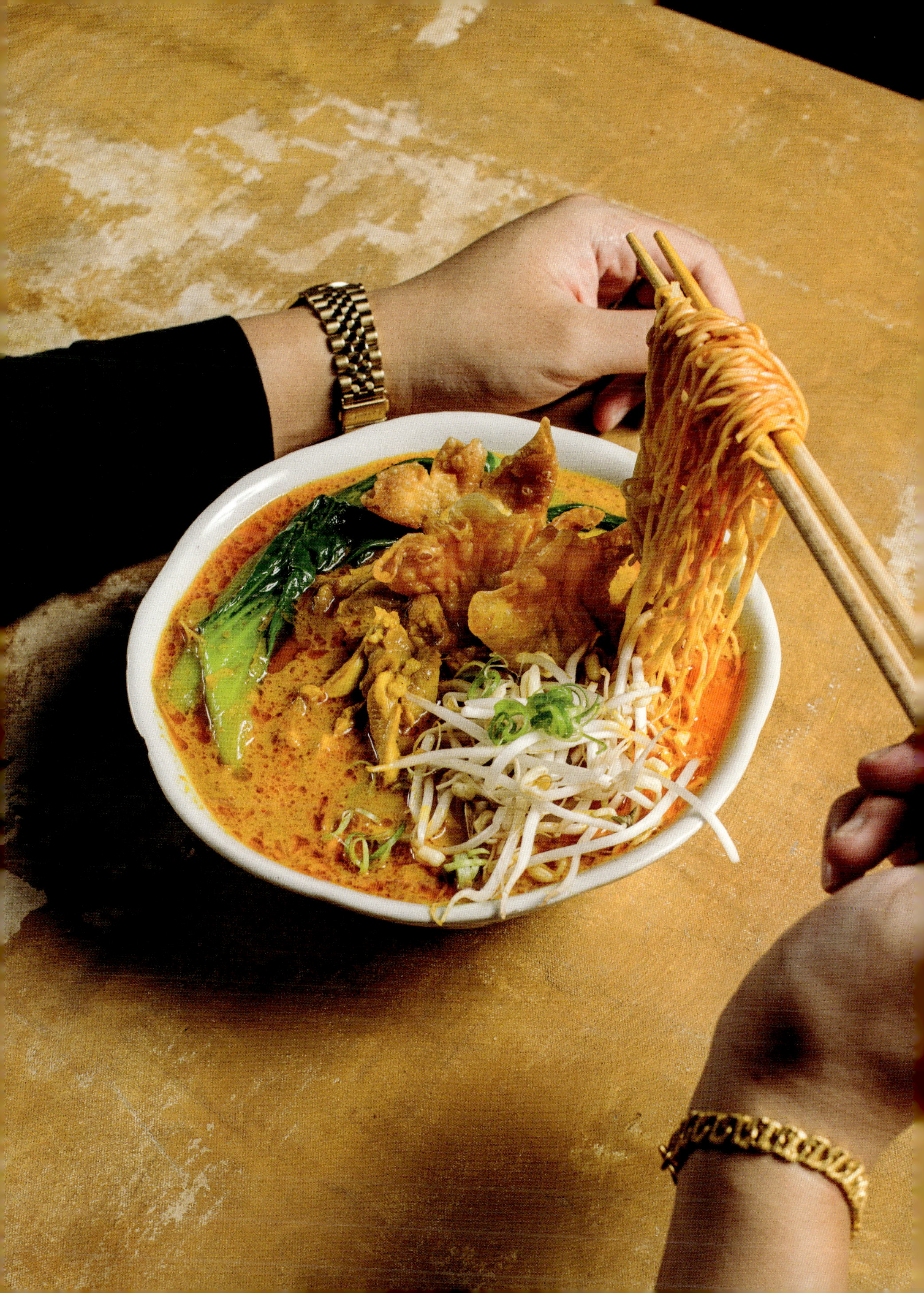

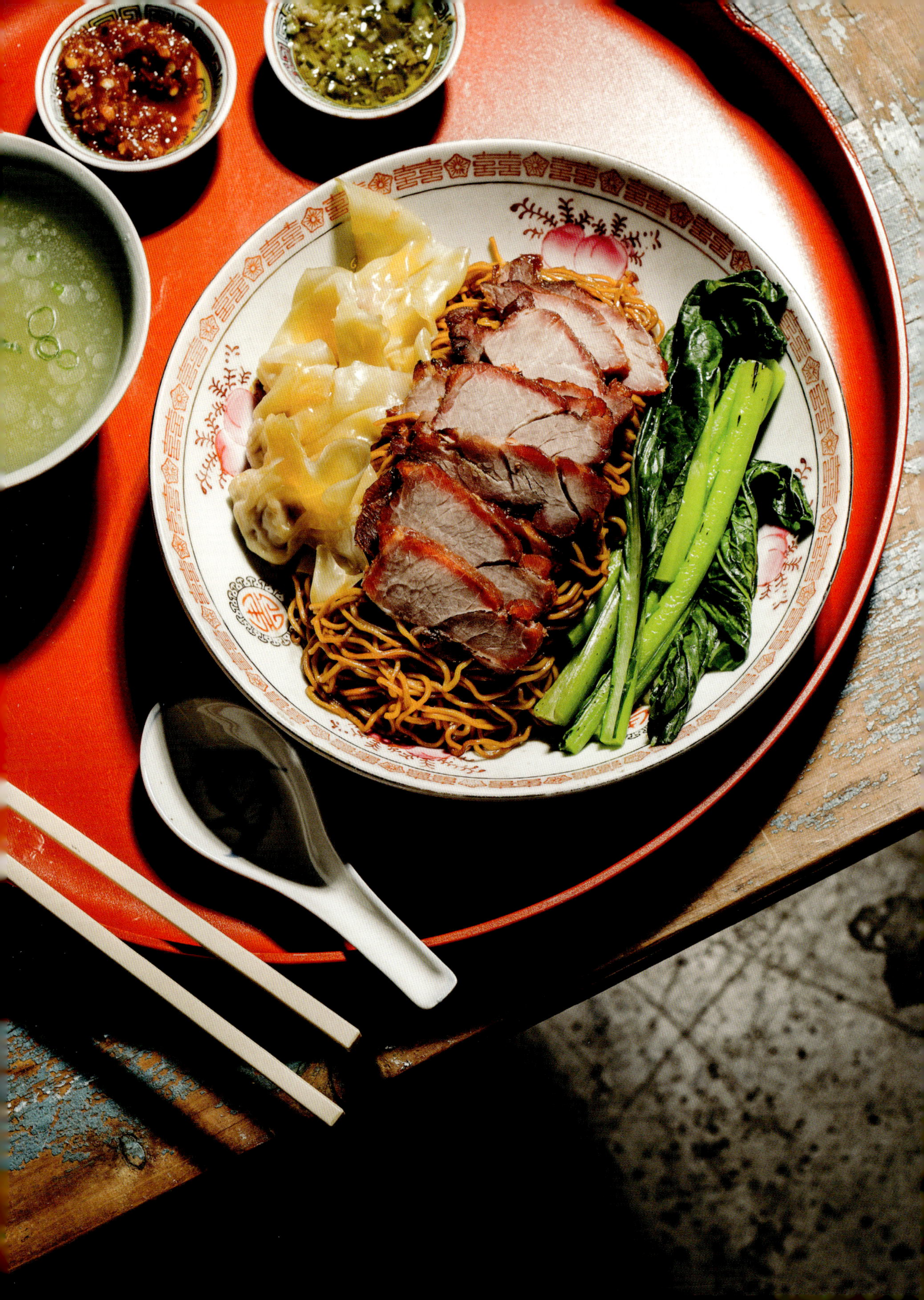

SERVES 2

KON LOH MEE

KON LOH MEE IS A COMFORTING CLASSIC IN CHINESE CUISINE – TENDER WONTONS AND SPRINGY NOODLES IN A RICH SAVOURY SAUCE. PAIRED WITH CRISP VEGETABLES AND AROMATIC SEASONINGS, IT'S A PERFECT BALANCE OF TEXTURE AND TASTE IN EVERY BITE. THIS IS POPULAR WITH THE WONTONS IN A SOUP, OR FRIED WITH THE DRY MIXED NOODLES. PICK YOUR FAVOURITE!

350 g (12½ oz) fresh egg noodles

choy sum (a few stalks), to serve

8 Pork and prawn wontons (page 40)

1 × quantity Easy char siu pork (page 179)

vegetable oil, for deep-frying

SAUCE

2 teaspoons sesame oil

2 teaspoons soy sauce

4 teaspoons kecap manis (sweet soy sauce)

2 tablespoons dark soy sauce

2 tablespoons water

2 tablespoons Ginger scallion oil (page 33)

pinch of salt

½ teaspoon sugar

FOR SOUP OPTION

Chicken stock (page 32 or shop-bought), enough to cover the wontons

pinch of salt

drizzle of sesame oil

Bring a pot of water to a boil and cook the egg noodles according to the package instructions. In the last minute of cooking, add the choy sum to the pot, cooking until the noodles are tender and the choy sum is just wilted. Drain both and set aside.

In a small bowl, mix together the sesame oil, soy sauce, kecap manis, dark soy sauce, water, ginger scallion oil, salt and sugar until well combined to create the sauce.

For the fried wonton option, fill a wok or large pot halfway full with oil and bring to 180°C (350°F) over medium–high heat (you can also test the oil with a wooden chopstick – if bubbles form around it, the oil is ready). Fry the wontons until golden brown and crispy, then drain them on paper towels.

For the soup wonton option, bring chicken stock to a simmer in a pot. Add the wontons and cook until they float to the top and are fully cooked, about 3–5 minutes. Season the broth with salt and a drizzle of sesame oil.

In a large bowl, toss the cooked noodles and choy sum with the prepared sauce until everything is evenly coated.

For the fried wonton option, serve the noodles in a bowl topped with the fried wontons and char siu slices on the side.

For the soup wonton option, serve the noodles in a bowl with char siu on the side, and the soup wontons in a separate bowl with the hot chicken stock.

NOODLES & RICE

SERVES 2

CHAR KWAY TEOW

CHAR KWAY TEOW IS A POPULAR STIR-FRIED NOODLE DISH FROM SOUTHEAST ASIA, KNOWN FOR ITS SMOKY FLAVOURS AND SATISFYING MIX OF FLAT RICE NOODLES, PRAWNS, CHINESE SAUSAGE AND BEAN SPROUTS. IT'S A STREET FOOD FAVOURITE, PACKED WITH BOLD FLAVOURS AND A DELICIOUS COMBINATION OF TEXTURES.

450 g (1 lb) fresh thick rice noodles

10 large prawns (shrimp)

½ teaspoon bicarbonate of soda (baking soda)

2 tablespoons pork lard or vegetable oil

2 lap cheong (Chinese sausages), thinly sliced on a diagonal

2 garlic cloves, diced

10 fish cakes, sliced

1 large egg (duck or chicken)

1 bunch garlic chives, cut into 4 cm (1½ in) lengths, plus extra to garnish (optional)

2 handfuls bean sprouts, plus extra to garnish (optional)

SAUCE

1 heaped tablespoon sugar

1 heaped tablespoon cooking caramel (karamel masakan)

1 teaspoon dark soy sauce

¼ teaspoon white pepper

1 teaspoon YumYum or MSG

½ teaspoon chicken bouillon powder

1 teaspoon oyster sauce

1 tablespoon water

Place the fresh rice noodles in a large microwave-safe bowl and cover with plastic wrap. Heat at 30-second intervals for 2 minutes, checking in between, until the noodles have softened. Separate the noodles by hand and set aside.

In a small bowl, combine the prawns with the bicarbonate of soda, mix well and set aside. In another bowl, mix all the sauce ingredients and set aside as well.

Heat a wok over high heat and add the pork lard or oil. Add the lap cheong slices and stir-fry until they release their oil and become slightly crispy. Remove the sausages from the wok and set them aside.

Using the same wok, add the diced garlic and stir-fry until fragrant. Add the prawns and cook until they turn pink, then remove and set them aside with the lap cheong.

Next, add the fish cake slices to the wok and stir-fry briefly. Add the rice noodles, separating them as you stir, ensuring they are evenly coated with the oil. Pour the sauce over the noodles and stir-fry until the noodles are well-coated and heated through.

Push the noodles to one side of the wok and crack the egg into the other side. Scramble the egg until fully cooked, then mix it into the noodles. Add the garlic chives, bean sprouts, prawns, and lap cheong back into the wok. Toss everything together until well-mixed and heated through.

Serve hot, garnished with extra garlic chives or bean sprouts, if desired.

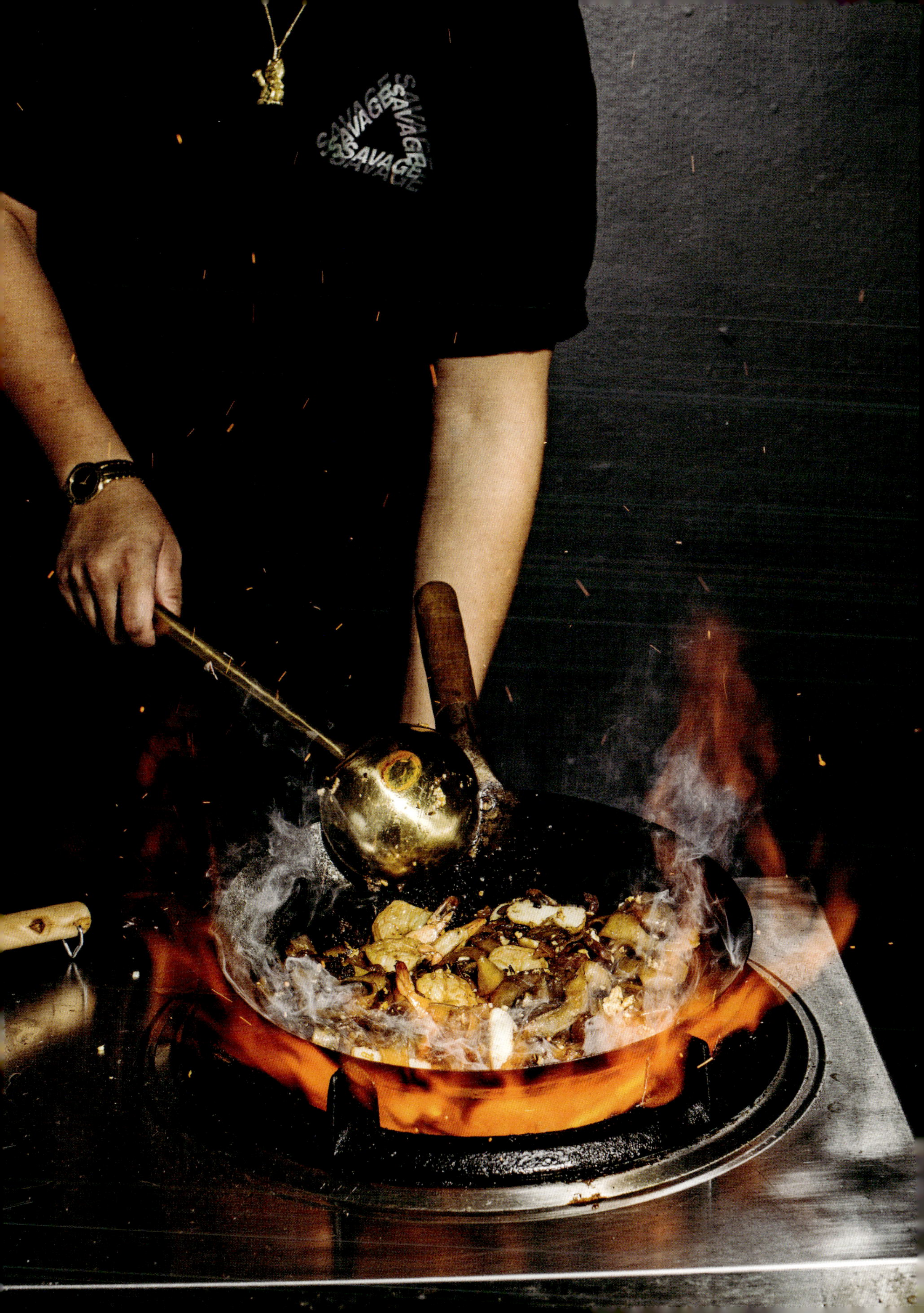
SAVAGE

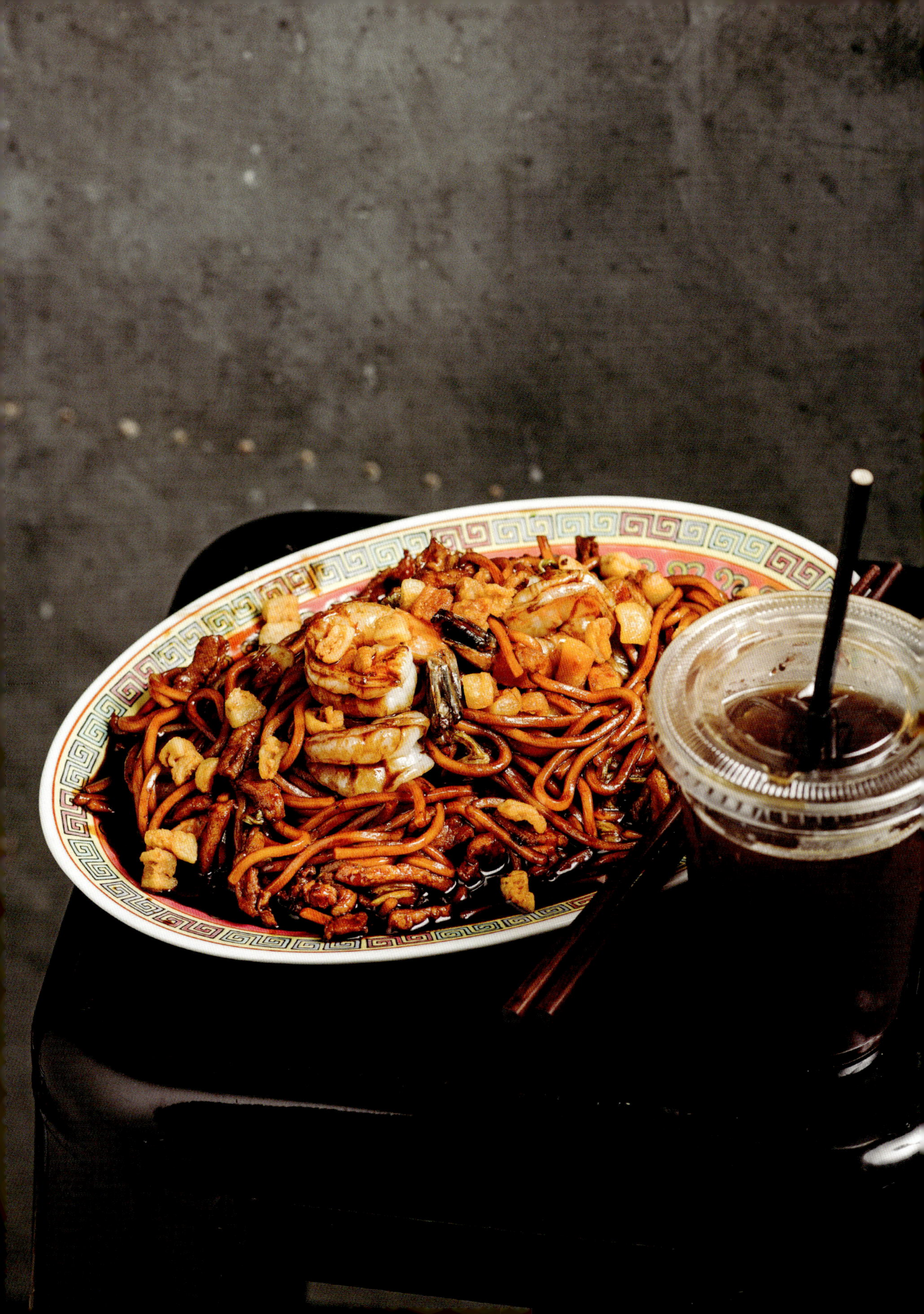

SERVES 2

HOKKIEN MEE

HOKKIEN MEE IS A POPULAR MALAYSIAN AND SINGAPOREAN STIR-FRIED NOODLE DISH, FEATURING EGG NOODLES, PRAWNS, SQUID, PORK AND A SAVOURY SOY-BASED SAUCE. THIS FLAVOURFUL STREET FOOD CLASSIC IS LOVED FOR ITS SMOKY, UMAMI-PACKED TASTE AND SATISFYING TEXTURE.

2 tablespoons pork lard or vegetable oil

50 g (1¾ oz) pork belly, thinly sliced

3 garlic cloves, finely chopped

250 g (9 oz) fresh thick Hokkien noodles, separated

2 leaves Chinese (Napa) cabbage, roughly chopped

1 fried fish cake, thinly sliced

240 ml (8 fl oz/1 cup) Chicken stock (page 32 or shop-bought)

crispy pork lard crackling, to finish (page 32), optional

PRAWNS

4 large prawns (shrimp)

¼ teaspoon bicarbonate of soda (baking soda)

SAUCE

1 tablespoon dark soy sauce

1 tablespoon oyster sauce

1 tablespoon cooking caramel (karamel masakan)

2 teaspoons granulated sugar

¼ teaspoon white pepper

½ teaspoon YumYum or MSG

240 ml (8 fl oz/1 cup) water

In a small bowl, combine the prawns with the bicarbonate of soda, mix well and set aside.

Heat a large wok or frying pan over medium–high heat and add the pork lard or vegetable oil, allowing it to heat up.

Add the pork belly to the wok and stir-fry for about 2–3 minutes until just cooked through. Next, add the finely chopped garlic and stir-fry for about 30 seconds until fragrant and lightly golden.

Toss the Hokkien noodles into the wok, stirring to combine with the pork belly and garlic. Then, add the roughly chopped Chinese cabbage and stir-fry for about 2 minutes, or until the cabbage starts to wilt.

Add the large prawns and the fish cake to the wok, continuing to stir-fry until the prawns turn pink and are cooked through. Pour in all the sauce ingredients and toss everything together to combine.

Turn the heat up to high and add the chicken stock, tossing the noodles until they have absorbed all the sauce. Once everything is well mixed and coated, transfer the Hokkien mee to serving plates or a large platter.

For extra crunch and added flavour, top the dish with crispy pork lard crackling.

NOODLES & RICE

SERVES 2

'PANDA EXPRESS' CHOW MEIN

THIS IS MY VERSION OF THE WELL-KNOWN PANDA EXPRESS CHOW MEIN, ADAPTED TO BRING OUT EVEN MORE FLAVOUR. MADE UP OF STIR-FRIED NOODLES, CABBAGE, ONIONS AND CELERY TOSSED IN A SAVOURY SAUCE, IT'S AN EASY, DELICIOUS TAKE ON THE TAKEAWAY CLASSIC.

200 g (7 oz) chow mein noodles
½ brown onion, thinly sliced
1 celery stalk, thinly sliced
1 white cabbage leaf, roughly chopped
spring onion (scallion), finely sliced, to garnish

SAUCE
3 tablespoons light soy sauce
1 heaped tablespoon sugar
1 tablespoon Shaoxing wine (Chinese cooking wine)
pinch of white pepper
1 tablespoon oyster sauce
1 teaspoon sesame oil
½ teaspoon YumYum or MSG
120 ml (4 fl oz/½ cup) Chicken stock (page 32 or shop-bought)

In a small bowl, mix together all the sauce ingredients. Stir until the sugar and YumYum are fully dissolved, then set the sauce aside.

Cook the chow mein noodles in boiling water for about 30 seconds, then drain and set them aside.

Heat a wok over medium–high heat and add a small amount of oil, swirling to coat the wok. Add the sliced onion, cabbage and celery, and stir-fry for 2–3 minutes until the vegetables begin to soften.

Next, add the cooked chow mein noodles to the wok with the vegetables. Pour the sauce over the noodles and toss everything together, ensuring the noodles and vegetables are evenly coated. Stir-fry for an additional 2–3 minutes until everything is heated through and well combined. Serve immediately.

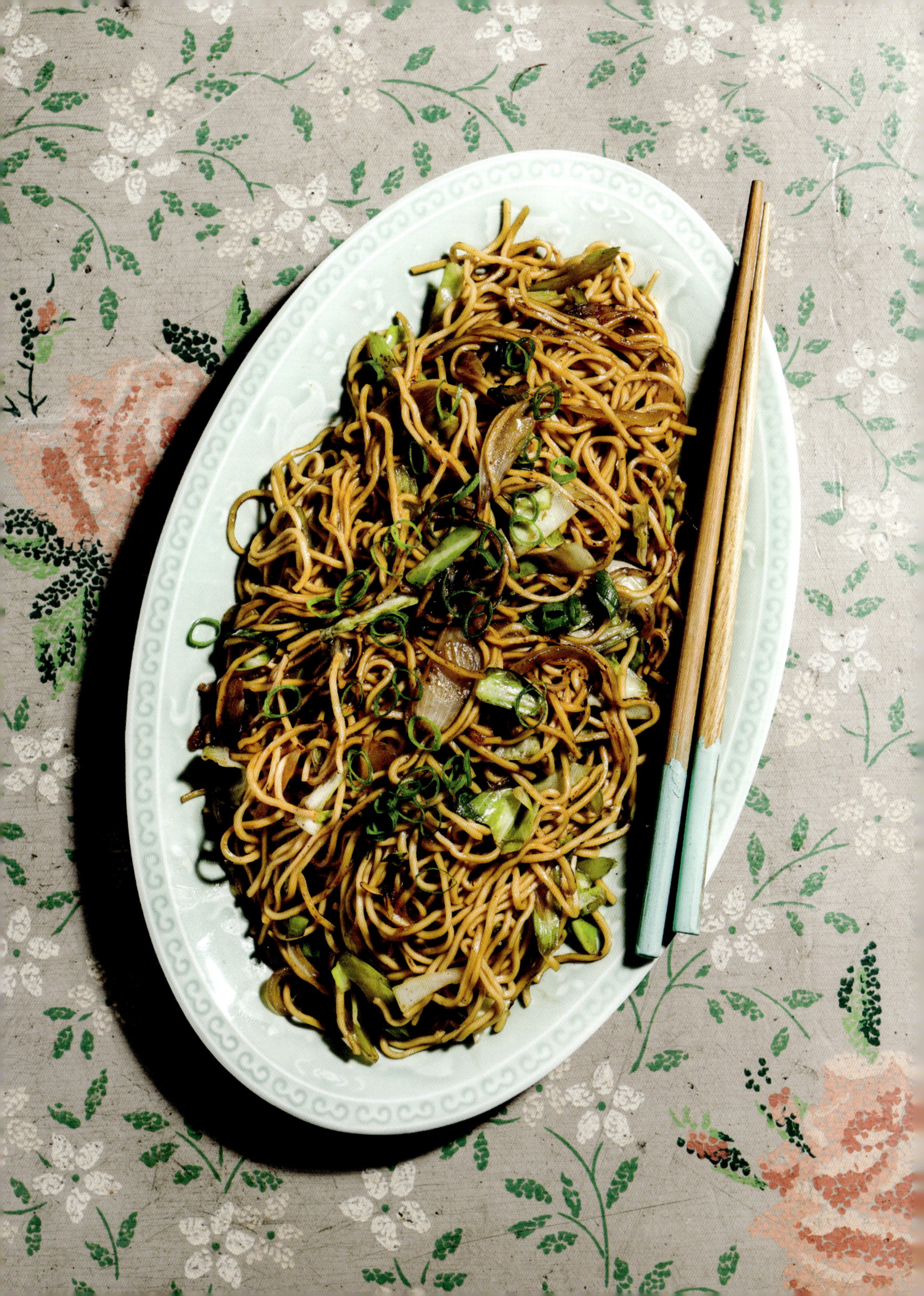

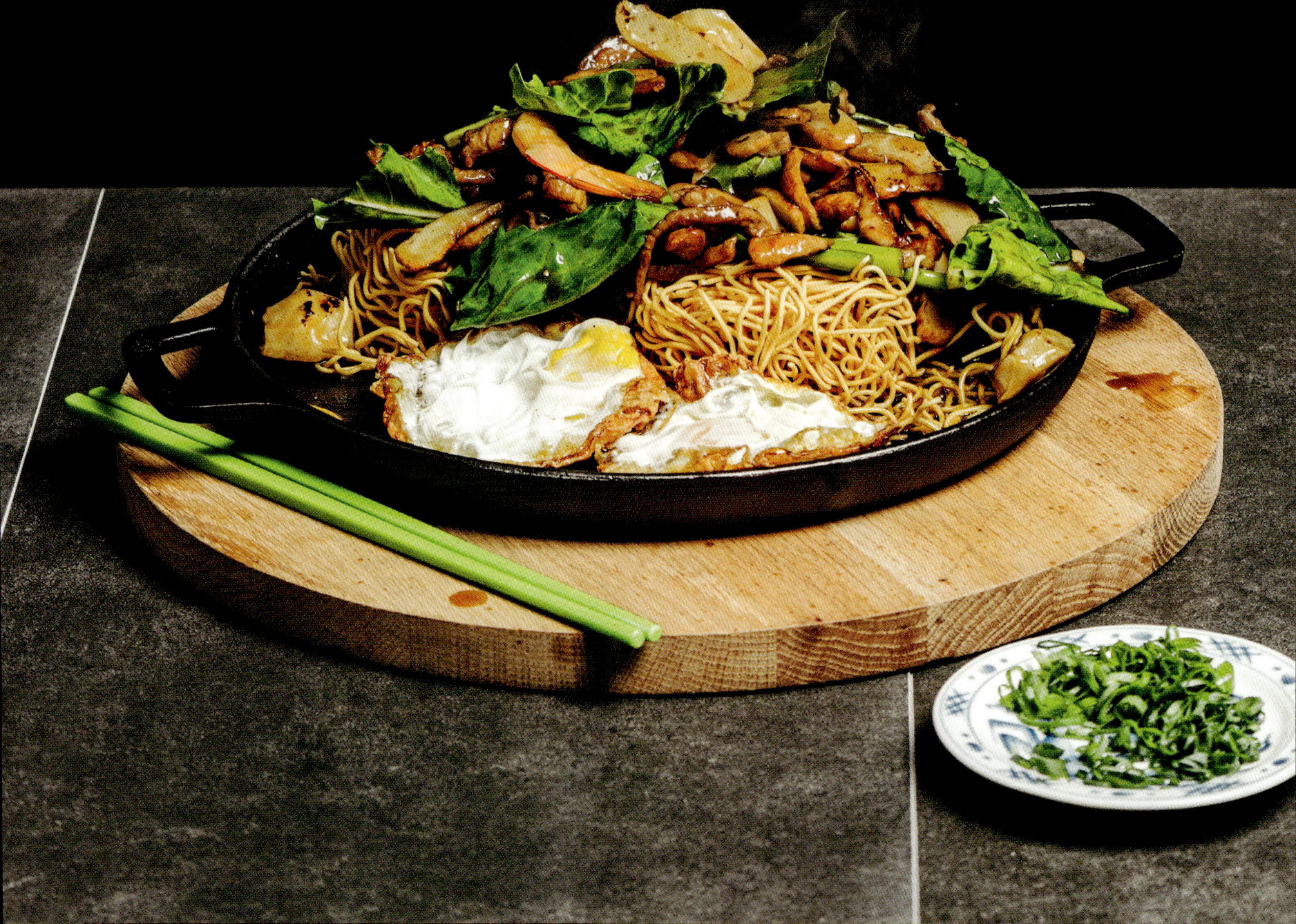

SERVES 1

SIZZLING YEE MEIN

SIZZLING YEE MEIN IS A FLAVOURFUL AND EXCITING DISH THAT COMBINES SOFT, CHEWY YEE MEIN NOODLES WITH SAVOURY SAUCE AND TOPPINGS, ALL SERVED ON A SIZZLING HOT PLATE. THE CRACKLING SOUND AND RICH AROMA MAKE THIS DISH A CROWD-PLEASER, PERFECT FOR A DRAMATIC AND DELICIOUS MEAL.

1 tablespoon oil, plus 1 tablespoon extra

3 prawns (shrimp), peeled and deveined

6 thin slices of fish cake

2 fish balls

70 g (2½ oz) pork belly, sliced into thin strips

2 teaspoons garlic, finely chopped

3 stalks choy sum

½ spring onion (scallion) stalk, finely chopped

1 yee mein (clay pot noodles) cluster (approx. 80 g/2¾ oz)

1 egg (optional)

SAUCE

1 tablespoon potato starch

240 ml (8 fl oz/1 cup) water

½ teaspoon chicken bouillon powder

½ teaspoon YumYum or MSG

½ teaspoon sugar

pinch of white pepper

½ teaspoon oyster sauce

1 teaspoon sesame oil

1 tablespoon Shaoxing wine (Chinese cooking wine)

1 teaspoon dark soy sauce

1 teaspoon Maggi seasoning sauce

Heat 1 tablespoon of the oil in a wok over high heat. Add the prawns, fish cake and fish balls, cooking and stirring for 3–4 minutes until they are cooked through. Remove from the wok and set them aside.

Place a cast-iron sizzling plate on your wok burner or in an oven preheated to 220°C (430°F) to heat up.

While the plate is heating up, in the same wok, heat another tablespoon of oil over high heat. Add the pork belly and garlic, cooking for 2–3 minutes until the pork is fully cooked. Remove the pork from the wok and set it aside with the other cooked ingredients.

In a jug, combine the potato starch and water, stirring until the starch is fully dissolved, then set it aside.

Reduce the heat to medium and add all the sauce ingredients and the potato starch slurry to the wok. Turn the heat back up to high and cook the sauce, stirring constantly, until it comes to a boil and thickens slightly.

By now, the sizzling plate should be hot. Carefully remove it from the heat and place it on a heatproof board. Arrange the noodles, cooked proteins and choy sum on the sizzling plate. Pour the prepared sauce over the top of them, then crack an egg on the side of the plate or top with a fried egg, if desired.

Serve immediately, allowing the sizzling plate to keep the dish hot and enhance the flavours.

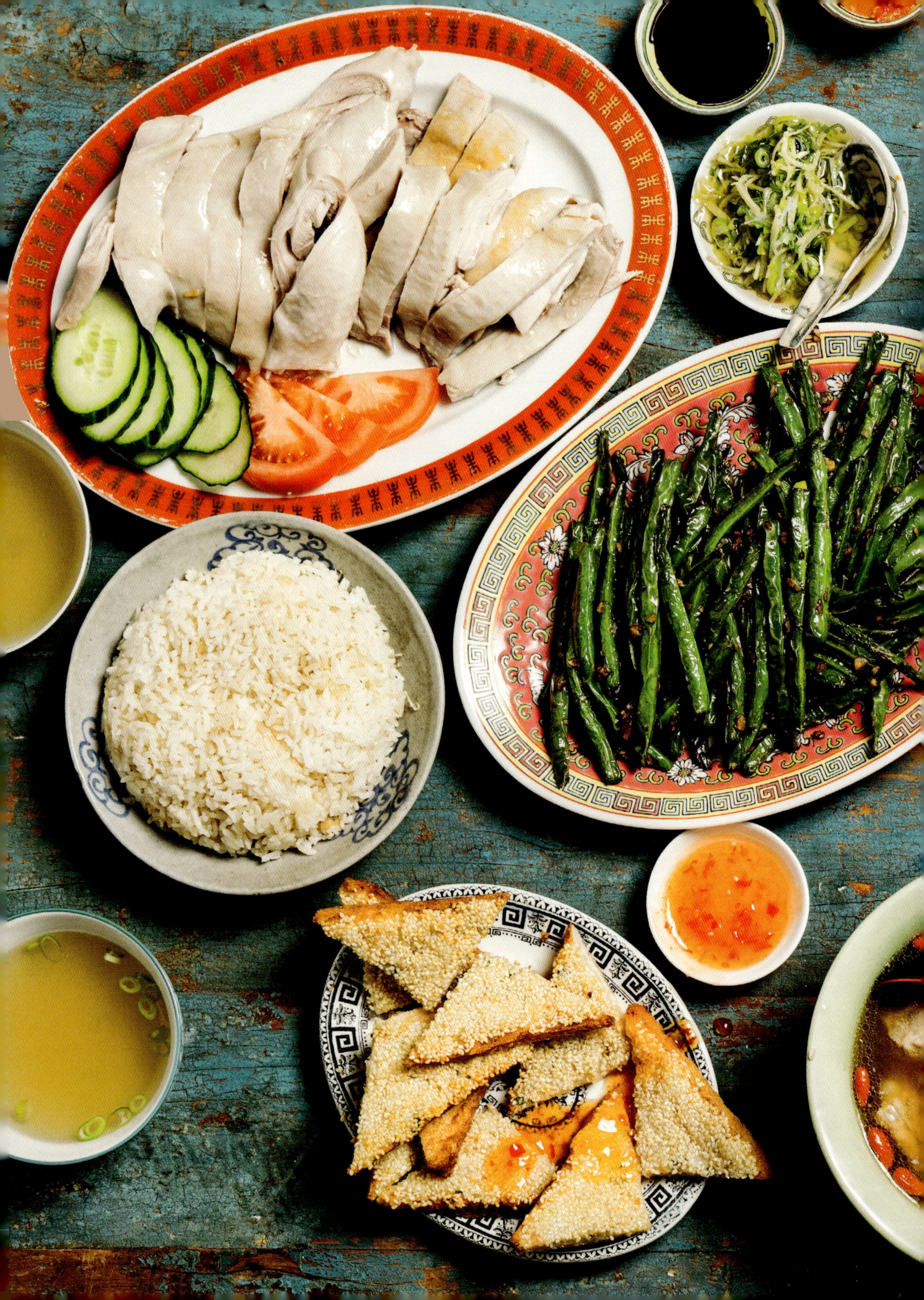

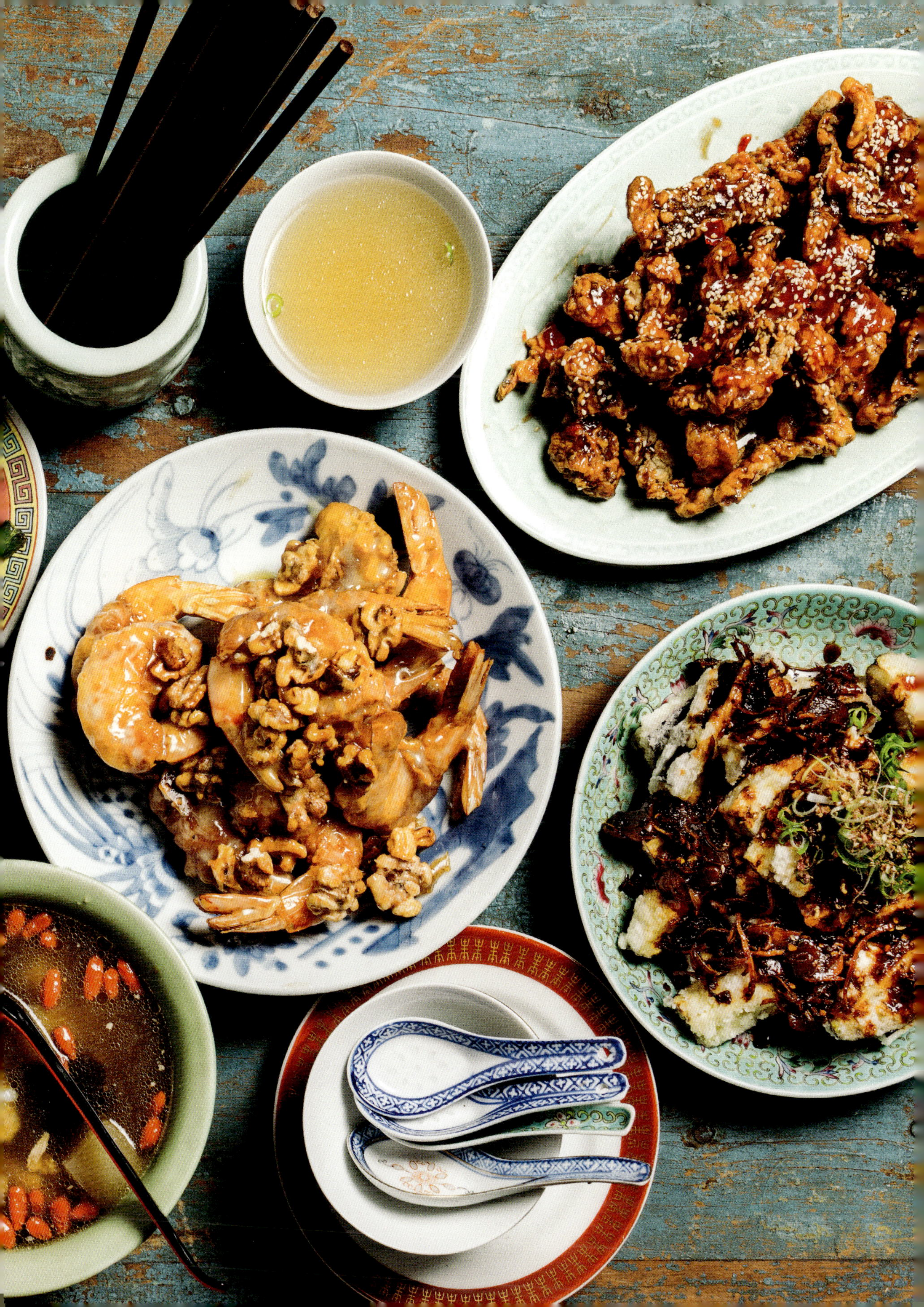

SERVES 2

WAT DAN HOR

WAT DAN HOR IS A COMFORTING CANTONESE NOODLE DISH FEATURING SILKY SMOOTH FLAT RICE NOODLES STIR-FRIED WITH A RICH, EGGY GRAVY. PACKED WITH TENDER SEAFOOD OR MEAT AND FRESH VEGETABLES, IT'S A POPULAR GO-TO FOR A SATISFYING MEAL.

400 g (14 oz/approx. half a pack) fresh flat rice noodles

2 tablespoons vegetable oil

½ teaspoon dark soy sauce

½ teaspoon light soy sauce

2 garlic cloves, minced

10 thin slices of fish cake

8 prawns (shrimp), peeled and deveined, tails intact

2 stalks choy sum, roughly chopped

2 tablespoons vegetable oil

PORK BELLY

50 g (1¾ oz) pork belly, thinly sliced

1 teaspoon cornflour (cornstarch)

2 teaspoons water

GRAVY

500 ml (17 fl oz/2 cups) Chicken stock (page 32 or shop-bought)

½ teaspoon chicken bouillon powder

½ teaspoon YumYum or MSG

¼ teaspoon white pepper, plus extra to garnish (optional)

1½ tablespoons potato starch

3 tablespoons water

1 egg

In a small bowl, combine the sliced pork belly with the cornflour and water, mixing until the water is fully absorbed by the pork. Set aside. Separate the fresh flat rice noodles by peeling each strand individually.

Heat half the oil in a wok over medium–high heat. Add the fresh noodles, followed by the dark soy sauce and light soy sauce. Stir-fry to ensure the noodles are evenly coated with the sauce, then let the noodles sit for a few seconds in the wok to develop a light char. Once done, transfer the noodles to a plate.

In the same wok, heat the remaining tablespoon of vegetable oil over medium-high heat. Add the minced garlic and stir-fry for about 30 seconds until fragrant. Add the pork belly and stir-fry until it starts to brown.

Next, add the fish cake slices and prawns to the wok, cooking until the prawns turn pink and the pork is fully cooked. Stir in the roughly chopped choy sum and stir-fry for about 30 seconds until it begins to wilt.

Pour in the chicken stock, then stir in the chicken bouillon powder, YumYum or MSG and white pepper. Bring the mixture to a simmer. Meanwhile, mix the potato starch and water to make a slurry.

When the sauce is simmering, add the potato starch slurry to thicken the gravy, stirring continuously until the sauce reaches just below your desired consistency, as the egg will also thicken the gravy. Slowly pour in the beaten egg, gently stirring to create egg ribbons in the gravy.

Serve the wat dan hor hot, and garnish with extra white pepper, if desired.

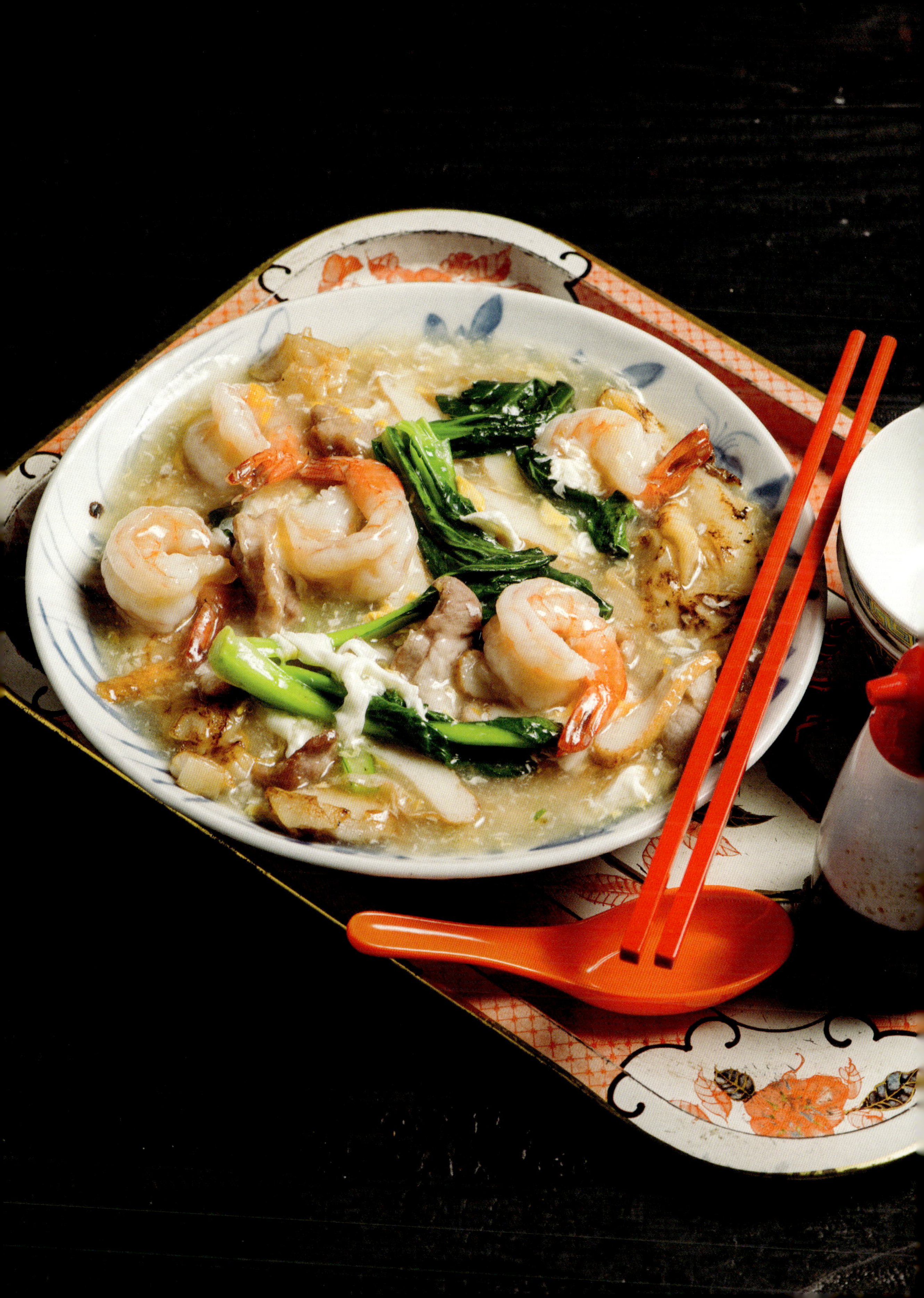

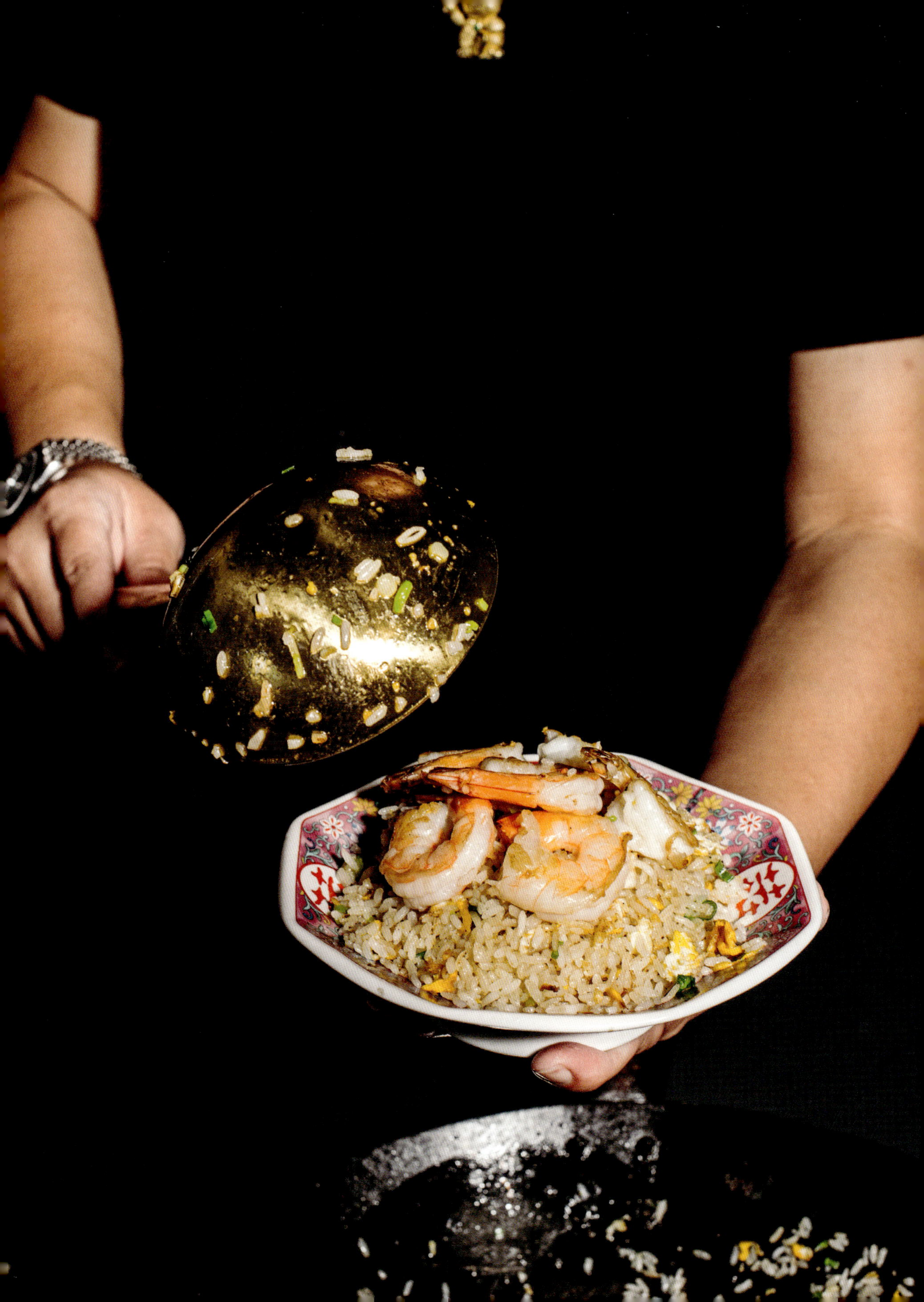

SERVES 1

DIN TAI FUNG FRIED RICE

DIN TAI FUNG FRIED RICE IS A SIMPLE YET FLAVOURFUL DISH, KNOWN FOR ITS PERFECTLY SEASONED RICE, TENDER EGGS AND SUBTLE AROMATICS. INSPIRED BY THE FAMOUS TAIWANESE RESTAURANT, THIS FRIED RICE IS A COMFORTING AND SATISFYING MEAL THAT'S BOTH EASY TO MAKE AND PACKED WITH UMAMI.

1½ cups medium-grain white rice

1 large egg

5 large prawns (shrimp), peeled and deveined

1 tablespoon vegetable oil, plus extra, if needed

1 spring onion (scallion), finely chopped, whites and greens separated

½ teaspoon YumYum or MSG

1 teaspoon chicken bouillon powder

pinch of white pepper

Cook the medium-grain rice in your rice cooker. Freshly cooked rice works best for this recipe, so there's no need to use chilled or day-old rice. Once the rice is ready, beat the egg in a bowl and add the cooked rice. Mix well until the rice is evenly coated with the egg.

Heat a tablespoon of oil in a large skillet or wok over medium–high heat. Add the prawns to the hot pan and cook for about 2–3 minutes per side, until they turn pink and opaque. Once cooked, remove the prawns from the pan and set them aside.

In the same pan, add a little more oil if necessary, then add the egg-coated rice. Stir-fry the rice for about a minute, allowing it to heat through. Add the sliced spring onion whites, then sprinkle the YumYum or MSG, chicken bouillon powder and white pepper over the rice. Stir-fry for another minute to evenly distribute the seasonings.

Return the cooked prawns to the pan and continue to stir-fry until the rice is fragrant and slightly dry, combining everything well.

To serve, arrange the prawns at the bottom of a medium-sized round bowl. Press the fried rice gently on top of the shrimp to form a firm shape. Place a plate over the bowl and carefully flip it over so the bowl is upside down on the plate. Lift the bowl to reveal the perfectly shaped rice with prawns on top.

Garnish with the spring onion greens and serve immediately.

SERVES 2

SPECIAL FRIED RICE

SPECIAL FRIED RICE IS A DELICIOUS AND VERSATILE DISH, PACKED WITH CHAR SIU, CHICKEN AND HAM. ITS RICH FLAVOURS AND FLUFFY TEXTURE COMPLEMENT A WIDE VARIETY OF DISHES, MAKING IT A STAPLE FOR ANY CHINESE MEAL – PAIR IT WITH CLASSICS LIKE HONEY CHICKEN (PAGE 138) OR PEPPER STEAK (PAGE 163) FOR A CLASSIC FEED.

300 g (10½ oz/2½ cups) jasmine rice, cooked

3 tablespoons vegetable oil

1 spring onion (scallion), thinly sliced, greens and whites separated

2 tablespoons Easy char siu pork (page 179)

2 tablespoons cooked chicken

2 tablespoons leg ham or tinned ham (e.g. Spam)

2 eggs, beaten

2 teaspoons chicken bouillon powder

1 teaspoon YumYum or MSG

2 teaspoons light soy sauce

1 teaspoon sesame oil

To begin, cook the jasmine rice in your rice cooker. Freshly cooked rice works best for this recipe, so there's no need to use chilled or day-old rice.

Heat the vegetable oil in a large wok over medium–high heat. Add the sliced spring onion whites and stir-fry until fragrant. Next, add the char siu pork, cooked chicken and ham to the wok, stir-frying for about 1–2 minutes until the proteins are heated through.

Push the meat to one side of the wok and add the beaten eggs to the other side. Let the eggs cook undisturbed for a few seconds, then gently scramble them until just set. Once the eggs are ready, add the freshly cooked jasmine rice to the wok. Let it sit for about 5 seconds, undisturbed, before giving the wok a quick toss. Use the back of your wok ladle to break up any clumps of rice.

Sprinkle the chicken bouillon powder and YumYum or MSG over the rice, tossing everything together to combine. Drizzle the light soy sauce around the edges of the wok, allowing it to sizzle and mix with the rice. Toss the rice once more to ensure even seasoning. Add the sliced spring onion greens, giving the dish a final toss to combine all the ingredients.

Finally, drizzle the sesame oil over the fried rice and give it one last toss before serving hot. Enjoy!

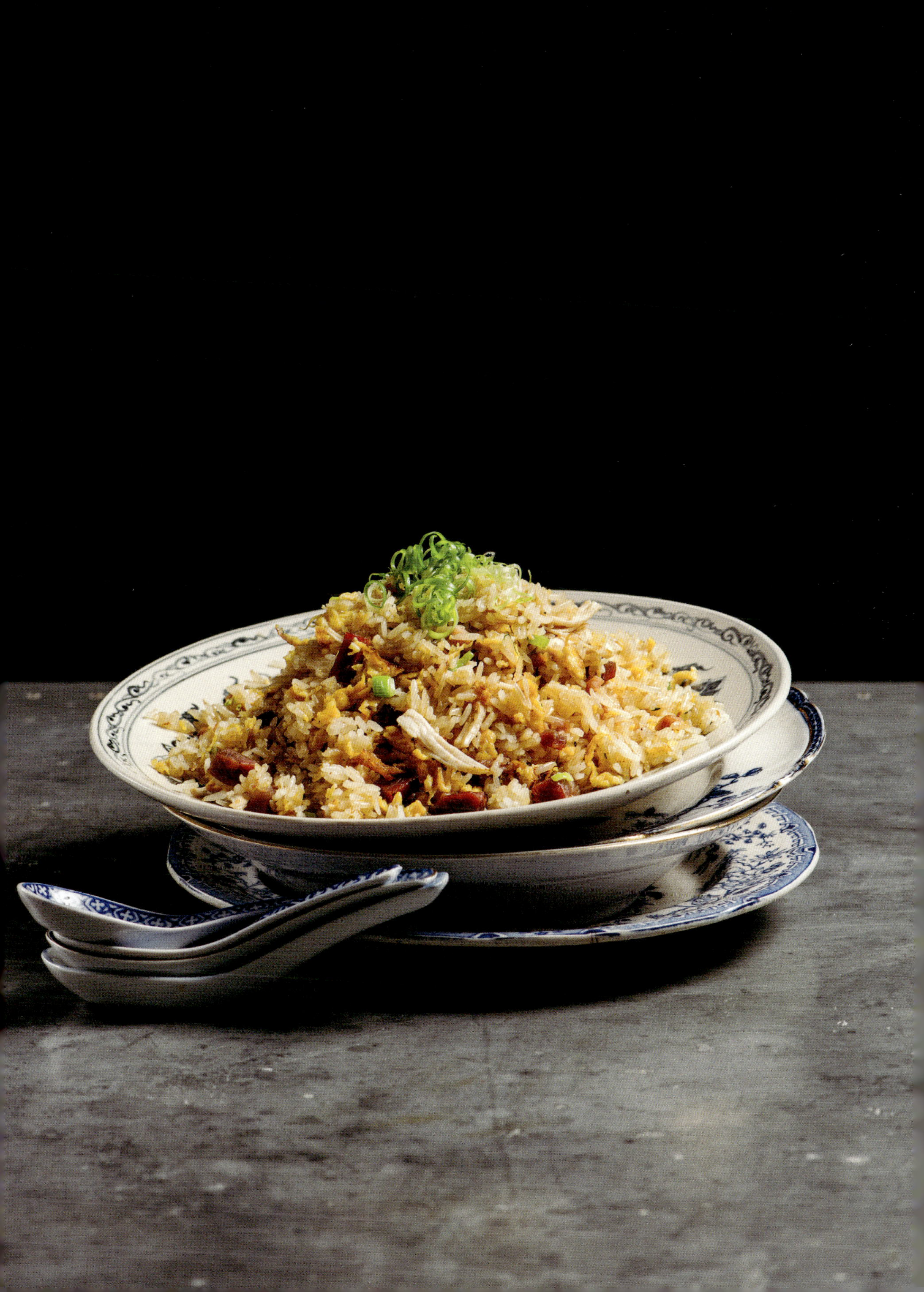

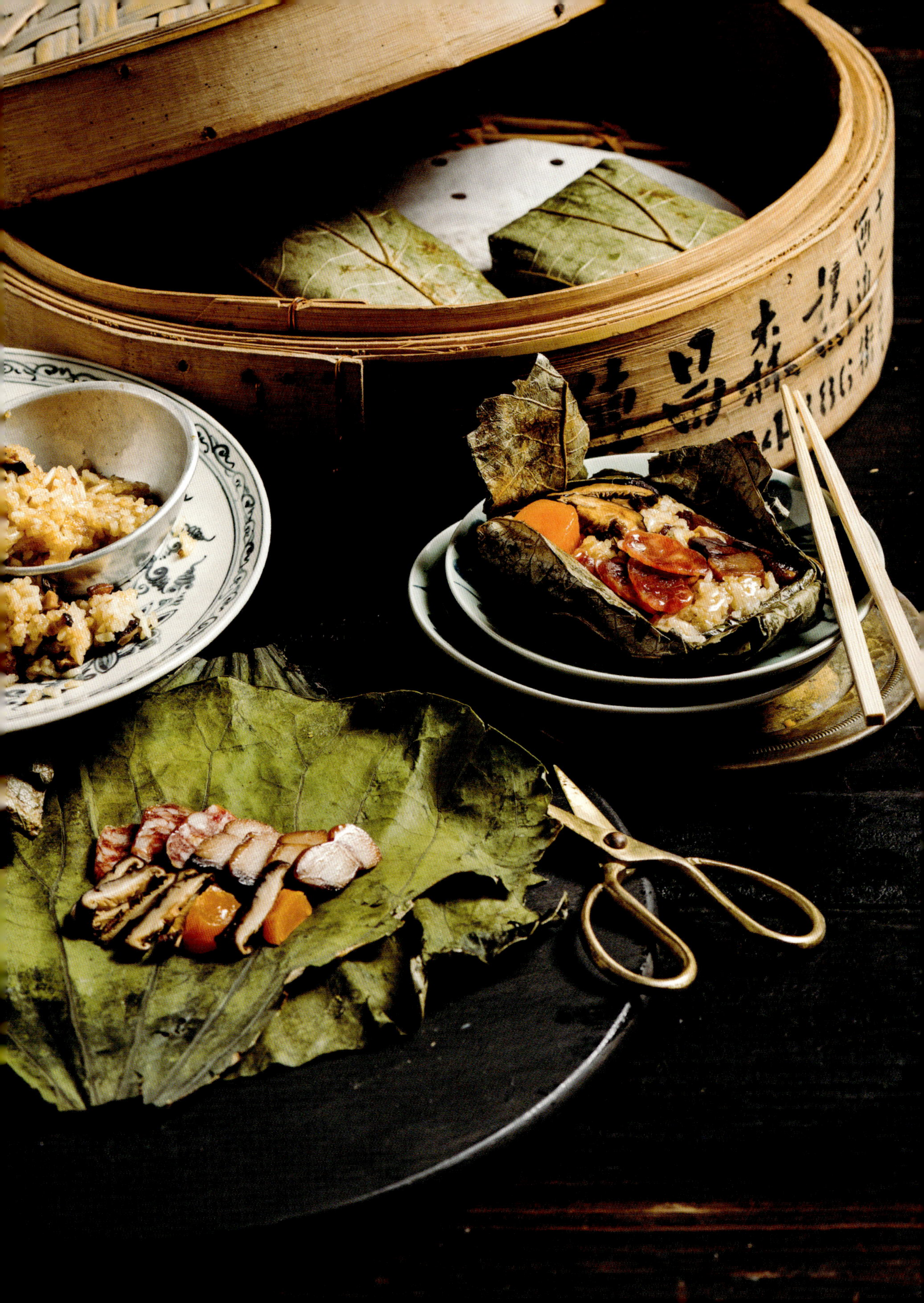

SERVES 2

LO MAI GAI

LO MAI GAI IS A CLASSIC DIM SUM DISH — STICKY RICE PACKED WITH FLAVOURFUL INGREDIENTS LIKE LUP YOOK (CHINESE CURED PORK BELLY), LAP CHEONG (CHINESE SAUSAGE) AND SALTED EGG YOLK. WRAPPED IN LOTUS LEAVES AND STEAMED, THIS DISH OFFERS THE FRAGRANT, SAVOURY EXPERIENCE CANTONESE CUISINE IS KNOWN FOR.

RICE

200 g (7 oz /1 cup) sticky rice

1 heaped tablespoon dried prawns (shrimp)

6 dried shiitake mushrooms

2 tablespoons vegetable oil, plus 1 teaspoon extra

2 lap cheong sausages (1 diced, 1 sliced diagonally)

6 garlic cloves, minced

1 tablespoon oyster sauce

240 ml (8 fl oz/1 cup) water

pinch of salt

2 dried lotus leaves

1 × 5 cm (2 in) piece lup yook (Chinese cured pork belly), thinly sliced

1 salted egg yolk, steamed and quartered (optional), see recipe introduction on page 114

SEASONINGS

½ teaspoon chicken bouillon powder

¼ teaspoon YumYum or MSG

¼ teaspoon sugar

¼ teaspoon salt

¼ teaspoon light soy sauce

pinch of white pepper

Wash the sticky rice at least three times, then let it soak in water, with the water level about 5 cm (2 in) above the rice, for at least 30 minutes. Meanwhile, soak the dried prawns and shiitake mushrooms in hot water for 10 minutes. Drain, dice two of the mushrooms, and slice the rest for topping.

In a pot, cook the soaked prawns over medium heat until all the water has evaporated. Add 2 tablespoons of oil, the lap cheong and garlic. Sauté until golden brown and fragrant. Add the diced mushrooms and the oyster sauce, stirring to combine.

Add the water to the pot along with all the seasoning ingredients. Bring to a simmer and stir well.

Transfer the seasoned mixture to a rice cooker along with the soaked sticky rice. Mix everything together, then cook in a rice-cooker on the regular rice setting.

While the rice is cooking, prepare the lotus leaves. Bring a pot of water to a boil, then add a pinch of salt and 1 teaspoon of oil. Submerge the lotus leaves, rotating them slowly for about 3–4 minutes. Drain the leaves once softened.

Cut the lotus leaves into four wedges in total. Place two of these on your work surface on top of each other, facing opposite directions with the pointy side facing either end. The inside of the leaves should be facing up, ready to wrap the rice. Begin by placing the lap cheong mixture, the lup yook and salted egg yolk (if using) in the centre of the leaves. Add the cooked rice mixture, pressing it down to pack it in.

Fold both sides of the lotus leaf over the centre, then fold the top and bottom over each other and place seam-side down in a steamer. Repeat this process with the remaining lotus leaf wedges.

Steam the wrapped rice parcels for about 15 minutes. Serve hot and enjoy!

SERVES 4–6

CENTURY EGG AND PORK RIB CONGEE

THIS IS A COMFORTING AND SAVOURY CHINESE PORRIDGE, COMBINING TENDER PORK RIBS WITH THE UNIQUE FLAVOUR OF CENTURY EGG. IT'S A HEARTY AND BELOVED STAPLE, OFTEN ENJOYED FOR BREAKFAST OR AS A SOOTHING MEAL DURING COOLER WEATHER.

500 g (1 lb 2 oz) pork spare ribs
200 g (7 oz/1 cup) jasmine rice
2½ litres (85 fl oz/10 cups) water
1 tablespoon salt, or to taste
1 tablespoon chicken bouillon powder
1 teaspoon YumYum or MSG
2 teaspoons sesame oil

TO SERVE
6 century eggs, quartered
spring onion (scallions), finely chopped, to serve
youtiao (Chinese fried crullers), for dipping

Begin by blanching the pork spare ribs in boiling water for a few minutes to remove impurities, then drain and set them aside. Rinse the jasmine rice under cold water until the water runs clear, then drain the rice.

In a large pot, bring the water to a boil. Add the rinsed rice and the blanched pork spare ribs. Reduce the heat to a simmer and cook the congee for 30–40 minutes, stirring occasionally, until it thickens to your desired consistency.

Season the congee with salt, chicken bouillon powder, YumYum or MSG and sesame oil. Taste and adjust the seasonings as needed.

Once ready, divide the congee between serving bowls and top each bowl with the quartered century eggs. Garnish with chopped spring onion and serve hot, accompanied by youtiao for dipping. Enjoy!

NOODLES & RICE

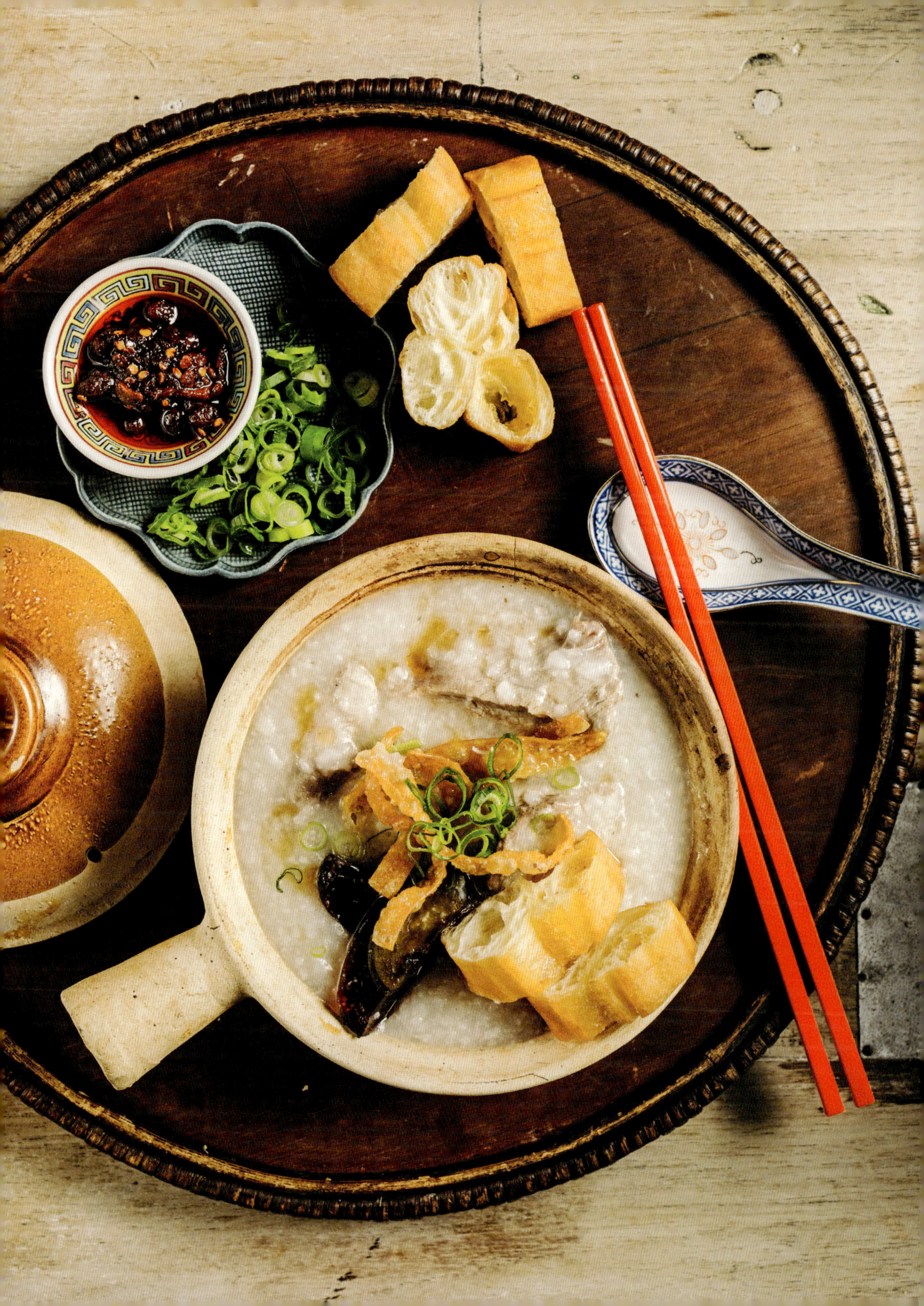

SEAFOOD

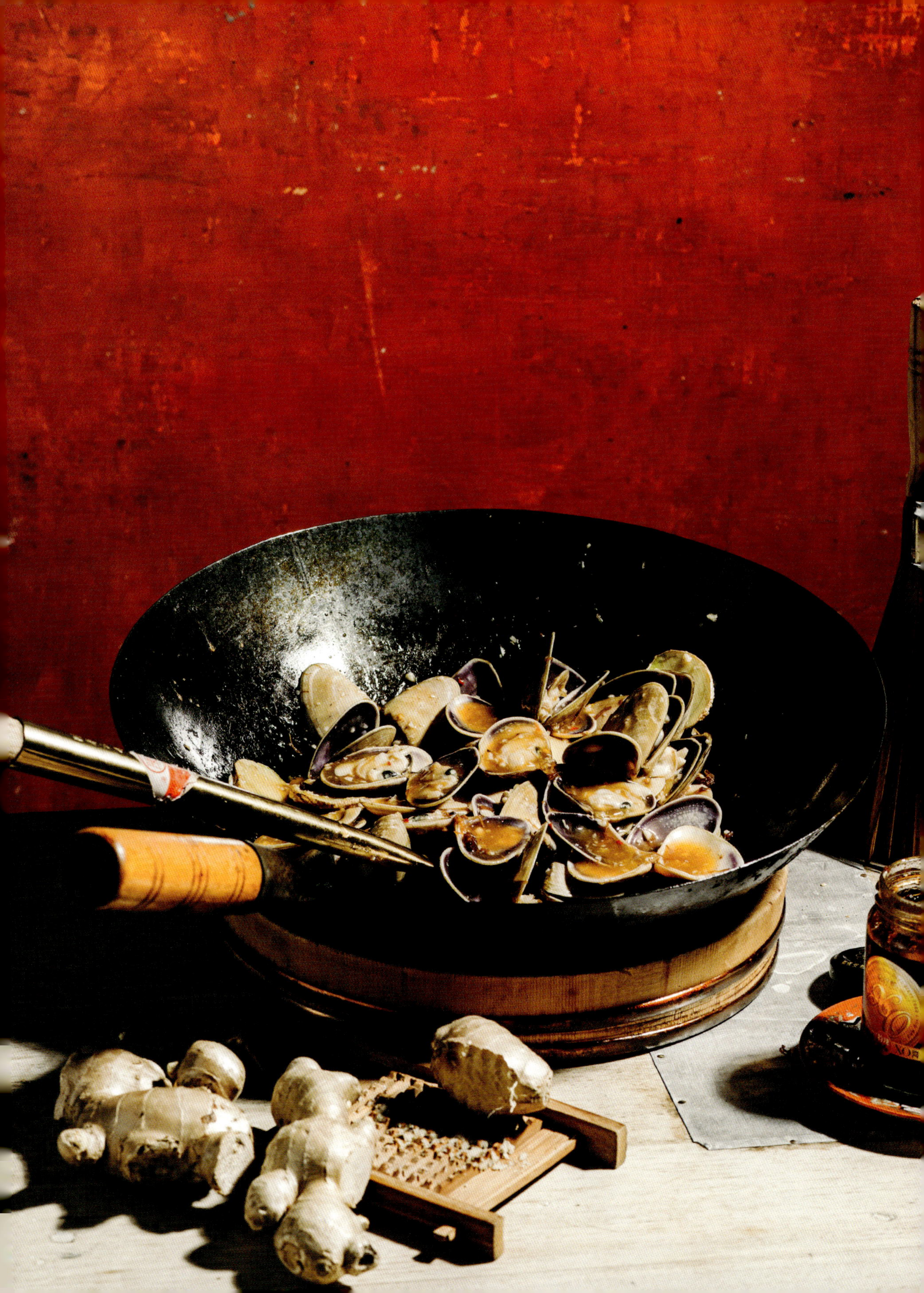

SERVES 3

XO PIPIS

XO PIPIS IS A FLAVOURFUL AND LUXURIOUS DISH MADE WITH TENDER PIPIS STIR-FRIED IN A RICH, SAVOURY XO SAUCE. KNOWN FOR ITS BOLD UMAMI FLAVOURS AND HINT OF SPICE, THIS SEAFOOD DELICACY IS A FAVOURITE AT CHINESE RESTAURANTS AND PERFECT FOR SHARING AT THE TABLE.

STIR-FRY

800 g (1 lb 12 oz) pipis or clams, preferably live
20 g (¾ oz) rice vermicelli noodles
3 tablespoons vegetable oil
1 tablespoon minced garlic
2 slices of ginger
1 tablespoon oyster sauce
4 tablespoons abalone sauce
1 tablespoon XO sauce
pinch of white pepper
½ teaspoon YumYum or MSG
600 ml (20½ fl oz/2½ cups) Chicken stock (page 32 or shop-bought)
1 tablespoon potato starch
2 tablespoons water
2 tablespoons Shaoxing wine (Chinese cooking wine)
1 teaspoon sesame oil

TO SERVE

half a spring onion (scallion), chopped
handful of coriander (cilantro) leaves

Before you start, place the pipis or clams in a large bowl of water to sit for 15 minutes to purge them of sand. Alternatively, you can leave them in the water overnight in the fridge.

Bring a pot of water to a boil and add the pipis or clams, boiling them for about 3 minutes. Once cooked, drain the pipis and rinse under cold water. Discard any unopened pipis. Then prepare the remaining pipis by using a paring knife to fully open each of them. Meanwhile, soak the vermicelli noodles in cold water for 15 minutes until softened, then drain them completely.

Heat the oil in a non-stick wok over medium heat. Add the softened vermicelli noodles and pan-fry them until golden and crispy on both sides. Once your noodle cake is crispy, remove it from the wok and set it aside to drain any excess oil.

In the same wok, add a little more oil if needed, and stir-fry the garlic and ginger until fragrant. Add the boiled pipis to the wok, then stir in the oyster sauce, abalone sauce, XO sauce, white pepper, YumYum or MSG and chicken stock. Mix everything together well and bring the mixture to a boil.

In a small bowl, mix the potato starch and water to make a slurry. Slowly pour the slurry into the wok while stirring continuously to thicken the sauce. Let the sauce cook for another 1–2 minutes until it thickens and the flavours meld together.

Finish by pouring in the Shaoxing wine and sesame oil, giving the dish a final toss to combine all the flavours. Cut the crispy noodle cake into quarters and place it on serving plates. Serve the pipis on top of the crispy vermicelli noodles, and garnish with chopped spring onion and coriander.

Serve immediately.

SERVES 6

STEAMED SCALLOPS WITH VERMICELLI

STEAMED SCALLOPS WITH VERMICELLI IS A DELICATE AND FLAVOURFUL DISH OF TENDER SCALLOPS TOPPED WITH GLASS NOODLES, GARLIC AND SAVOURY SAUCES. IT'S A POPULAR CHINESE APPETISER THAT'S BOTH LIGHT AND SATISFYING, PERFECT FOR ANY SEAFOOD LOVER.

40 g (1½ oz) mung bean vermicelli

12 scallops on the half-shell

10 g (¼ oz ginger), thinly sliced

3 tablespoons finely chopped garlic

SAUCE

1 teaspoon sugar

¼ teaspoon white pepper

1 teaspoon chicken bouillon powder

1 teaspoon sesame oil

1 tablespoon Shaoxing wine (Chinese cooking wine)

2 tablespoons light soy sauce

¼ teaspoon YumYum or MSG

60 ml (2 fl oz/¼ cup) water

1 tablespoon vegetable oil

TO SERVE

60 ml (2 fl oz/¼ cup) vegetable oil, to finish

spring onion (scallions), thinly sliced

coriander (cilantro) leaves

ginger, thinly sliced into matchsticks

Soak the mung bean vermicelli in warm water for about 10 minutes until softened, then drain and set aside. Clean the scallops thoroughly, ensuring they are free of any sand or grit, and place each scallop on its half shell.

In a small saucepan, combine all the sauce ingredients. Bring the mixture to a boil, stirring until the sugar and chicken bouillon powder are completely dissolved. Once the sauce is ready, remove it from the heat and set it aside.

Top each scallop with a small portion of the softened vermicelli. Add a few slices of ginger and a small amount of chopped garlic on top of the vermicelli-covered scallops. Arrange the scallops in a single layer on a steaming tray.

Steam the scallops over high heat for about 5–7 minutes, or until they are just cooked through. Carefully remove the steaming tray from the heat and spoon the prepared sauce over each scallop.

Heat the vegetable oil until smoking hot, then carefully pour a small amount over each scallop to release the aroma and add a finishing touch.

Serve the steamed scallops hot, garnished with spring onions, fresh coriander and ginger.

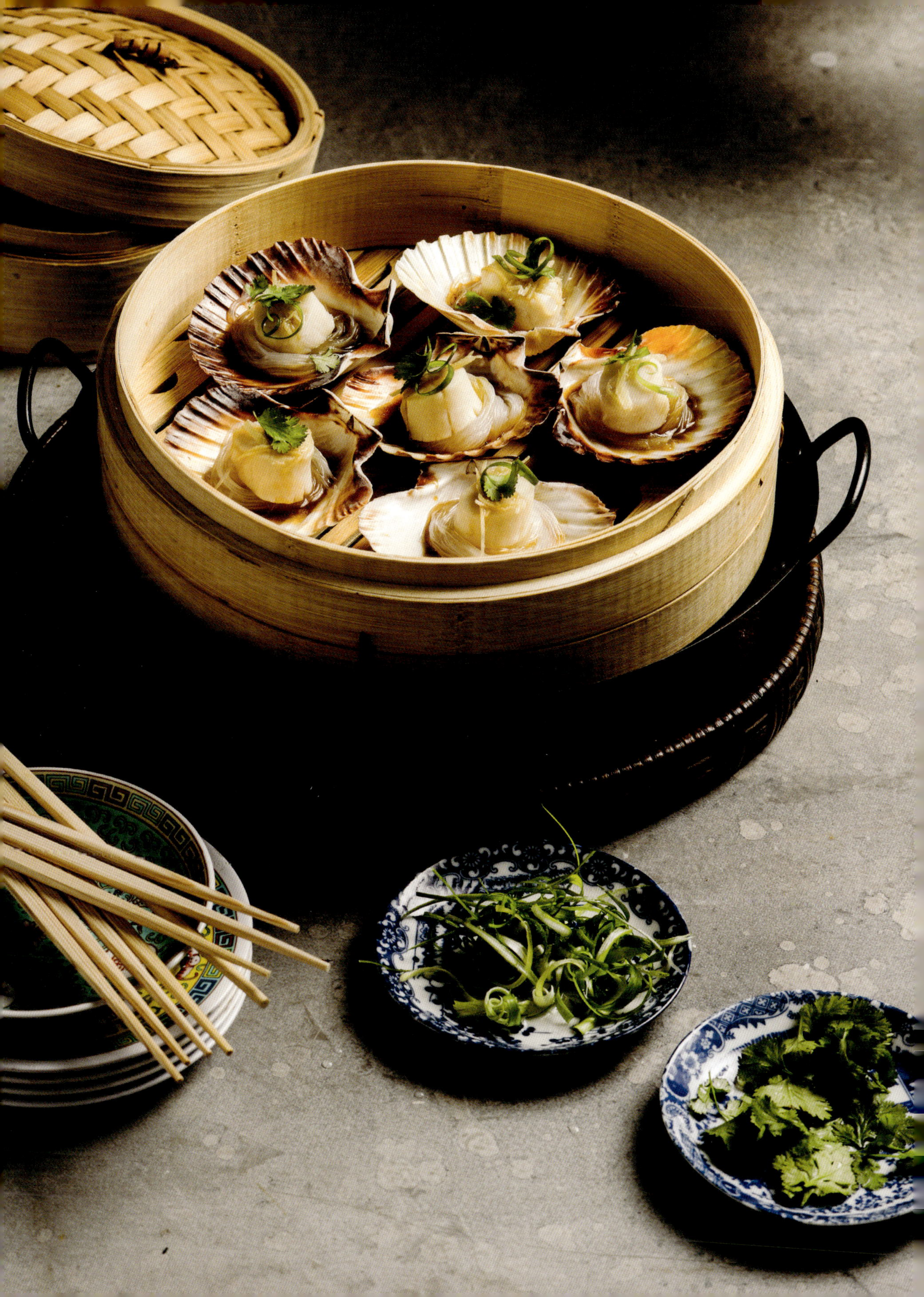

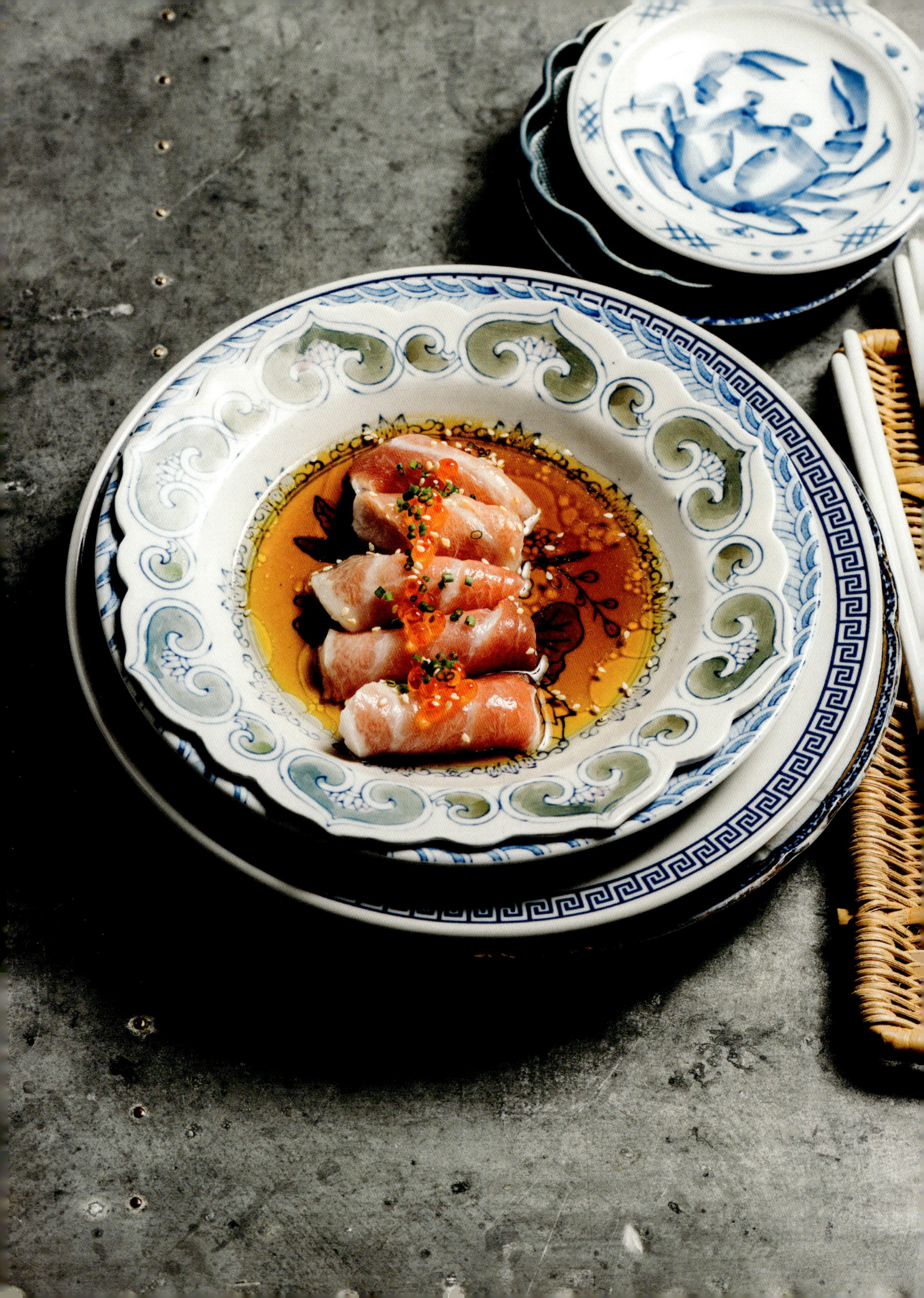

SERVES 3

TORO TORO

TORO TORO, TUNA SASHIMI, IS ALWAYS A SIGNATURE DISH AT MY POP-UPS. THIS DISH BRINGS A LUXURIOUS TWIST TO TRADITIONAL SASHIMI, OFFERING A PERFECT BALANCE OF SIMPLICITY AND INDULGENCE. THE FLAVOURS ARE FRESH AND CLEAN WITH RICHNESS FROM THE TRUFFLE OIL, A MUST TRY FOR SASHIMI LOVERS.

250 g (9 oz) sashimi-grade toro (tuna belly) or tuna

SAUCE
80 ml (2½ fl oz/⅓ cup) white soy sauce (shiro shoyu)
1 tablespoon liquid kombu
1 tablespoon truffle oil
4 tablespoons mirin
1 tablespoon sugar
1 tablespoon ponzu
2 teaspoons shallot oil

TO SERVE
chives, finely chopped
sesame seeds, toasted
salmon roe

In a bowl, combine the white soy sauce, kombu, truffle oil, mirin, sugar, ponzu and shallot oil, stirring well to thoroughly mix the ingredients. Thinly slice the toro (tuna) into sashimi pieces, roll into small cylinders, and arrange them neatly on a plate.

Pour the sauce over the tuna, allowing the flavours to complement the fish. Top the tuna slices with finely chopped chives, sesame seeds and salmon roe for added texture and flavour. This tastes best eaten fresh, so serve immediately.

SEAFOOD

SERVES 2–3

STEAMED GINGER-SHALLOT CORAL TROUT

THIS IS A CLASSIC WAY TO PREPARE FISH IN CHINESE CUISINE, CELEBRATING THE NATURAL FLAVOURS OF THE FISH WITH MINIMAL SEASONING. THIS TRADITIONAL METHOD OF STEAMING, COMBINED WITH AROMATIC GINGER AND SHALLOTS, ENHANCES THE TROUT'S DELICATE TEXTURE WHILE KEEPING IT MOIST AND TENDER.

SAUCE

2 teaspoons sugar
½ teaspoon white pepper
2 teaspoons chicken bouillon powder
2 teaspoons sesame oil
2 tablespoons Shaoxing wine (Chinese cooking wine)
4 tablespoons light soy sauce
120 ml (4 fl oz/½ cup) water
½ teaspoon YumYum or MSG

FISH

1 × 1.2–1.5 kg (2 lb 10 oz– 3 lb 5 oz) whole red coral trout, or fish of your choice

TO SERVE

1 knob ginger, thinly sliced into matchsticks
½ spring onion (scallion), thinly sliced into matchsticks
handful of coriander (cilantro) leaves
3 tablespoons vegetable oil

Combine all the sauce ingredients in a small saucepan. Bring the mixture to a simmer over medium heat, adjusting the seasoning to taste. Once the sauce is well balanced, set it aside.

Prepare the fish by scoring it four times on a diagonal on each side and place it in a steamer. Steam the fish over high heat for 10 minutes. Next, turn off the heat and let the fish rest in the steamer for an additional 2 minutes, allowing the residual heat to finish cooking. Check the doneness by gently inserting a fork into the thickest part of the fish. If it's not fully cooked, steam for another 3 minutes.

Once the fish is cooked, arrange the sliced ginger, spring onion and coriander leaves on top. Pour the prepared sauce over the fish, letting it soak into the flesh.

In a small saucepan, heat the vegetable oil until it's steaming hot. Carefully pour the hot oil over the ginger, spring onion and coriander garnish to release the aromatic flavours. Serve the steamed fish immediately.

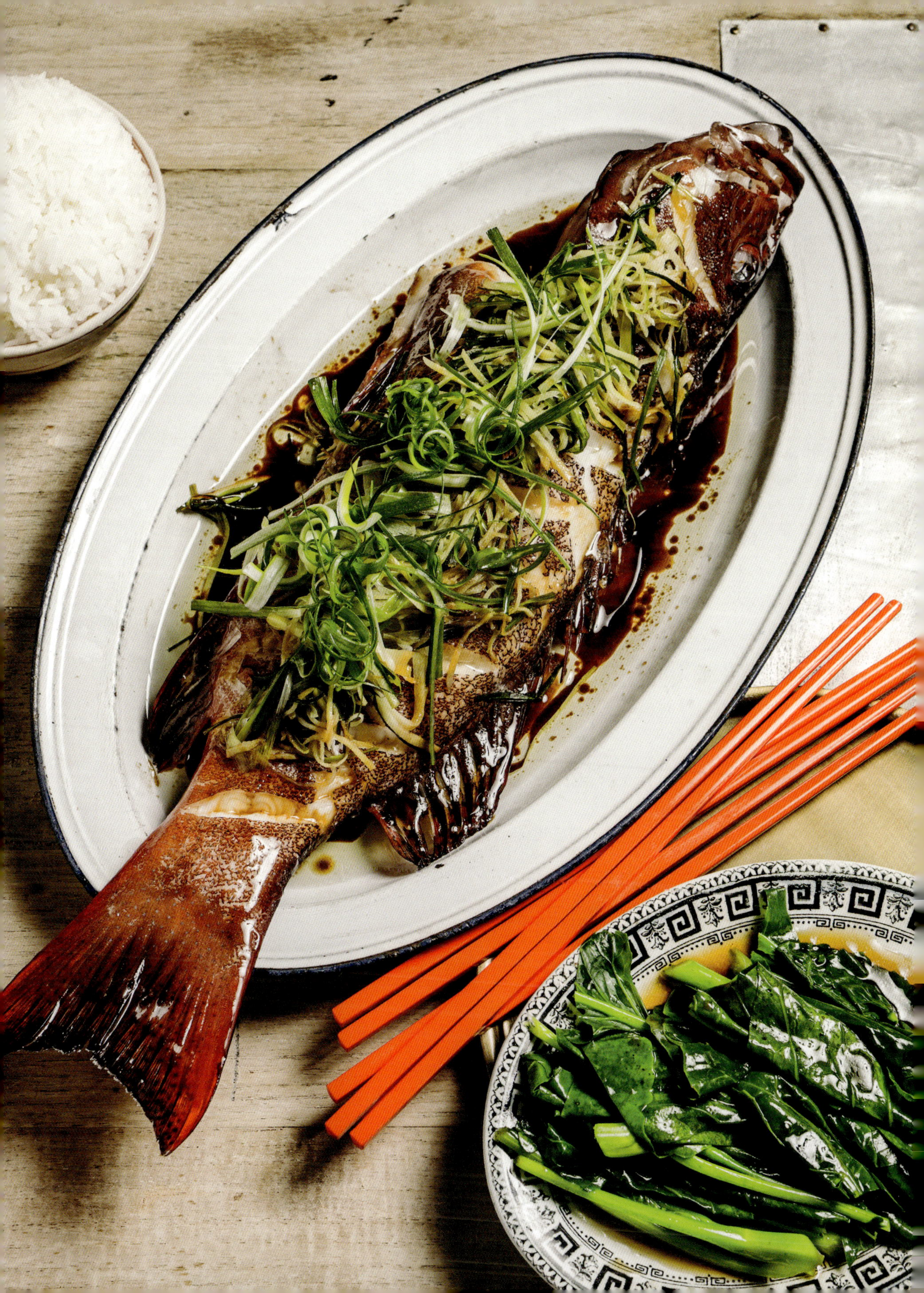

SERVES 4

FLYING LOBSTER NOODLES

I INVENTED THIS DISH. GROWING UP, LOBSTER WAS A RARE TREAT RESERVED FOR SPECIAL OCCASIONS. I WANTED TO BRING A CRAZY ELEMENT TO THIS CLASSIC CHINESE FAVOURITE, AND THAT'S HOW MY FLYING LOBSTER NOODLES WERE BORN. CRISPY NOODLES, TOPPED WITH JUICY CHUNKS OF LOBSTER AND FRESH PIPIS IN AN UMAMI SEAFOOD SAUCE – A REAL TREAT FOR YOUR NEXT SPECIAL OCCASION.

---

12 large pipis, or clams, preferably live

FLYING NOODLES

375 g (13 oz/1 pack) thin fresh egg noodles (e.g. MC Yee Foods)

2 pairs of high-quality disposable wooden chopsticks

vegetable oil, for deep-frying

LOBSTER

1.3 kg (2 lb 14 oz) live red rock lobster (or your lobster of choice), deconstructed

180 g (6½ oz/1½ cups) cornflour (cornstarch)

3 tablespoons oil

6 slices of ginger

8 garlic cloves, peeled and finely chopped

4 spring onions (scallions), cut into 3 cm (1¼ in) pieces

SAUCE

3 tablespoons Shaoxing wine (Chinese cooking wine)

60 ml (2 fl oz/¼ cup) water

1 heaped tablespoon potato starch

700 ml (23½ fl oz) Chicken stock (page 32 or shop-bought)

2 tablespoons sesame oil

Bring a wok of water to a boil and blanch the live pipis or clams for 1–2 minutes, or until they open. Drain them and use a paring knife to fully open the shells. Set the pipis aside for later use.

Fill a wok or large pot half full with oil and heat to 180°C (350°F) over medium–high heat (you can also test the oil with a wooden chopstick – if bubbles form around it, the oil is ready). Place the noodles in a mesh strainer. To create the illusion of noodles suspended in mid air, twirl about half the noodles between two chopsticks, twisting them so they stay in place. Leave the rest of the noodles hanging down into the strainer. Rest the strainer over the wok, hold the chopsticks in place and ladle the oil over the noodles several times, frying them until they are golden brown and firm enough to suspend the chopsticks in the air. Set the noodles aside on a wire rack to cool. Repeat the process with the remaining chopsticks and noodles.

To humanely dispatch the lobster, place it on a sturdy surface and use a sharp knife to quickly pierce the cross on the top of its head, cutting straight down. Next, deconstruct the lobster by removing the head and separating the body. Clean out the gills and innards from the head, retaining 2 full-length antennae for presentation. Cut the body into 8 pieces, each with a leg attached. Remove the spikes from the tail, then cut the tail into 3 cm (1¼ in) chunks, keeping it whole for presentation. Pat the lobster pieces dry.

In a large bowl, evenly coat the lobster pieces with cornflour, shaking off any excess. Reheat the oil from the noodles to 180°C (350°F). Once hot, add the lobster head and tail, ladling hot oil over the head until fully cooked. Remove and set aside. Fry the remaining lobster pieces for about 2 minutes, or until they turn deep orange. Remove and place on paper towels to drain. Set the remaining oil aside for future use.

SEASONINGS

½ teaspoon white pepper
2 teaspoons chicken bouillon powder
1 teaspoon sugar
2 teaspoons YumYum or MSG
½ teaspoon salt

TO SERVE

coriander (cilantro) leaves
spring onion (scallion), thinly sliced

In the empty wok, heat the 3 tablespoons of oil over high heat. Cook the ginger and garlic for 1 minute until fragrant, then add the lobster pieces (excluding the head and tail) and toss with Shaoxing wine. In a small bowl, combine the water and potato starch to make a slurry. Add the spring onions, pipis and chicken stock to the wok, along with all the seasoning ingredients. Bring to a simmer, then stir in the potato starch slurry to thicken the sauce. Finish by adding the sesame oil.

To plate, place the lobster head in the centre of your serving platter, with the tail at the back. Position one flying noodle structure in the back left and the other in the front right of the lobster head. Pour the lobster pieces, pipis and sauce over and around the noodles. Garnish with coriander and spring onions and serve immediately.

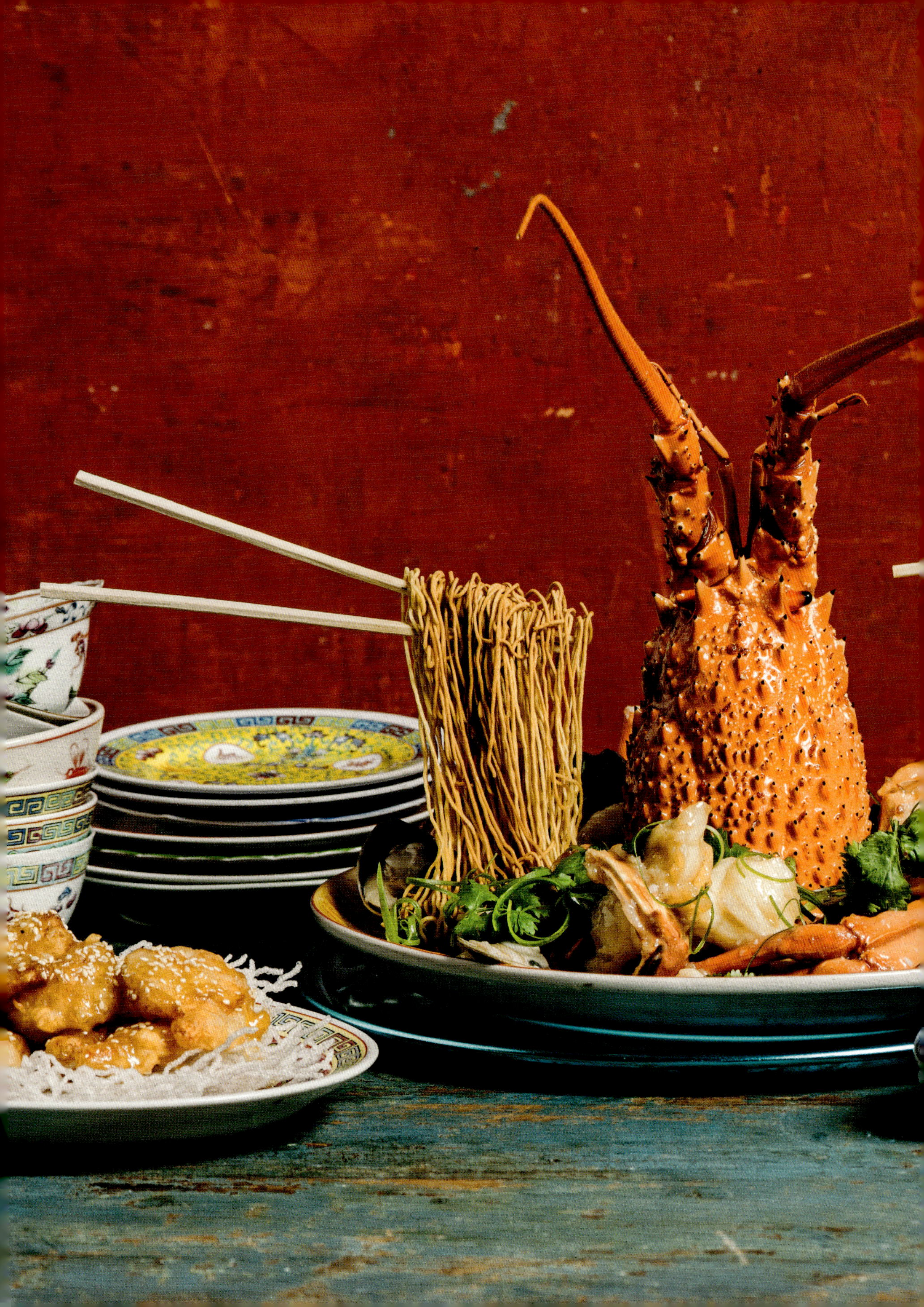

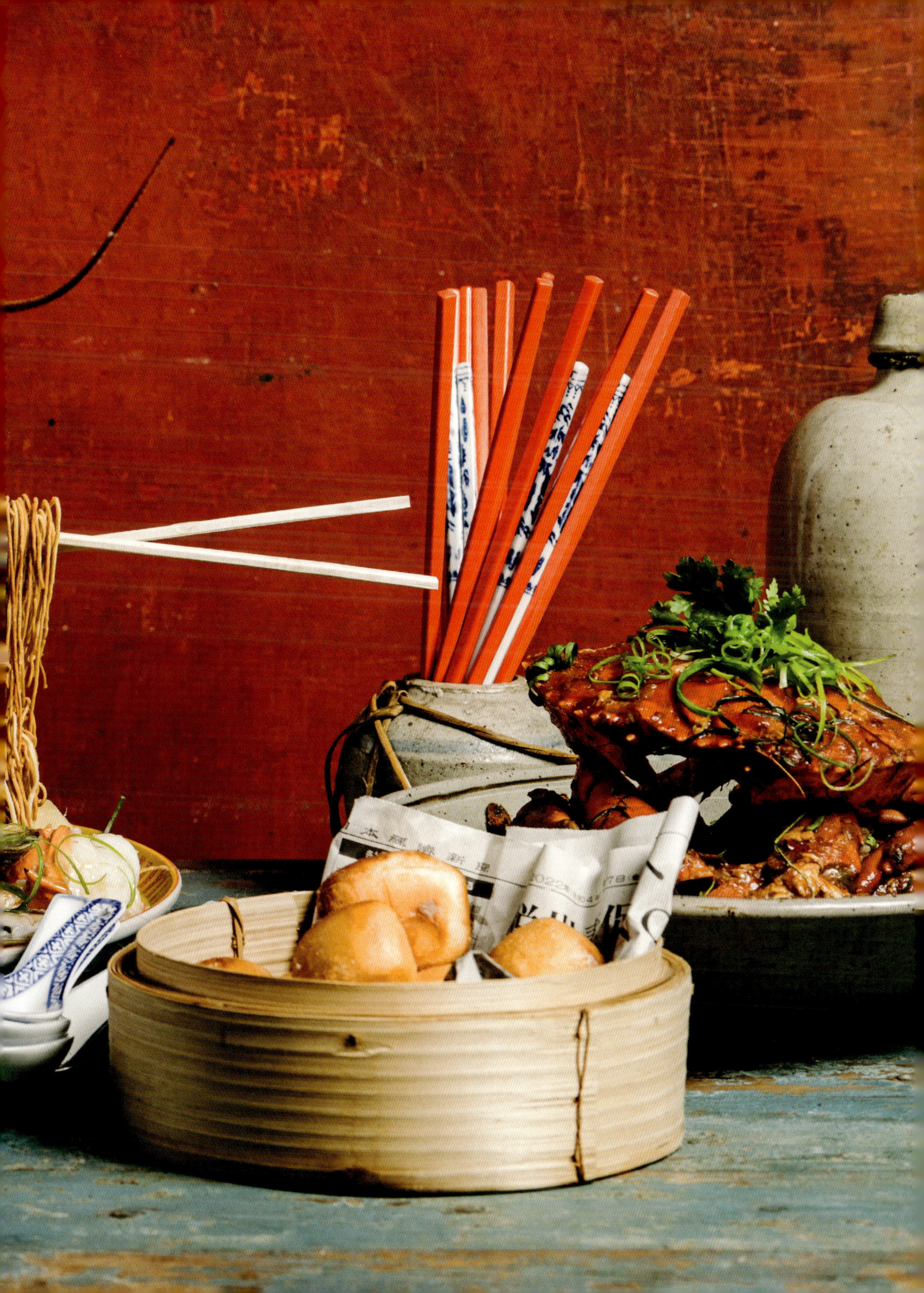

SERVES 4

SALTED EGG YOLK LOBSTER

SALTED EGG YOLK LOBSTER IS A LUXURIOUS AND RICH DISH THAT COMBINES THE SWEETNESS OF TENDER LOBSTER WITH THE SAVOURY, CREAMY FLAVOUR OF SALTED EGG YOLK. SALTED DUCK EGG YOLKS CAN BE BOUGHT PRECOOKED, OR YOU CAN BUY RAW SALTED DUCK EGGS AND REMOVE THE YOLKS, THEN STEAM FOR 5 TO 10 MINUTES, OR UNTIL FULLY COOKED.

1.3 kg (2 lb 14 oz) live red rock lobster

vegetable oil, for deep-frying

125 g (4½ oz/1 cup) cornflour (cornstarch)

6 salted duck egg yolks, steamed (see recipe introduction)

1 tablespoon unsalted butter

2 tablespoons minced garlic

½ teaspoon YumYum or MSG

1 teaspoon chicken bouillon powder

½ teaspoon sugar

Humanely dispatch the lobster using the method on page 110. Then, deconstruct the lobster by removing the head. Clean out the gills and innards from the lobster head. Cut the body into 8 pieces, each with a leg attached. Trim off the spikes from the tail, remove the membrane, and cut the tail into 3 cm (1¼ in) chunks, keeping it intact for presentation. Pat the lobster pieces dry to ensure a crispy fry.

Pour enough oil into a wok to fully cover the lobster, and bring it to 180°C (350°F) over medium heat (you can also test the oil with a wooden chopstick – if bubbles form around it, the oil is ready). Lightly coat the chopped lobster pieces, excluding the head and tail, in cornflour. Fry the lobster head and tail first until the shell turns orange, then set aside to drain on paper towels. Then, fry the remaining lobster pieces in batches for about 3 minutes, or until fully cooked. Strain the lobster pieces from the oil and place them on paper towels to drain. Reserve the leftover oil for future deep-frying.

In the now-empty wok, mash the steamed salted duck egg yolks with a fork until smooth. Over medium–low heat, melt the butter and stir in the mashed egg yolks, cooking until the mixture becomes a smooth, foamy sauce. Add the minced garlic, YumYum or MSG, chicken bouillon powder and sugar, stirring everything well to combine with the egg yolk mixture.

Toss the cooked lobster pieces into the wok, ensuring each piece is generously coated in the salted egg yolk sauce. Once well coated, transfer the lobster to a serving platter, arranging the lobster head and tail at either end.

Serve the salted egg yolk lobster immediately.

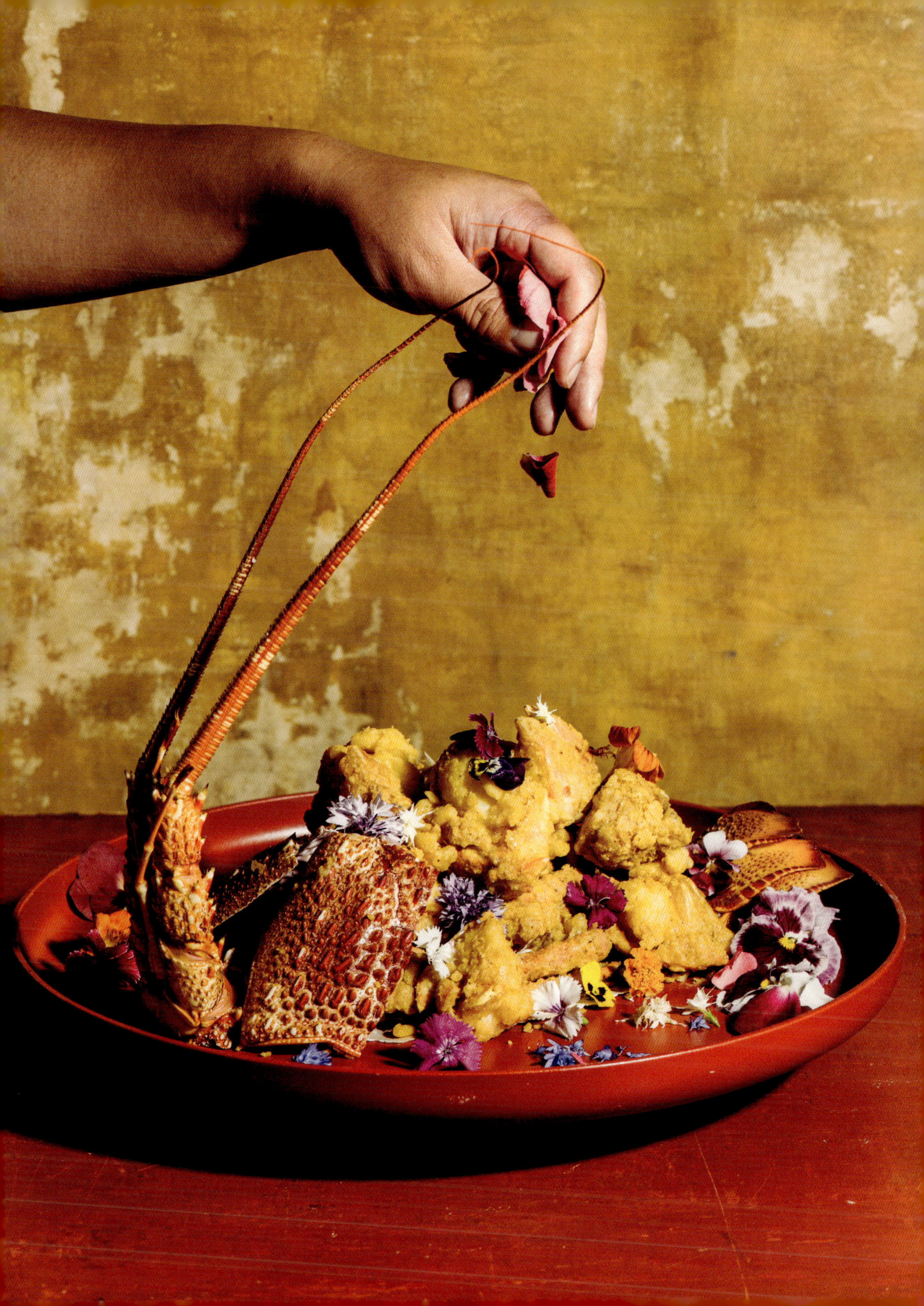

SERVES 4

SINGAPORE CHILLI CRAB

SINGAPORE CHILLI CRAB IS A MUST-TRY FOR SEAFOOD LOVERS, WITH ITS SWEET CRAB AND SPICY, TANGY SAUCE THAT'S PACKED WITH FLAVOUR. IT'S A MESSY BUT DELICIOUS DISH, ESPECIALLY WHEN YOU SCOOP UP THAT SAUCE WITH SOME FRIED MANTOU (CHINESE BUNS)!

3 tablespoons tomato sauce (ketchup)

1 heaped tablespoon sugar

1½ teaspoons tau cheo (fermented bean paste)

1 teaspoon YumYum or MSG

2 teaspoons chicken bouillon powder

2 teaspoons unsalted butter

1 teaspoon potato starch

625 ml (21 fl oz/2½ cups) Chicken stock (page 32 or shop-bought)

1 egg, beaten

REMPAH (SPICE PASTE)

1 tablespoon belacan (firm shrimp paste)

3 shallots

3 garlic cloves

2 red chillies

1 bird's eye chilli (optional)

2 whole dried chillies

1 coriander (coriander) root

½ thumb-sized piece of galangal (approx. 5 g/⅛ oz)

¼ lemongrass stalk, inner white part only

juice of ¼ lime or calamansi

CRAB AND SAUCE

500 g–1 kg (1 lb 2 oz –2 lb 3 oz) mud crab, live

vegetable oil, for deep-frying, plus ½ cup extra

125 g (4½ oz/1 cup) cornflour (cornstarch)

TO SERVE

coriander (cilantro) leaves

chillies, sliced

spring onions (scallions), chopped

mantou (Chinese steamed buns), deep-fried until golden brown

Toast the belacan by heating a wok over medium heat without any oil. Break up the belacan and place it directly in the wok, pressing it slightly with a spatula to ensure even contact. Allow it to toast for about 3–5 minutes, turning it occasionally until it becomes dry, crumbly, and releases a strong, deep aroma. Once it's toasted to your liking, remove it from the wok and let it cool slightly.

To humanely dispatch the mud crab, place it belly-side up on a sturdy surface. Insert the tip of a sharp knife into the centre of its underside, just below the triangular apron, and push down firmly (to sever the nerve centre). Once dispatched, lift the apron flap and remove the top shell with the tip of a cleaver to expose the internal organs. Discard the inedible gills (known as 'dead man's fingers') on each side. Next, grip each claw and leg at the joint, then using the cleaver's heel, carefully press and twist to detach them without damaging the meat. Position the crab upright and use a firm chop with the cleaver to split the body in half, creating easy access to the meat. Finally, crack the claws and legs by giving them a gentle tap with the cleaver's back edge to break the shell without crushing the meat, making it ready for cooking or further preparation.

In a food processor, combine the shallots, garlic, red chillies, bird's eye chilli (if using), dried chillies, coriander root, galangal, lemongrass, lime juice and toasted belacan. Blitz the mixture until it forms a fine paste.

Heat enough oil in a wok to fully cover the crab, bringing it to 190°C (375°F) over medium–high heat. If you don't have a thermometer, test the oil with a wooden chopstick – bubbles should form around it immediately. Fry the crab shell for about 30 seconds, or until it turns orange, then remove and set aside. Combine the cornflour and remaining crab pieces in a large bowl and toss to coat. Fry the coated crab pieces for 30–60 seconds, or until cooked through. Carefully strain the crab pieces from the oil and place them on paper towels to drain. Reserve the leftover oil for future use.

In the now-empty wok, heat ½ cup of oil over medium–high heat until very hot. Add the rempah and fry until fragrant. Stir in the tomato sauce, sugar, tau cheo, YumYum or MSG, chicken bouillon powder and butter, and combine well.

In a small bowl, dissolve the potato starch in the chicken stock and add it to the wok, stirring to thicken the sauce. Add the fried crab pieces to the wok and stir well to coat them with the sauce.

Slowly pour the beaten egg into the sauce, gently stirring to create egg ribbons. Simmer for another 10 seconds before turning off the heat.

Pour the chilli crab and sauce onto a serving platter, place the fried shell on top, and garnish with coriander leaves, sliced chillies and chopped spring onions. Serve hot with deep-fried mantou for dipping.

SERVES 2

HONEY PRAWNS

WITH JUICY PRAWNS (SHRIMP) COATED IN A LIGHT BATTER AND TOSSED IN A STICKY HONEY SAUCE, THIS IS A LONG-TIME CHINESE FAVOURITE. IT'S SWEET, SAVOURY AND CRISPY ALL AT ONCE, AND A REAL CROWD-PLEASER TO WHIP UP AT HOME.

BATTER

125 g (4½ oz/1 cup) self-raising flour
60 g (2 oz/½ cup) cornflour (cornstarch)
270 ml (9 fl oz) water

PRAWNS

1 × quantity Velveted prawns (shrimp) (page 31)
vegetable oil, for deep-frying

SAUCE

175 g (6 oz/½ cup) honey
6 tablespoons water
1 tablespoon custard powder
3 tablespoons sugar
pinch of salt
¾ teaspoon YumYum or MSG

toasted sesame seeds, to serve

In a large bowl, mix together the self-raising flour and cornflour. Gradually add water while whisking until the batter is smooth. Add the prawns to the batter and stir until they are fully coated.

Fill a wok or large pot halfway full with oil and heat to 180°C (350°F) over high heat (you can also test the oil with a wooden chopstick – if bubbles form around it, the oil is ready). One by one, drop the battered prawns into the hot oil and fry for 3–5 minutes, or until they are golden brown and cooked through. Carefully strain the prawns from the oil and drain them on paper towels. Reserve the leftover oil for future deep-frying.

In the now-empty wok or large pot, combine all the sauce ingredients. Heat the mixture over high heat until it begins to bubble and slightly thickens into a sauce.

Once the sauce is ready, add the fried prawns and toss them until they are well coated in the honey sauce. Serve immediately, sprinkling with toasted sesame seeds.

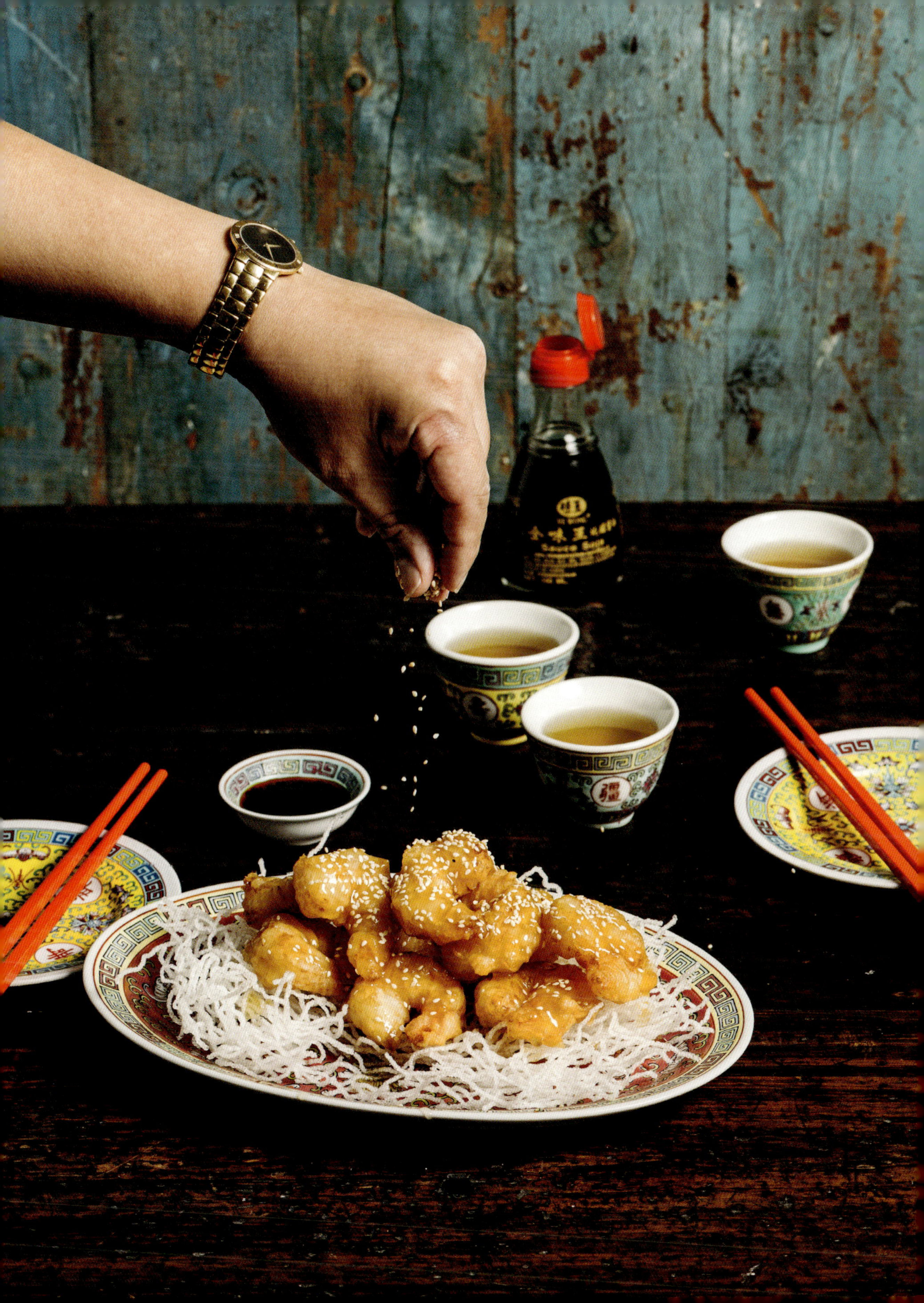

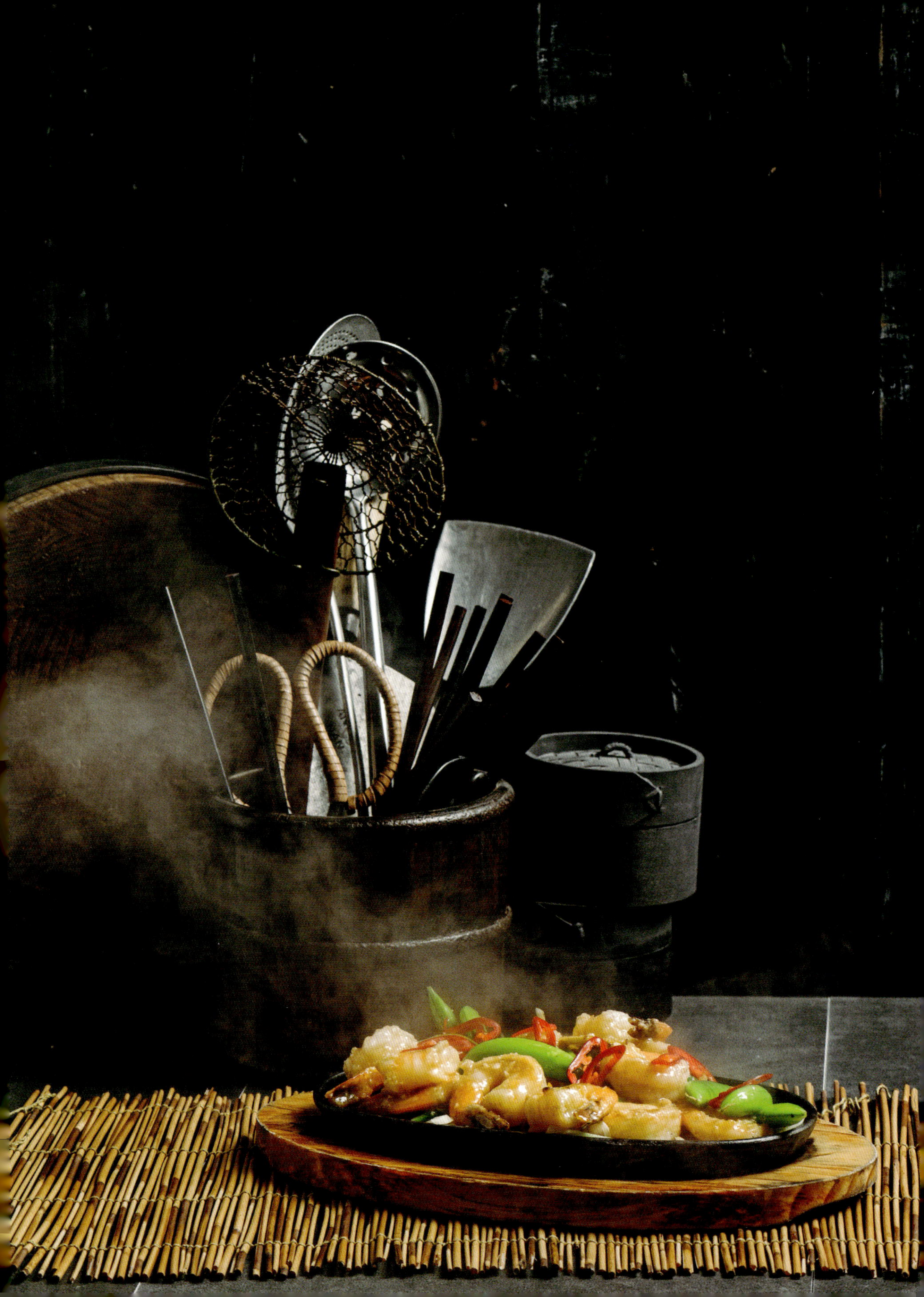

SERVES 2

SIZZLING GARLIC PRAWNS

SIZZLING GARLIC PRAWNS (SHRIMP) IS A FLAVOURFUL DISH OF JUICY PRAWNS WITH A RICH, GARLICKY SAUCE, SERVED ON A HOT, SIZZLING PLATE. THE AROMA AND CRACKLE OF THE DISH AS IT HITS THE TABLE MAKES IT AN EXCITING AND DELICIOUS CHOICE FOR SEAFOOD LOVERS.

STIR-FRY

vegetable oil for flash-frying, plus 1 tablespoon extra

1 × quantity Velveted prawns (page 31)

6 sugar-snap peas

1 spring onion (scallion), cut into 6 cm (2½ in) lengths

10 garlic cloves, minced

2 slices of ginger

120 ml (4 fl oz/½ cup) Chicken stock (page 32 or shop-bought)

3 teaspoons Shaoxing wine (Chinese cooking wine)

1 teaspoon sesame oil

¼ teaspoon white pepper

1 teaspoon potato starch

2 teaspoons water

½ brown onion, thinly sliced

red chilli slices, to garnish (optional)

Fill a wok or large pot one-third full with oil and heat to 190°C (375°F) over a medium–high heat. Flash-fry the velveted prawns until they are almost cooked through. Add the sugar-snap peas with the spring onion and fry for an additional 30 seconds. Carefully strain the prawns and spring onion from the oil, placing them in a sieve or on a plate lined with paper towels to drain. Set the leftover oil aside for future use.

Meanwhile, place a cast-iron sizzling plate over your wok burner or in an oven preheated to 220°C (430°F) to heat.

In the empty wok or frying pan, heat 1 tablespoon of vegetable oil over medium heat. Add the minced garlic and ginger slices, stir-frying until fragrant. Pour in half of the chicken stock, followed by the prawns. Stir in the Shaoxing wine, sesame oil, white pepper, and the remaining chicken stock, bringing the mixture to a boil.

In a small bowl, mix the potato starch and water to make slurry. Slowly pour the slurry into the boiling sauce, stirring continuously until the sauce thickens to your desired consistency. Remove from the heat once thickened.

By this time, the sizzling plate should be hot. Carefully remove it from the heat and place it on a heatproof board. Arrange the thinly sliced raw onion evenly over the hot plate, then immediately pour the finished garlic prawns and sauce over the top. The dish should sizzle as it makes contact with the plate.

Serve the sizzling garlic prawns immediately.

SEAFOOD

SERVES 2

SALT AND PEPPER SQUID

SALT AND PEPPER SQUID IS A BELOVED DISH IN CHINESE CUISINE, KNOWN FOR ITS CRISPY, GOLDEN EXTERIOR AND TENDER, FLAVOURFUL SQUID. LIGHTLY SEASONED WITH A PUNCHY MIX OF SALT, PEPPER AND AROMATIC SPICES, THIS RECIPE BRINGS RESTAURANT-QUALITY SQUID TO YOUR TABLE IN NO TIME.

SQUID

1 × 400 g (14 oz) squid, whole

1 tablespoon Shaoxing wine (Chinese cooking wine)

1 tablespoon potato starch

pinch of white pepper

STIR-FRY

1 tablespoon oil

¼ red capsicum (bell pepper), thinly sliced

1 red bird's eye chilli, thinly sliced

1 spring onion (scallion), chopped

4 garlic cloves, thinly sliced

2 teaspoons Five-spice salt and pepper (page 33)

BATTER

125 g (4½ oz/1 cup) self-raising flour

60 g (2 oz/½ cup) cornflour (cornstarch)

270 ml (9 fl oz) water

pinch of salt

1 teaspoon vegetable oil, plus extra for deep-frying

TO SERVE

spring onion (scallion), thinly sliced

chilli, thinly sliced

Rinse the squid well under cold water. Pull the head and tentacles away from the body, removing the clear quill from inside the squid's body and discarding it. Peel off the outer skin and discard that as well. Rinse the squid tube and tentacles to remove any remaining innards. Slice down one side of the squid to form one large sheet. Using a sharp knife, gently score the surface of the squid in a crosshatch pattern. Cut the squid tube into 6 cm (2½ in) long diamonds. Pat the pieces of squid dry with paper towels.

In a bowl, combine the squid pieces and tentacle sections with the Shaoxing wine, potato starch, and white pepper. Toss well to coat the squid evenly and let it marinate for 10–15 minutes.

In a separate bowl, make the batter by whisking together the self-raising flour, cornflour, water, salt and oil until smooth. Set aside.

Fill a wok or large pot halfway full with oil and heat to 180°C (350°F) over medium–high heat (you can also test the oil with a wooden chopstick – if bubbles form around it, the oil is ready).

Dip each piece of marinated squid into the batter, letting any excess drip off, and carefully add the squid to the hot oil in batches. Fry for 2–3 minutes or until the squid is golden and crispy. Remove the squid from the oil and drain on paper towels. Strain the used oil and reserve for future use.

Heat 1 tablespoon of oil in the wok or pot over medium heat. Add the red capsicum, red chilli, spring onion and garlic, stir-frying for 2–3 minutes until the vegetables are fragrant and slightly softened.

Return the fried squid to the wok, tossing everything together quickly over high heat. Sprinkle with the five-spice salt and pepper mix, tossing to coat the squid evenly. Taste and adjust the seasoning as desired.

Transfer the salt and pepper squid to a serving plate and garnish with additional chopped spring onion or chilli.

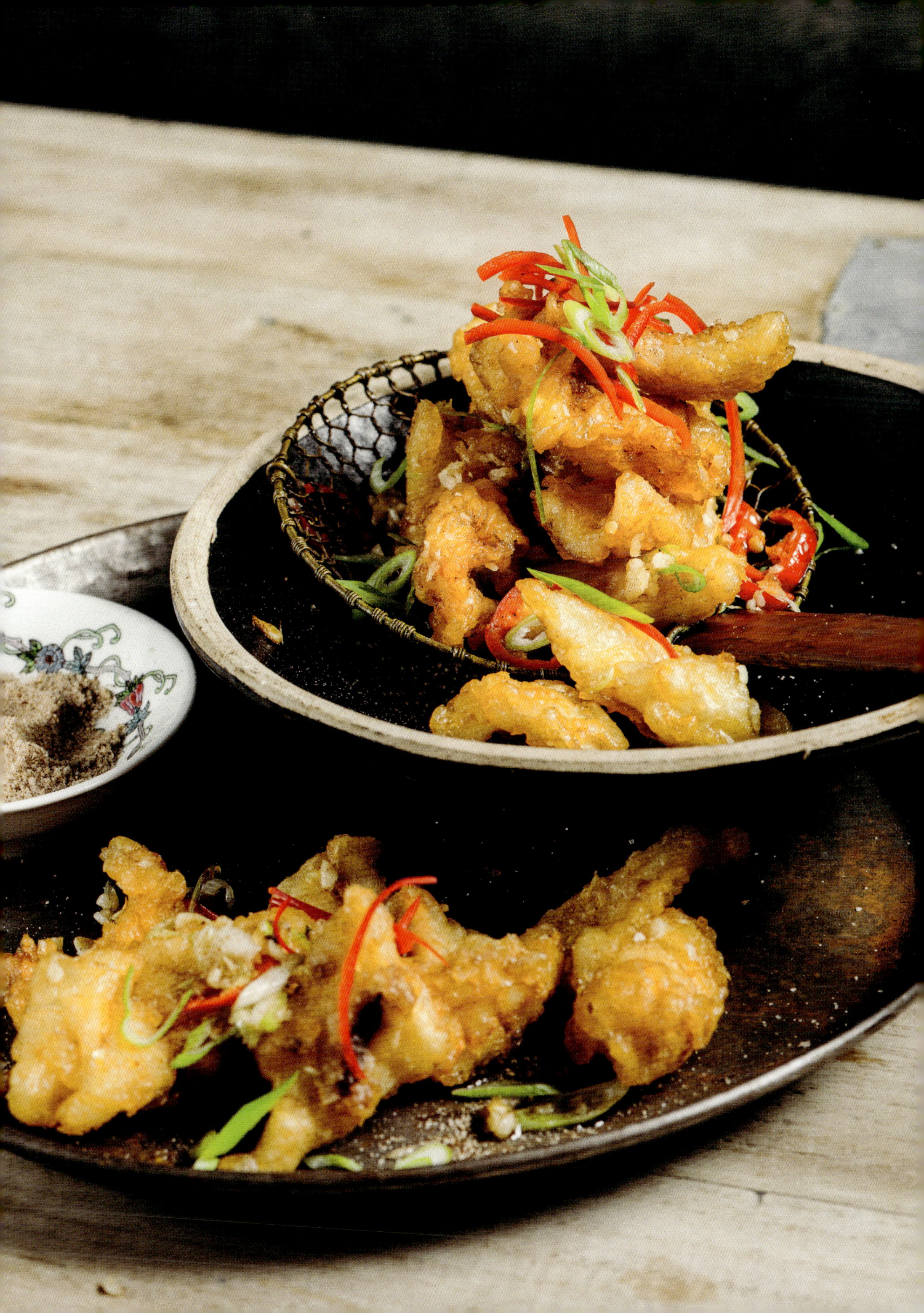

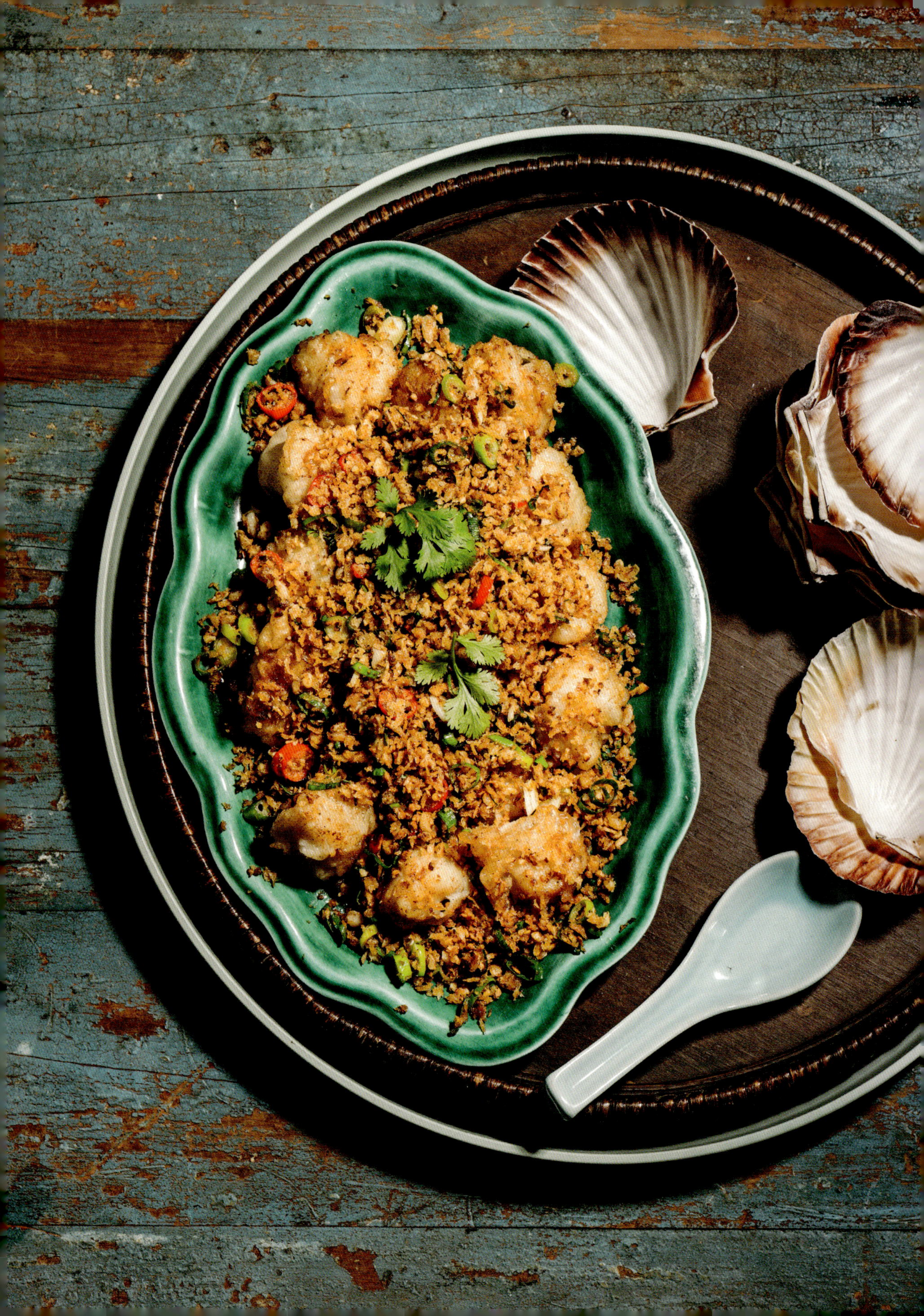

SERVES 3

TYPHOON SHELTER SCALLOPS

TYPHOON SHELTER SCALLOPS ARE A BOLD AND FLAVOURFUL DISH INSPIRED BY THE FAMOUS HONG KONG STREET FOOD, TYPICALLY MADE WITH PRAWNS (SHRIMP). WITH TENDER SCALLOPS TOSSED IN CRISPY GARLIC, CHILLI AND FRAGRANT SPICES, IT'S A WINNING MIX OF TEXTURES AND SAVOURY GOODNESS.

20 garlic cloves, minced

vegetable oil for deep-frying, plus 2 tablespoons extra

3 dried chillies, roughly chopped

¼ teaspoon paprika

400 g (14 oz) scallops

30 g (1 oz/½ cup) panko breadcrumbs

¼ teaspoon white pepper

2 teaspoons Shaoxing wine (Chinese cooking wine)

2 slices of ginger, finely chopped

2 spring onions (scallions), finely chopped, plus extra to garnish

2 red chillies, finely chopped

pinch of salt

¼ teaspoon sugar

1 teaspoon chicken bouillon powder

¼ teaspoon YumYum or MSG

green and red chilli, thinly sliced, to serve

BATTER

75 g (2¾ oz/½ cup) self-raising flour

30 g (1 oz/¼ cup) cornflour (cornstarch)

135 ml (4½ fl oz) water

Place the minced garlic in a sieve and submerge it in a wok half-filled with cold oil, ensuring there is enough oil to completely cover the sieve. Cook over low heat, stirring constantly, until the garlic turns a light blonde colour. Add the chopped dried chillies to the garlic and fry for 30 seconds. Remove the sieve from the oil, drain, and set the garlic-chilli mixture aside. Stir in the paprika to combine.

To make the batter, combine the self-raising flour and cornflour in a separate bowl. Gradually add water while whisking until the batter is smooth and free of lumps.

Fill a wok or large pot halfway full with vegetable oil and bring to 180°C (350°F) over medium–high heat. You can also test the oil with a wooden chopstick – if bubbles form around it when lowered in, it's hot enough. Once the oil is hot, add the scallops to the batter, stirring to coat each scallop evenly. One by one, carefully lower the scallops into the hot oil, frying them in batches to avoid overcrowding the pot. Fry the scallops for 4–5 minutes, or until golden brown and crispy. Remove the scallops with a slotted spoon and drain in a sieve or on paper towels to remove any excess oil. Reserve the leftover oil for future use.

In the now-empty wok, heat 2 tablespoons of oil over medium heat. Add the panko breadcrumbs and toss them continuously until golden brown. Then add the white pepper, Shaoxing wine, chopped ginger, spring onions, red chillies, salt, sugar, chicken bouillon powder and YumYum or MSG, tossing everything until fragrant and well combined.

Return the fried garlic mixture and the scallops to the wok, lightly tossing to combine all the flavours. Garnish with additional spring onions or green and red chilli and serve immediately.

SERVES 2

SLIPPERY SHRIMP

SLIPPERY SHRIMP COMES FROM THE ICONIC YANG CHOW RESTAURANT IN LOS ANGELES' CHINATOWN, WHERE IT QUICKLY BECAME A SIGNATURE DISH. WITH ITS CRISPY PRAWNS (SHRIMP) TOSSED IN A TANGY, SWEET AND SLIGHTLY SPICY SAUCE, IT'S NOW A BELOVED FAVOURITE IN CHINESE-AMERICAN CUISINE.

PRAWNS

2 × quantity Velveted prawns (shrimp) (page 31)

120 g (4½ oz/1 cup) cornflour (cornstarch)

vegetable oil, for deep-frying

SAUCE

3 tablespoons tomato sauce (ketchup)

60 ml (2 fl oz/¼ cup) rice vinegar or distilled white vinegar

60 ml (2 fl oz/¼ cup) rice wine

2 teaspoons sesame oil

3 tablespoons sugar

2 teaspoons salt

2 teaspoons potato starch

60 ml (2 fl oz/¼ cup) water

STIR-FRY

2 tablespoons vegetable oil

5 garlic cloves, minced

2 teaspoons minced ginger

large pinch of chilli flakes

4 spring onions (scallions), finely chopped, plus extra for garnish

coriander (cilantro) leaves, to garnish

In a bowl, toss the prawns in the cornflour until fully coated, then set them aside. In a separate bowl, mix together the tomato sauce, rice vinegar, rice wine, sesame oil, sugar and salt to make the sauce. Stir until the sugar is fully dissolved, then set the sauce aside.

Fill a wok or large pot halfway full with the oil and bring to 180°C (350°F) over medium–high heat. Carefully add the cornflour-coated prawns to the hot oil and fry for 2–3 minutes, or until they are golden and crispy. Once fried, strain the prawns from the oil and place them in a sieve or on a plate lined with paper towels to drain. Set the leftover oil aside for future deep-frying.

In the now-empty wok, heat 2 tablespoons of oil over medium heat. Add the minced garlic, ginger and chilli flakes, stir-frying for about 30 seconds until fragrant. Reduce the heat to low and pour in the tomato sauce mixture, bringing the sauce to a simmer.

In a small bowl, mix the potato starch and water to make a slurry. Slowly pour the slurry into the simmering sauce, stirring continuously until the sauce thickens to your desired consistency. Once the sauce has thickened, add the fried prawns to the wok and toss them until they are evenly coated and heated through.

Add the spring onions to the wok and give everything a final toss. Serve the slippery shrimp hot, garnished with coriander leaves and extra spring onions.

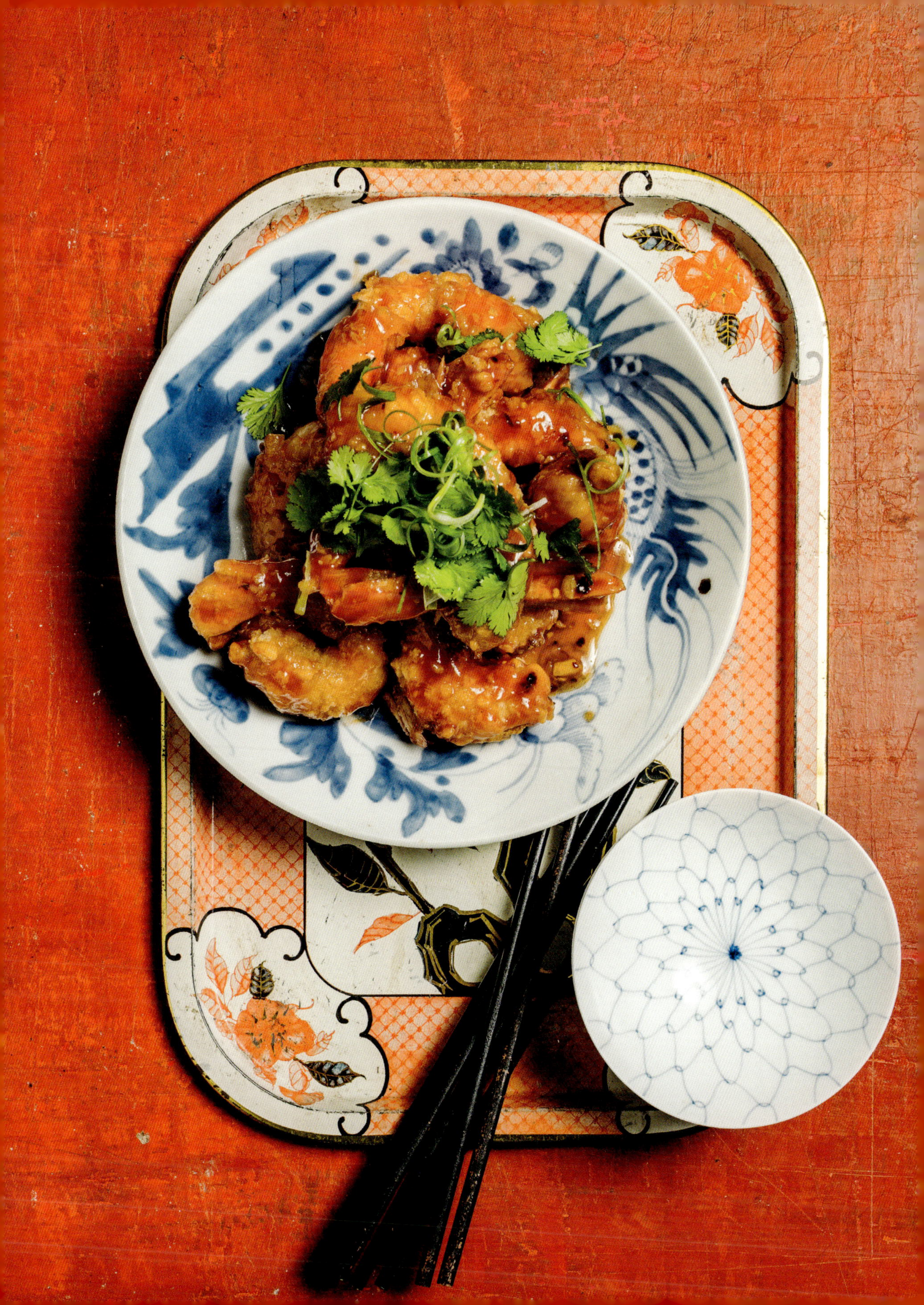

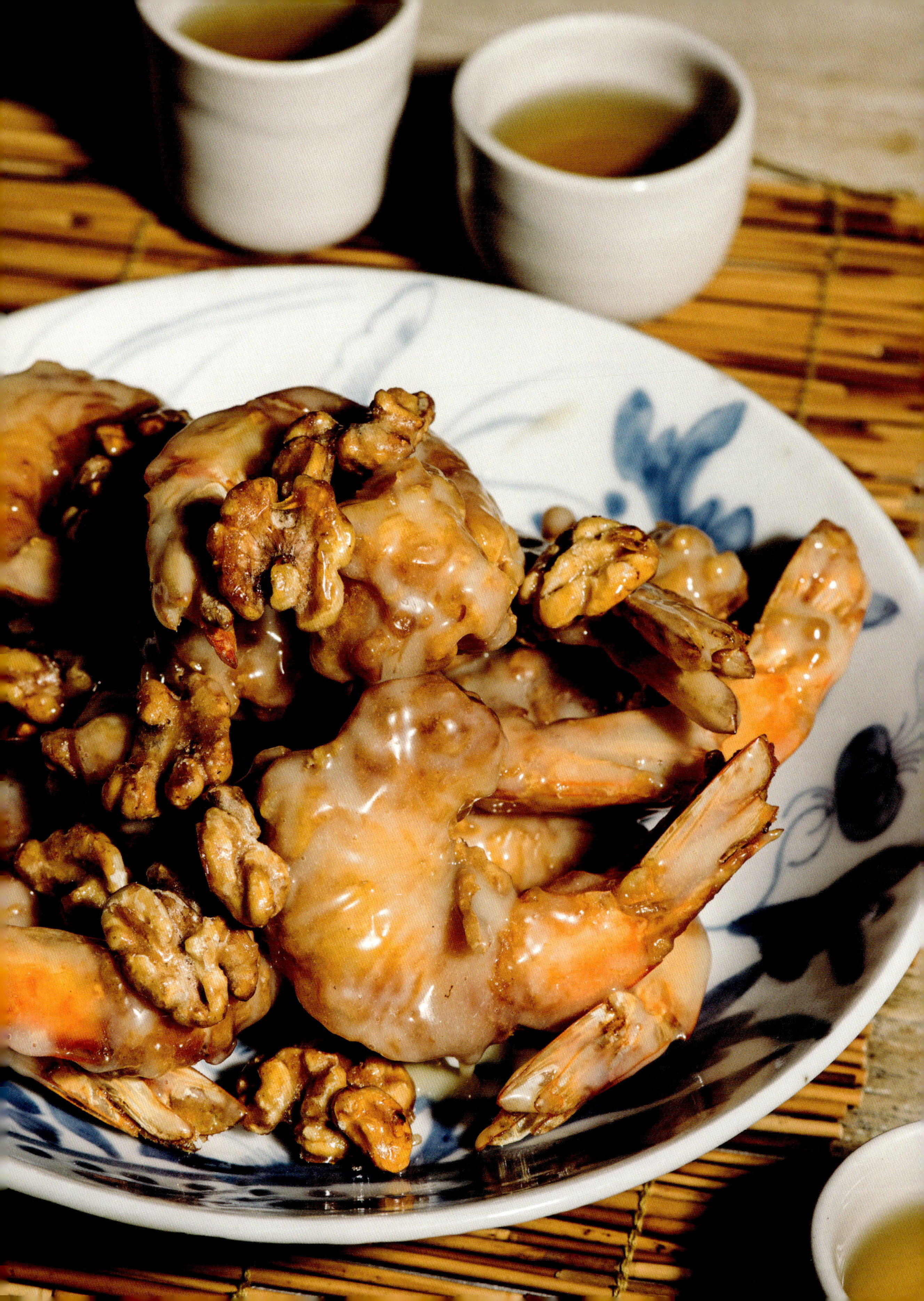

SERVES 2
HONEY WALNUT SHRIMP

HONEY WALNUT SHRIMP IS A FAN FAVOURITE AT AMERICAN-CHINESE CHAIN PANDA EXPRESS. IT'S SWEET, CREAMY AND CRUNCHY, AND EQUALLY FUN TO MAKE AND ENJOY AT HOME.

CANDIED WALNUTS

30 g (1 oz/¼ cup) walnut halves
3 tablespoons sugar
1 tablespoon water

PRAWNS

125 g (4½ oz/1 cup) self-raising flour
60 g (2 oz/½ cup) cornflour (cornstarch)
270 ml (9 fl oz) water
1 × quantity Velveted prawns (page 31)
vegetable oil, for deep-frying

SAUCE

70 g (2½ oz/¼ cup) Japanese mayonnaise (e.g. Kewpie) or regular mayonnaise
3 tablespoons sweetened condensed milk
2 tablespoons honey
1 tablespoon freshly squeezed lemon juice

TO SERVE

lemon slices (optional)
spring onion (scallion), thinly sliced, optional

In a small saucepan, combine the walnut halves, sugar and water. Cook over medium heat, stirring frequently, until the sugar dissolves and coats the walnuts. Continue cooking until the walnuts are caramelised and golden brown. Transfer the candied walnuts to a sheet of parchment paper to cool, and set them aside.

In a large bowl, mix the self-raising flour and cornflour. Gradually whisk in the water until the batter is smooth.

Fill a wok or large pot halfway full with oil and heat to 180°C (350°F) over medium–high heat (you can also test the oil with a wooden chopstick – if bubbles form around it, the oil is ready). Dip the velveted prawns into the batter, ensuring they are fully coated. Carefully drop the prawns into the hot oil one at a time and fry them for 3–5 minutes, or until golden brown and cooked through. Once fried, carefully strain the prawns from the oil and set them aside in a sieve or on a plate lined with paper towels to drain. Set the leftover oil aside for future deep-frying.

In the empty wok or large pot over low heat, combine the Japanese mayonnaise, sweetened condensed milk, honey and lemon juice, stirring until well combined. Add the fried prawns to the sauce and gently toss to coat them evenly.

Transfer the coated prawns to a serving plate and sprinkle the candied walnuts on top. Serve the honey walnut shrimp immediately, garnished with lemon slices or spring onions if desired.

XO BUTTER STEAMED OYSTERS

SERVES 4

THIS IS A DELICIOUS MIX OF TENDER OYSTERS, BUTTERY RICHNESS AND SAVOURY XO SAUCE. IT'S AN EASY-YET-FANCY DISH THAT'S PERFECT FOR A SPECIAL MEAL OR WHEN YOU WANT TO ENJOY SOMETHING A LITTLE EXTRA AT HOME.

80 ml (2½ fl oz/⅓ cup) XO sauce

125 g (4½ oz/½ cup) unsalted butter, softened

¼ teaspoon YumYum or MSG

12 oysters

spring onion (scallion), thinly sliced, to serve

In a bowl, combine the XO sauce, softened butter and YumYum or MSG, mixing until smooth and well combined. Arrange the oysters on a plate that fits inside your steamer, and top each oyster with a teaspoon of the XO butter mixture.

Prepare a steamer and steam the oysters over high heat for about 7 minutes, or until fully cooked. Once steamed, garnish the oysters with thinly sliced spring onion and serve immediately.

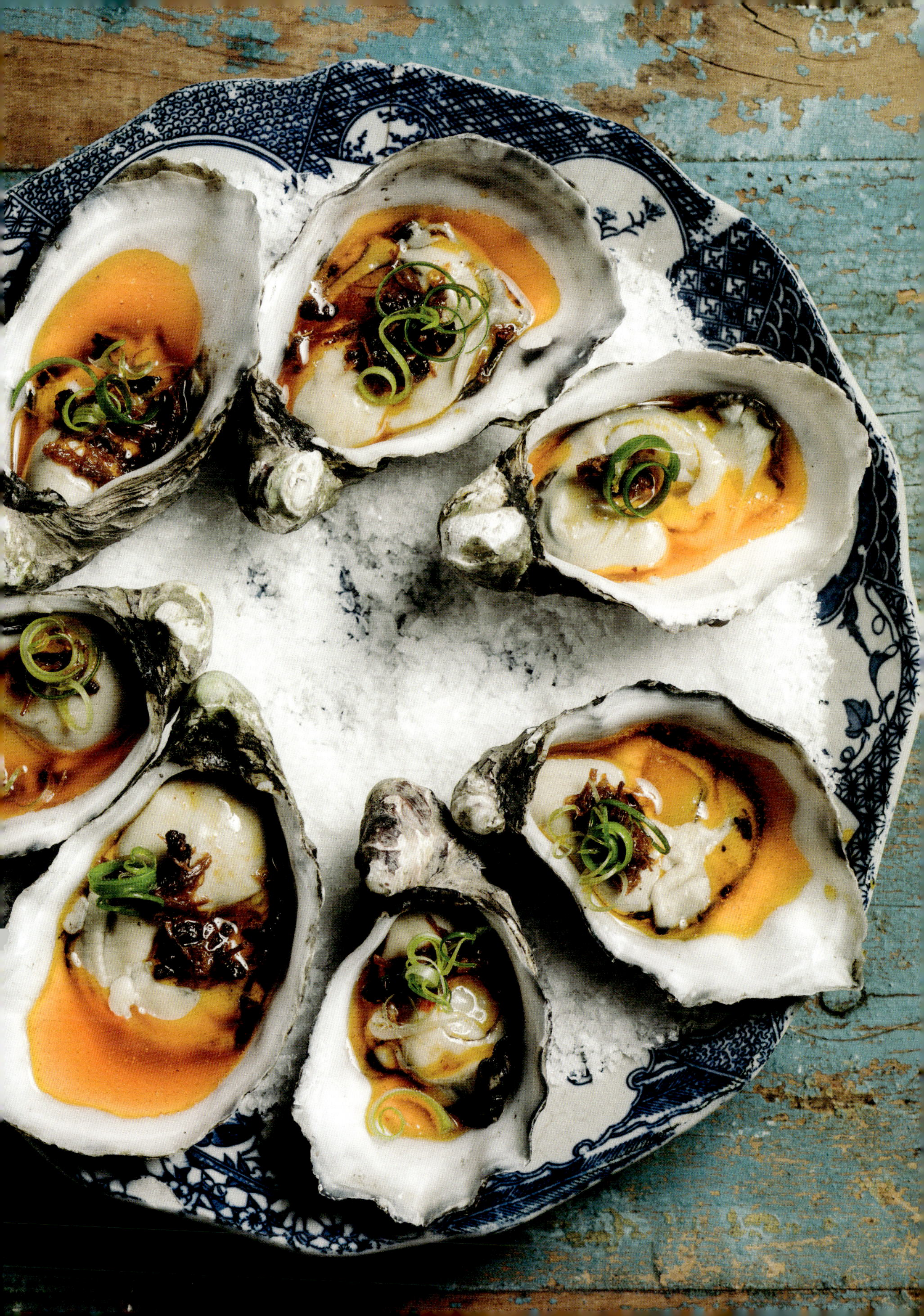

POULTRY

SERVES 3–4

KUNG PAO CHICKEN

KUNG PAO CHICKEN IS A SPICY STIR-FRIED DISH THAT'S A STAPLE IN SICHUAN CUISINE, KNOWN FOR ITS BOLD FLAVOURS AND SIGNATURE KICK OF HEAT. WITH TENDER CHICKEN, CRUNCHY PEANUTS AND A TANGY SAUCE, IT'S DELICIOUSLY SAVOURY, SPICY, AND SLIGHTLY SWEET. THIS RECIPE USES COOKING CARAMEL (KARAMEL MASAKAN — AVAILABLE AT ASIAN SUPERMARKETS) TO GIVE THE DISH DEPTH, AS WELL AS ITS SIGNATURE RICH, BROWN COLOUR.

CHICKEN

200 g (7 oz) boneless, skinless chicken thighs, cut into bite-sized cubes

1 teaspoon chicken bouillon powder

½ teaspoon white pepper

1 tablespoon Shaoxing wine (Chinese cooking wine)

1 tablespoon sesame oil

¼ teaspoon salt

1 tablespoon cornflour (cornstarch)

vegetable oil, for flash-frying

½ onion, cut into 3 cm (1¼ in) chunks

1 spring onion (scallion), cut into 4 cm (1½ in) batons

SAUCE

1 tablespoon vegetable oil

2 slices of ginger

12 garlic cloves, minced

10 dried chillies

2 teaspoons cooking caramel (karamel masakan)

2 teaspoons sugar

½ teaspoon dark soy sauce

½ teaspoon salt

1 tablespoon oyster sauce

½ teaspoon YumYum or MSG

1 teaspoon chicken bouillon powder

2 teaspoons potato starch

60 ml (2 fl oz/¼ cup) water

2 teaspoons Shaoxing wine (Chinese cooking wine)

¼ cup peanuts, roasted

TO SERVE

sesame seeds (optional)

spring onions (scallions), optional

In a bowl, combine the chicken with the chicken bouillon powder, white pepper, Shaoxing wine, sesame oil, salt and cornflour. Mix thoroughly, ensuring the chicken is evenly coated, and let it marinate for at least 15–20 minutes to absorb the flavours.

Fill a wok one-third full with vegetable oil and heat to 190°C (375°F) over a medium–high heat. You can also test the oil with a wooden chopstick – if bubbles form around it when lowered in, the oil is hot enough. Once the oil is hot, flash-fry the marinated chicken pieces for 5–7 minutes, or until cooked through. Add the onion and spring onion and cook for a further 1 minute. Carefully strain the chicken and onions from the oil using a slotted spoon, and place on a sieve or plate lined with paper towels to drain. Set aside the leftover oil to use for future use.

In a clean wok, heat 1 tablespoon of vegetable oil over medium heat. Add the ginger slices, minced garlic and dried chillies, stir-frying for 1–2 minutes until fragrant. Next, add the cooking caramel, sugar, dark soy sauce, salt, oyster sauce, YumYum or MSG and chicken bouillon powder. Stir in the sauce mixture until everything is well combined, letting the flavours meld together.

In a small bowl, mix the potato starch and water to make a slurry. Pour the slurry into the wok and stir until the sauce thickens. Once the sauce has reached the desired consistency, add the fried chicken pieces to the wok, tossing them to ensure they are evenly coated with the sauce.

Add the Shaoxing wine to the wok and stir for another 30 seconds to let the flavour sink in, then toss through the roasted peanuts. Remove the kung pao chicken from the heat, transfer it to a serving plate, and garnish with sesame seeds and spring onions, if desired. Enjoy!

SERVES 2—3

ORANGE CHICKEN

ORANGE CHICKEN IS PANDA EXPRESS'S SIGNATURE DISH AND A STAPLE IN AMERICAN CHINESE CUISINE. WITH ITS CRISPY FRIED CHICKEN TOSSED IN A SWEET, TANGY ORANGE GLAZE, IT BLENDS BOLD CITRUSY FLAVOUR WITH SAVOURY GOODNESS, MAKING IT A CROWD FAVOURITE ACROSS THE COUNTRY.

CHICKEN

200 g (7 oz) boneless, skinless chicken thighs, cut into bite-sized cubes

1 teaspoon chicken bouillon powder

1 teaspoon minced ginger

¼ teaspoon white pepper

1 tablespoon Shaoxing wine (Chinese cooking wine)

1 tablespoon sesame oil

¼ teaspoon salt

1 tablespoon cornflour (cornstarch)

vegetable, for deep-frying

BATTER

75 g (2¾ oz/½ cup) self-raising flour

30 g (1 oz/¼ cup) cornflour (cornstarch)

135 ml (4½ fl oz) water

ORANGE SAUCE

120 ml (4 fl oz/½ cup) fresh orange juice

2 teaspoons light soy sauce

2 tablespoons sweet chilli sauce

2 tablespoons sugar

1 tablespoon rice vinegar

4 garlic cloves, minced

½ teaspoon minced ginger

¼ teaspoon YumYum or MSG

3 teaspoons potato starch

TO SERVE

sesame seeds

spring onions (scallions), thinly sliced

In a large bowl, mix the chicken cubes with the chicken bouillon powder, minced ginger, white pepper, Shaoxing wine, sesame oil, salt and cornflour. Ensure the chicken is evenly coated and let it marinate for at least 30 minutes to absorb the flavours.

To make the batter, combine the self-raising flour and cornflour in a separate bowl. Gradually add the water while whisking until the batter is smooth and free of lumps.

Fill a wok or large pot halfway full with the oil and bring to 180°C (350°F) over medium–high heat. You can also test the oil with a wooden chopstick – if bubbles form around it when lowered in, the oil is hot enough. Once the oil is hot, dip the marinated chicken pieces into the batter, ensuring they are well coated. Carefully lower the battered chicken into the hot oil in batches, making sure not to overcrowd the pot. Fry each batch for about 5–7 minutes, or until the chicken is golden brown and crispy.

Once cooked, remove the chicken from the oil using a slotted spoon and set it aside on a sieve or plate lined with paper towels to drain. Save the leftover oil for future frying.

In a jug, combine all the sauce ingredients. Pour this mixture into the empty wok or pot and bring it to a boil over medium heat, stirring continuously until the sauce thickens.

Once the sauce is ready, add the fried chicken and toss it in the sauce until the pieces are evenly coated. Serve immediately, garnished with sesame seeds and spring onions.

SERVES 2–3

HONEY CHICKEN

HONEY CHICKEN IS A POPULAR DISH IN AUSTRALIA, OFTEN FOUND AT LOCAL CHINESE TAKEAWAYS. WITH ITS CRISPY FRIED CHICKEN COATED IN A SWEET AND STICKY HONEY GLAZE, IT'S ONE OF THOSE NOSTALGIC COMFORT FOODS THAT WINDS BACK THE CLOCK WITH EVERY BITE.

BATTER

125 g (4½ oz/1 cup) self-raising flour
60 g (2 oz/½ cup) cornflour (cornstarch)
300 ml (10 fl oz) water

CHICKEN

1 × quantity Velveted chicken (page 30)
vegetable oil, for deep-frying

SAUCE

3 tablespoons honey
180 ml (6 fl oz/¾ cup) water
1 teaspoon custard powder
2 tablespoons sugar, or more honey
pinch of salt
2 teaspoons potato starch
60 ml (2 fl oz/¼ cup) water

TO SERVE

fried thin vermicelli noodles
toasted sesame seeds

To make the batter, mix the self-raising flour and cornflour together in a large bowl. Gradually add the water, whisking until the batter is smooth. Add the velveted chicken to the batter and stir until each piece is completely coated. Set the mixture aside.

Fill a wok or large pot halfway full with vegetable oil and bring to 180°C (350°F) over medium–high heat. You can also test the oil with a wooden chopstick – if bubbles form around it when lowered in, the oil is hot enough. Hold a handful of battered chicken and gently drop it into the oil in chunks around the wok. Use the ladle to push the chunks away from each other so that they don't stick. Break any big chunks of chicken in half with your ladle. Fry the battered chicken in batches for about 10 minutes, or until golden brown and cooked through. Remove the chicken with a slotted spoon and place it on paper towels to drain. Set aside the leftover oil for future use.

In the empty wok or a frying pan, combine the honey, water, custard powder, sugar (or more honey) and salt. Heat the mixture over high heat, stirring until it starts to bubble.

In a small bowl, mix the potato starch and water to make a slurry. Gradually add the slurry to the sauce, stirring continuously until the sauce reaches the desired thickness.

Add the fried chicken to the sauce, tossing to ensure the pieces are well coated. Serve immediately with fried vermicelli noodles and sprinkle with toasted sesame seeds.

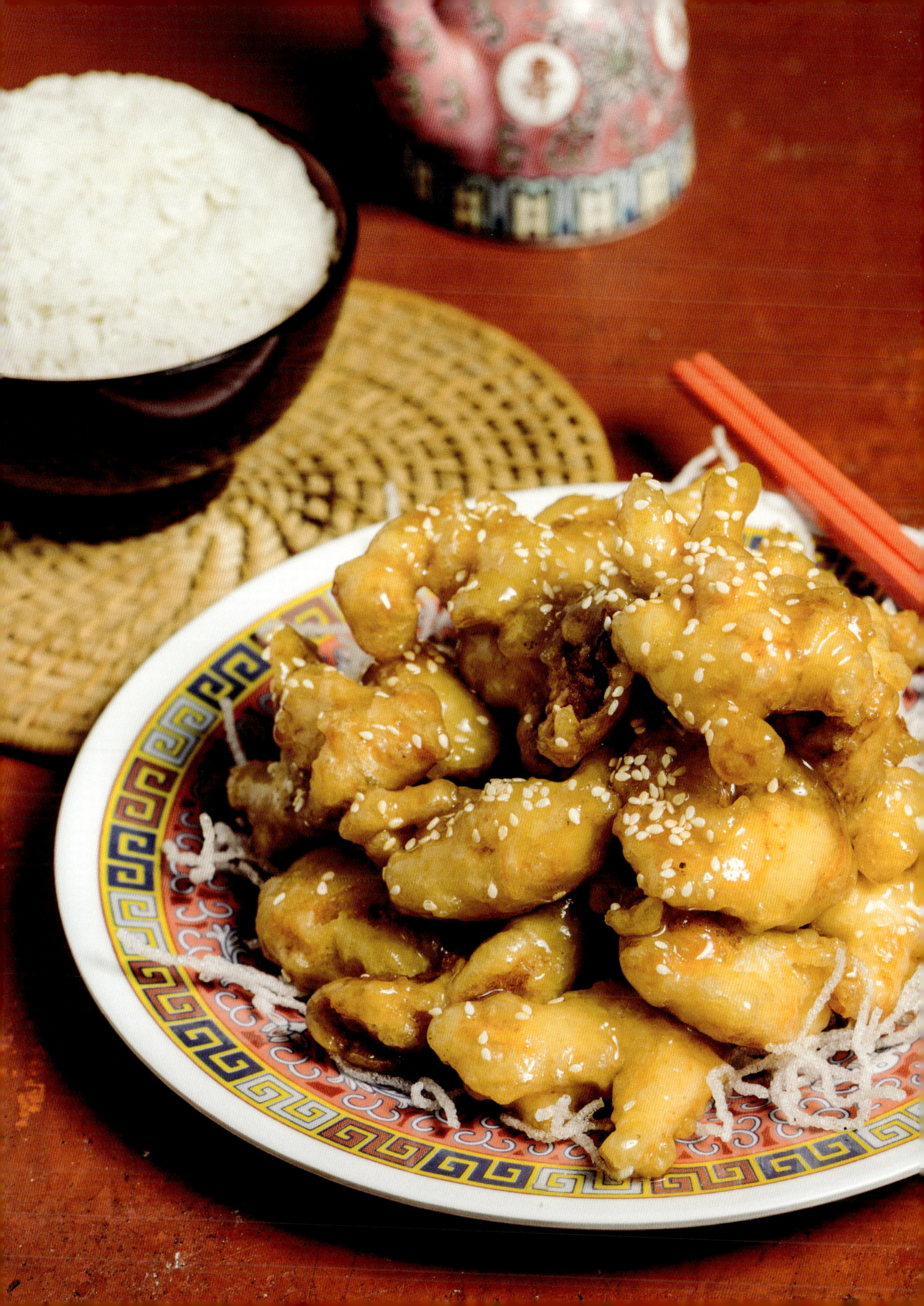

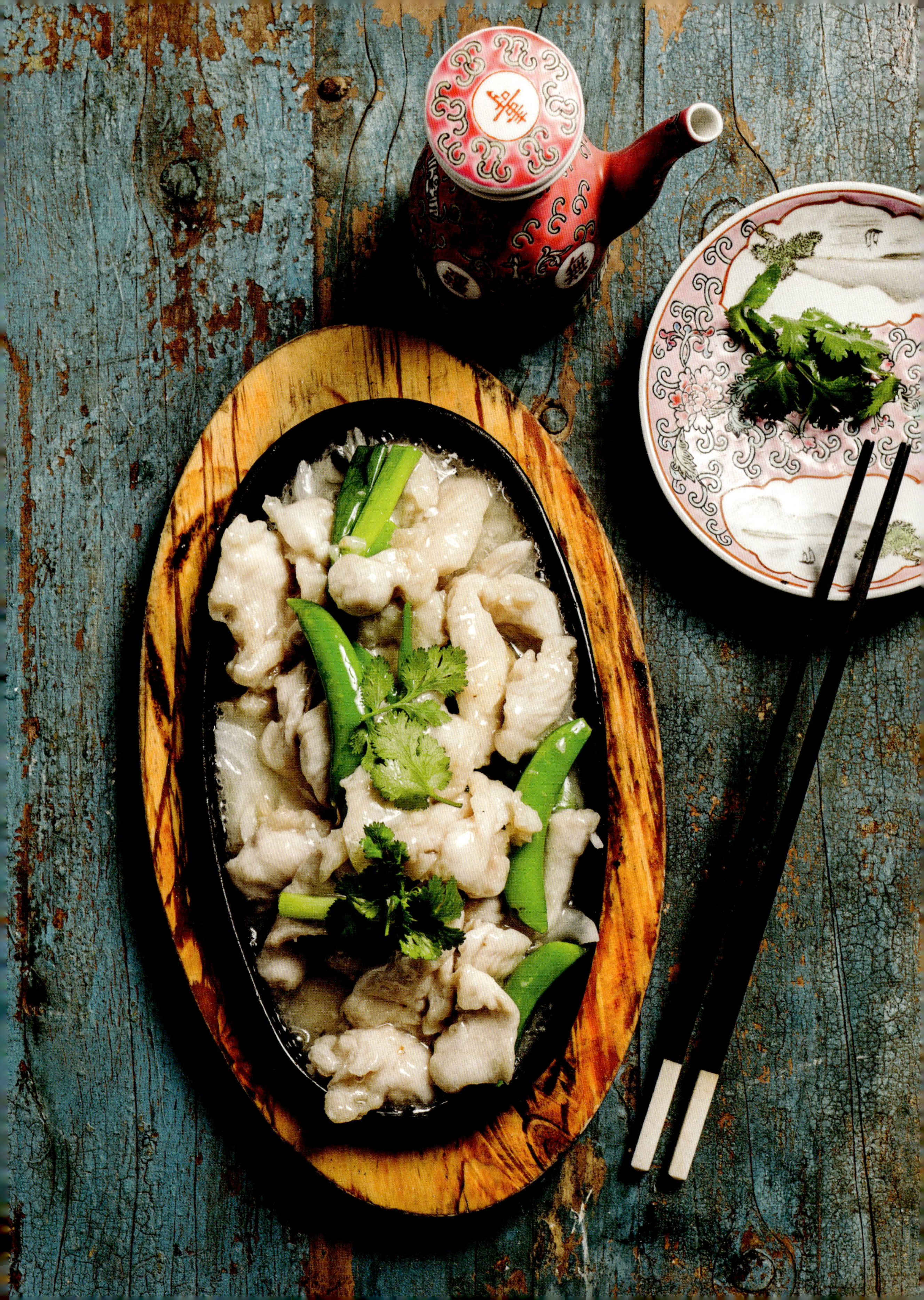

SERVES 1–2

SIZZLING GARLIC CHICKEN

SIZZLING GARLIC CHICKEN KNOWS HOW TO MAKE AN ENTRY. AS SOON AS THE CHICKEN HITS THE PLATE, YOU GET THAT AMAZING SIZZLE AND RICH GARLIC AROMA THAT MAKES THE WHOLE DISH POP.

CHICKEN

1 × quantity Velveted chicken (page 30)

vegetable oil for flash-frying, plus 1 tablespoon for stir-frying

6 sugar-snap peas

1 spring onion (scallion), cut into 6 cm (2½ in) lengths

12 garlic cloves, minced

2 slices of ginger

240 ml (8 fl oz/1 cup) Chicken stock (page 32 or shop-bought)

2 teaspoons potato starch

60 ml (2 fl oz/¼ cup) water

1 tablespoon Shaoxing wine (Chinese cooking wine)

2 teaspoons sesame oil

½ teaspoon white pepper

½ brown onion, thinly sliced

coriander (cilantro) leaves, to garnish

Fill a wok or deep fryer halfway full with oil and heat to 190°C (375°F) over medium–high heat (you can also test the oil with a wooden chopstick – if bubbles form around it, the oil is ready). Flash-fry the velveted chicken until it's cooked, then add the sugar-snap peas and spring onion to the oil, frying for an additional 10 seconds. Carefully strain the chicken and vegetables from the oil and set them aside in a sieve or on a plate lined with paper towels to drain. Set the leftover oil aside for future use.

Place a cast-iron sizzling plate over a burner or in an oven preheated to 220°C (430°F) to heat. Meanwhile, in the empty wok or a frying pan, heat 1 tablespoon of vegetable oil over medium heat. Add the chopped garlic and ginger slices, stir-frying until fragrant. Add the chicken stock and bring to a boil, then add the cooked chicken and vegetables.

In a small bowl, mix the potato starch and water to make a slurry. Slowly pour the slurry into the boiling sauce, stirring continuously until the sauce thickens. After thickening, finish the dish with Shaoxing wine, sesame oil and white pepper. Remove from heat.

By this time, the sizzling plate should be hot. Carefully remove it from the heat and place it on a heatproof board. Scatter an even layer of thinly sliced onion onto the plate, then immediately spoon the garlic chicken and its sauce over the top. It should sizzle as it makes contact with the hot plate. Garnish with coriander and serve immediately.

SERVES 2

LEMON CHICKEN

LEMON CHICKEN IS A POPULAR FOOD IN CHINESE-AMERICAN CUISINE, WITH A BRIGHT, TANGY SAUCE THAT OFFERS A FRESH TWIST ON TRADITIONAL SWEET-AND-SOUR DISHES. WHEN I WAS A KID, MY PARENTS NEVER LET ME ORDER IT BECAUSE IT WAS CONSIDERED A WESTERNISED CHINESE DISH — SO WHEN I OPENED MY RESTAURANT, I MADE SURE I HAD THE BEST LEMON CHICKEN IN THE WORLD.

CHICKEN

2 chicken breasts, skin on

¼ teaspoon salt

1 teaspoon chicken bouillon powder

1 tablespoon cornflour (cornstarch)

1 teaspoon custard powder

¼ teaspoon bicarbonate of soda (baking soda)

¼ teaspoon white pepper

1 teaspoon YumYum or MSG

1 tablespoon Shaoxing wine (Chinese cooking wine)

1 tablespoon sesame oil

BATTER

125 g (4½ oz/1 cup) self-raising flour

60 g (2 oz/½ cup) cornflour (cornstarch)

270 ml (9 fl oz) soda water

½ teaspoon chicken bouillon powder

¼ teaspoon salt

vegetable oil, for deep-frying

LEMON SAUCE

½ lemon

110 g (4 oz/½ cup) sugar

60 ml (2 fl oz/¼ cup) white vinegar

120 ml (4 fl oz/½ cup) water, plus 60 ml (2 fl oz/¼ cup) extra

1 teaspoon custard powder

2 tablespoons honey

pinch of salt

½ teaspoon light soy sauce

2 teaspoons potato starch

TO SERVE

2 lemon slices

Butterfly the chicken breasts and gently score the bottom side with a crosshatch pattern. With the back of your knife, lightly beat the chicken flat to a thickness of about 1.5 cm (½ in). In a large bowl, combine the chicken with the salt, chicken bouillon powder, cornflour, custard powder, bicarbonate of soda, white pepper, YumYum or MSG, Shaoxing wine and sesame oil. Coat the chicken evenly and let it marinate for at least 30 minutes, or for the best results, cover and refrigerate overnight.

In another large bowl, make the batter by whisking together the self-raising flour, cornflour, soda water, chicken bouillon powder and salt until smooth. Add the marinated chicken to the batter, stirring until the chicken is fully coated, then set aside.

Fill a wok or large pot halfway full with vegetable oil and heat to 180°C (350°F) over medium–high heat. You can also test the oil with a wooden chopstick – if bubbles form around it, the oil is hot enough. Fry the battered chicken in batches for 6–7 minutes, or until golden brown. Carefully remove the chicken from the oil using a slotted spoon and place it in a sieve or on a plate lined with paper towels to drain. Set aside the leftover oil for future deep-frying.

Once the chicken has cooled slightly, cut it into 2 cm (¾ in) thick pieces. For clean cuts, chop quickly and firmly to avoid breaking the crispy crust.

To make the lemon sauce, juice the lemon half and scoop out the pulp, removing any seeds. Roughly chop the pulp and set it aside. In the now-empty wok or pot, combine the lemon juice, chopped pulp, sugar, white vinegar, 120 ml (4 fl oz) water, custard powder, honey, salt and soy sauce. Bring the mixture to a light simmer over medium heat.

In a small bowl, mix the potato starch and 60 ml (2 fl oz) water to make a slurry. Slowly pour the slurry into the simmering lemon sauce while stirring continuously until the sauce thickens to the desired consistency.

Pour the lemon sauce over the crispy chicken pieces, top with the lemon slices and serve immediately.

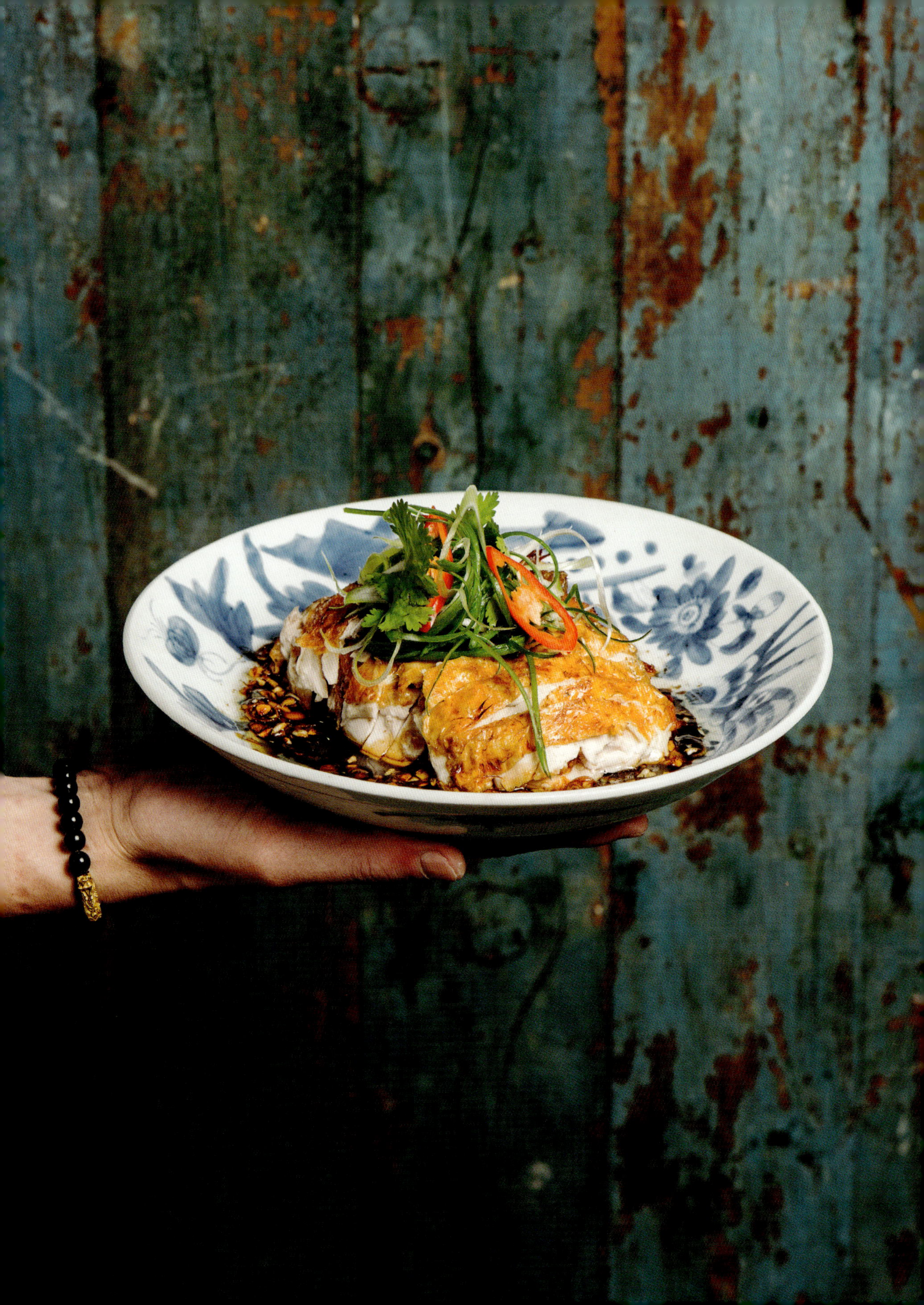

SERVES 4

SHANDONG CHICKEN

SHANDONG CHICKEN IS A CRISPY FRIED DISH FROM CHINA'S SHANDONG PROVINCE THAT'S ALL ABOUT BOLD, SIMPLE FLAVOURS. THE CHICKEN IS PERFECTLY GOLDEN AND TOPPED WITH A TANGY, VINEGAR-BASED SAUCE THAT'S BOTH REFRESHING AND SAVOURY, MAKING IT A MUST-TRY FOR FANS OF CHINESE FOOD. THE TRICK TO ACHIEVING THE CRISPY SKIN IS IN USING RED VINEGAR AND MALTOSE SYRUP.

CHICKEN

1 × 1.5 kg (3 lb 5 oz) whole chicken

3 litres (101 fl oz/12 cups) Chicken stock (page 32 or shop-bought)

240 ml (8 fl oz/1 cup) red vinegar

2 tablespoons maltose syrup

vegetable oil, for deep-frying

SAUCE

6 garlic cloves, minced

4 tablespoons broth from boiling the chicken

2 teaspoons dark soy sauce

1 teaspoon fish sauce

¼ teaspoon white peppercorns, smashed

1 tablespoon Shaoxing wine (Chinese cooking wine)

1 tablespoon Chinese red vinegar

1 teaspoon Chinkiang vinegar (black vinegar)

1 teaspoon sugar

1 tablespoon sesame oil

½ teaspoon YumYum or MSG

white part of spring onion (scallion), finely sliced

1 teaspoon chicken bouillon powder

1 bird's eye chilli, thinly sliced

spring onions (scallions), thinly sliced, to garnish

Boil the whole chicken in the chicken stock for about 1 hour. Once cooked, remove the chicken and set it aside, reserving 4 teaspoons of the broth for the sauce, and storing the rest for another use. In a large pot or wok, combine the red vinegar and maltose, heating over low heat until the maltose fully melts into the vinegar.

Place the chicken in a strainer and carefully ladle the vinegar-maltose mixture over it, ensuring the chicken is completely coated. Transfer the chicken to a wire rack and refrigerate, uncovered, for 2 days to allow the skin to dry out.

Fill a wok or large pot halfway full with vegetable oil and heat to 180°C (350°F) over medium–high heat. You can also test the oil with a wooden chopstick – if bubbles form around it, the oil is hot enough. Slowly lower the chicken into the hot oil, using a ladle to repeatedly pour the oil over the surface of the chicken until it turns golden brown. Remove the chicken from the oil and place it on a wire rack to drain. Strain the remaining oil, reserving 1 tablespoon for the next step and storing the rest for future deep-frying.

In the now-empty wok or a saucepan, heat the 1 tablespoon of reserved deep-frying oil over medium heat. Add the garlic and stir-fry for 1 minute, or until fragrant. Increase the heat to high and add the remaining sauce ingredients. Cook on high for 2 minutes, or until the ingredients have dissolved and combined.

Use a cleaver to cut the chicken or debone it as desired. Arrange the chicken pieces on a serving plate and pour the prepared sauce over the top. Garnish with thinly sliced spring onion and serve immediately.

SERVES 4

EMERGENCY HAINANESE CHICKEN

LIVING FAR FROM ANYWHERE THAT SERVES A DELICIOUS PLATE OF CHICKEN RICE, I'VE FOUND THAT INSTEAD OF MAKING THE LONG TRIP, I CAN CREATE AN EQUALLY FLAVOURFUL VERSION RIGHT AT HOME USING INGREDIENTS I ALWAYS HAVE ON HAND. THAT'S HOW THIS QUICK AND EASY HAINANESE CHICKEN RICE CAME TO BE. WITH A FEW SIMPLE SHORTCUTS AND KEY INGREDIENTS, YOU CAN WHIP UP THIS BELOVED DISH QUICKLY WITHOUT LOSING ANY OF ITS SIGNATURE FLAVOUR.

CHICKEN

2 teaspoons sea salt, for rubbing

4 litres (135 fl oz/16 cups) Chicken stock (page 32 or shop-bought) or water, for poaching

4 chicken leg quarters (or whole chicken, about 680 g/1½ lb)

4 slices of ginger

2 spring onions (scallions), cut into 6 cm (2½ in) lengths

1 teaspoon salt, for seasoning

iced water, for chilling

CHILLI SAUCE

6 long red chillies, coarsely chopped

3 slices of ginger

4 garlic cloves, coarsely chopped

2 tablespoons lime juice

2 tablespoons sugar

1 teaspoon salt

1 teaspoon vegetable oil

¼ teaspoon chicken bouillon powder

80 ml (2½ fl oz/⅓ cup) water

Start by preparing the chicken. Cut off about 2 tablespoons of excess chicken fat and set aside to use in the rice. Rub the chicken leg quarters (or whole chicken) with 2 teaspoons of sea salt, ensuring you coat both the inside and outside thoroughly. Let the chicken sit at room temperature for 30–40 minutes to soften the skin and remove the 'goosebumps'.

Next, poach the chicken. In a large pot, combine the chicken stock or water with the ginger, spring onions and 1 teaspoon of salt, and bring the mixture to a boil. Once boiling, add the chicken to the pot, bring the stock back to a boil, reduce the heat to low, and let the chicken simmer for 45 minutes.

Once the chicken is cooked, carefully remove it from the stock (reserving the stock to use later in the recipe), drain it well, and immediately plunge it into a bath of iced water. Let the chicken chill for 20–25 minutes to tighten the skin, then set it aside to come to room temperature.

To make the chilli sauce, use a food processor to blitz the chillies, ginger and garlic into a coarse paste. Add the lime juice, sugar, salt, vegetable oil, chicken bouillon powder and water, and stir until combined. Set the sauce aside. Any leftovers can be stored in the refrigerator for up to 2 weeks.

For the rice, start by chopping the reserved chicken fat and heating it in a wok over medium heat for 3–4 minutes until the fat renders. Discard any solids, then add the sliced shallots to the wok and cook until golden, about 5–6 minutes. Stir in the minced garlic and fry until fragrant. Add the washed jasmine rice to the wok and stir-fry until the rice starts to pop. Transfer the rice to a saucepan and add the pandan leaves along with enough reserved chicken stock to cover the rice by about 1 cm (½ in). Bring the rice to a boil over high heat, then reduce the heat to low, cover the saucepan, and cook for 11–12 minutes until the liquid is absorbed.

CHICKEN RICE

2 tablespoons chicken fat, reserved from the chicken, or 2 tablespoons vegetable oil
5 golden shallots, thinly sliced
3 garlic cloves, minced
550 g (1 lb 3 oz/3 cups) Thai jasmine rice, washed and drained well
2 pandan leaves, tied into a knot

SOY DRESSING

1 tablespoon oil
2 tablespoons light soy sauce
1 teaspoon sugar
1 tablespoon sesame oil
¼ teaspoon YumYum or MSG
¼ teaspoon white pepper

TO SERVE

Ginger scallion oil (page 33)
sliced Lebanese (short) cucumber
coriander (cilantro) sprigs

While the rice is cooking, prepare the soy dressing. In a small pan, heat 1 tablespoon of oil over medium heat. Add the soy sauce, sugar, YumYum or MSG and white pepper, bringing it to a gentle boil. Stir in 120 ml (4 fl oz/½ cup) of the reserved chicken stock and the sesame oil, then remove the sauce from the heat.

To serve, use a cleaver to deconstruct or debone the chicken as desired and arrange the pieces on a serving plate. Spoon the soy dressing over the chicken, and garnish with sliced cucumber and coriander sprigs. Serve the chicken alongside the fragrant rice, with the chilli sauce on the side for dipping. Enjoy your emergency Hainanese chicken rice!

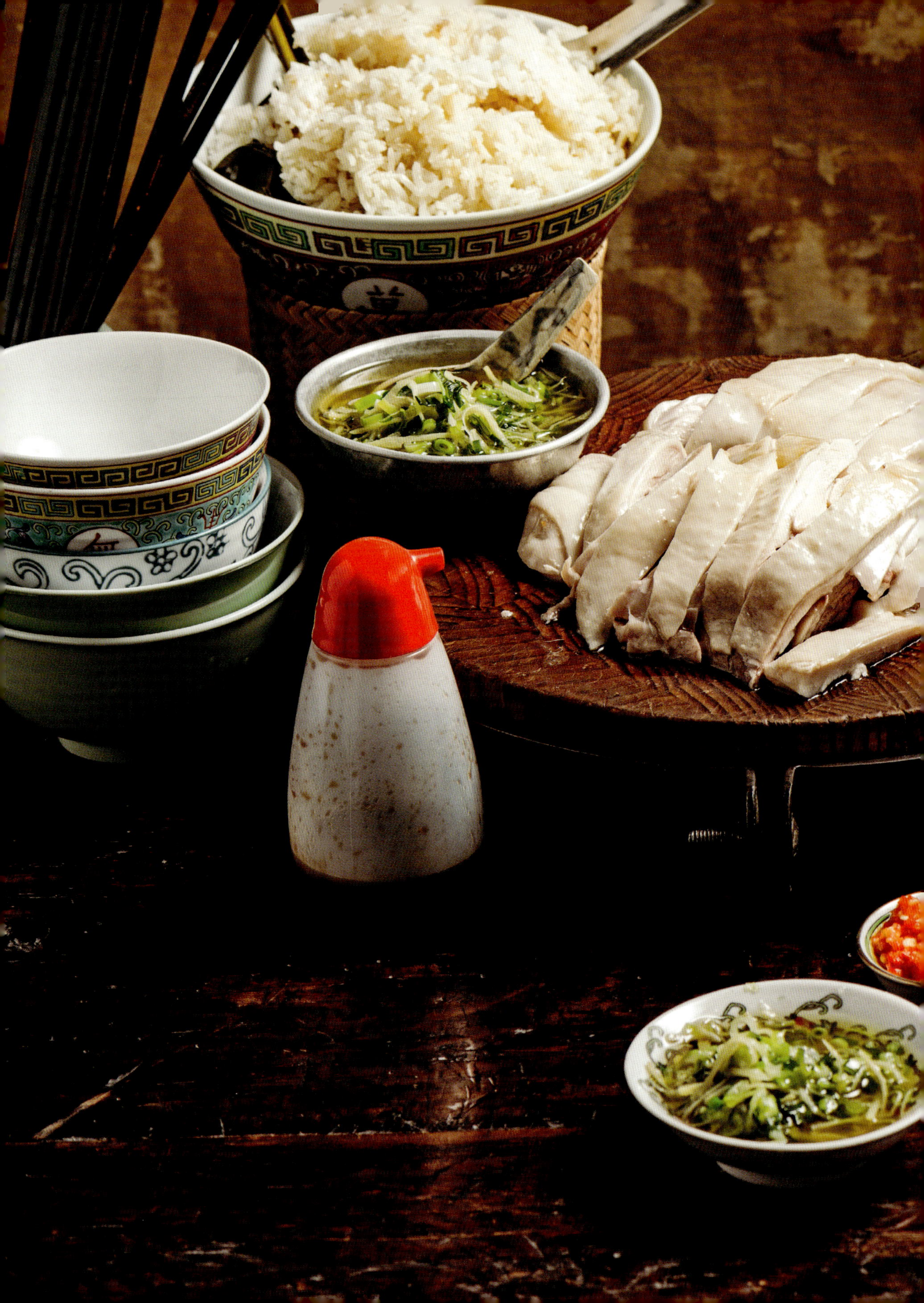

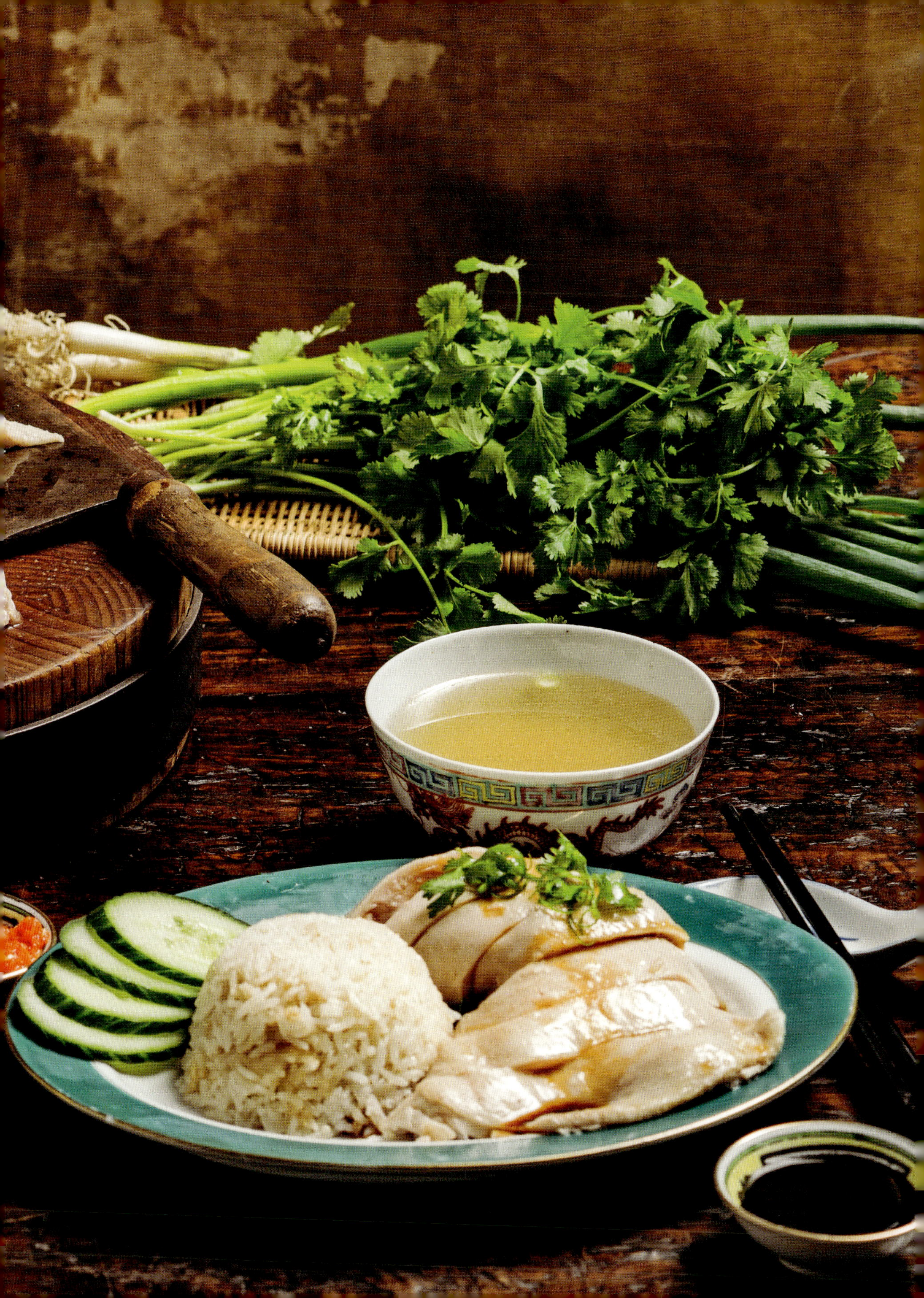

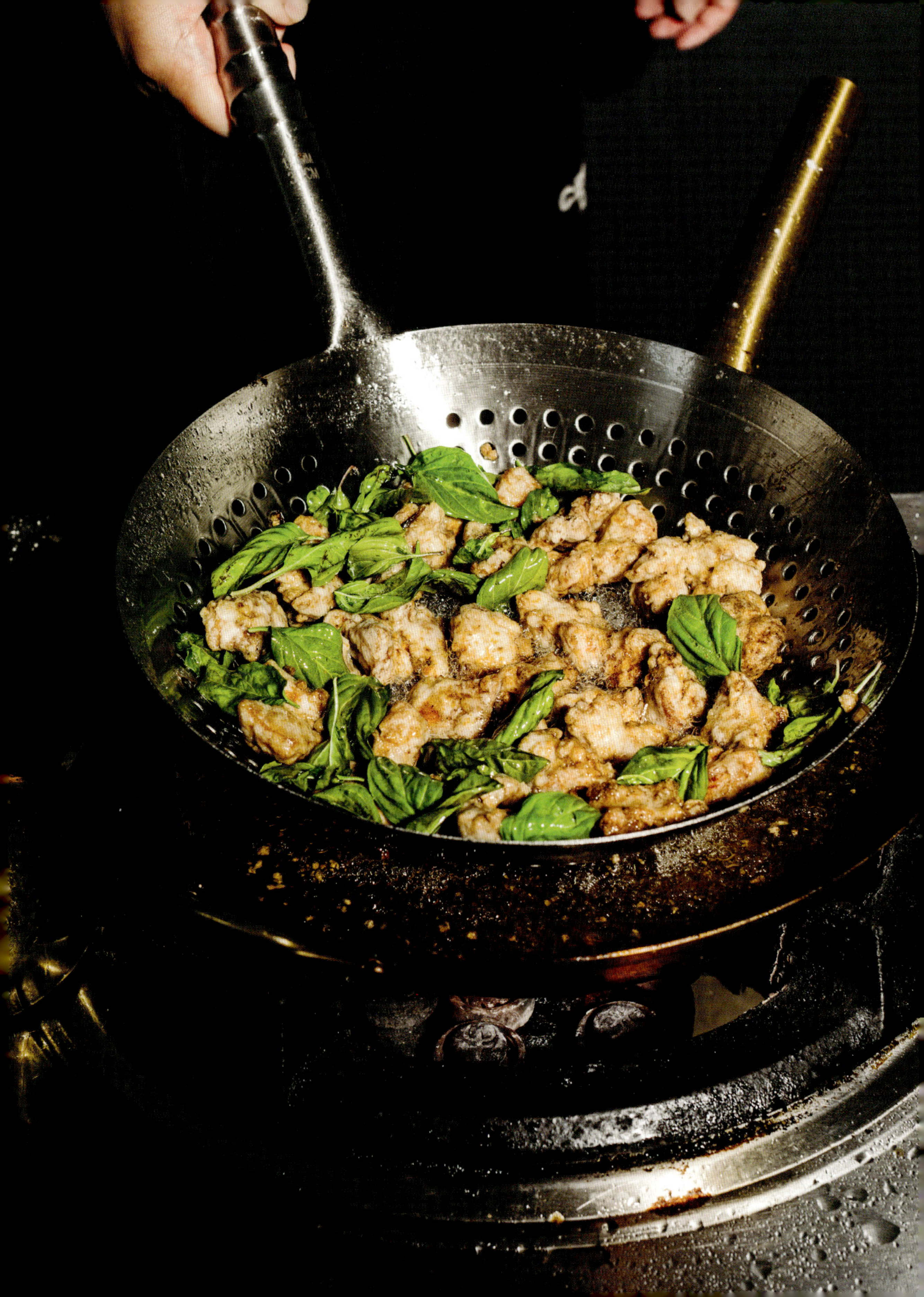

SERVES 3

TAIWANESE FRIED CHICKEN

CRISPY, GOLDEN FRIED CHICKEN IS A STREET FOOD STAPLE ACROSS TAIWAN. WHAT SETS IT APART IS THE FRAGRANT ADDITION OF CRUNCHY, DEEP-FRIED THAI BASIL. THIS IS A MUST-TRY FOR ANY FRIED-FOOD LOVER.

CHICKEN

450 g (1 lb) boneless, skinless chicken thighs, cut into bite-sized pieces

2 tablespoons Shaoxing wine (Chinese cooking wine)

1 tablespoon light soy sauce

1 teaspoon Chinese five-spice powder

½ teaspoon white pepper

SEASONING

3 teaspoons Five-spice salt and pepper (page 33) or to taste

FOR FRYING

60 g (2 oz/½ cup) potato starch

vegetable oil, for deep-frying

15 Thai basil leaves

In a large bowl, combine the chicken pieces with the Shaoxing wine, light soy sauce, Chinese five-spice powder and white pepper. Mix thoroughly to ensure the chicken is evenly coated with the marinade. Cover the bowl and refrigerate for at least 30 minutes, or up to 2 hours if you want to enhance the flavour further.

When ready to cook, remove the marinated chicken from the refrigerator and add the potato starch, tossing the pieces to coat them evenly. Fill a wok or large pot halfway full with oil and heat to 180°C (350°F) over medium–high heat (you can also test the oil with a wooden chopstick – if bubbles form around it, the oil is ready).

Carefully lower the chicken pieces into the hot oil in batches, making sure not to overcrowd the pan. Fry the chicken for 5–7 minutes, or until golden brown and crispy. Use a slotted spoon to remove the fried chicken from the oil, then place it on a wire rack or paper towels to drain.

If you're using Thai basil, quickly fry the leaves in the same hot oil for about 10–15 seconds, until they turn crispy. Remove the basil leaves and drain them on paper towels.

While the chicken is still hot, sprinkle it with the five-spice salt and pepper, adjusting the seasoning to your taste. Serve the fried chicken topped with the crispy Thai basil leaves.

SERVES 3–4

GENERAL TAO CHICKEN

GENERAL TAO'S CHICKEN IS A STAPLE OF CHINESE-AMERICAN CUISINE, BELIEVED TO HAVE BEEN CREATED IN 70S NEW YORK. WITH ITS SWEET, TANGY AND MILDLY SPICY SAUCE, IT HITS ALL THE RIGHT NOTES, AND HAS KEPT PEOPLE COMING BACK FOR MORE EVER SINCE.

CHICKEN

250 g (9 oz) boneless, skinless chicken thighs, cut into bite-sized cubes

1 teaspoon chicken bouillon powder

1 teaspoon minced ginger

pinch of white pepper

1 tablespoon Shaoxing wine (Chinese cooking wine)

1 tablespoon sesame oil

¼ teaspoon salt

1 tablespoon cornflour (cornstarch)

vegetable oil, for deep-frying

BATTER

75 g (2¾ oz/½ cup) self-raising flour

30 g (1 oz/¼ cup) cornflour (cornstarch)

135 ml (4½ fl oz) water

SAUCE

2 tablespoons minced garlic

8 whole dried chillies

2 spring onions (scallions), cut into 4 cm (1½ in) batons

3 teaspoons cooking caramel (karamel masakan)

1 tablespoon sugar

1 tablespoon oyster sauce

½ cup Chicken stock (page 32 or shop-bought)

1 teaspoon chicken bouillon powder

½ teaspoon dark soy sauce

pinch of YumYum or MSG (optional)

TO SERVE

sesame seeds (optional)

spring onion (scallion), thinly sliced (optional)

In a large bowl, combine the cubed chicken thighs with the chicken bouillon powder, minced ginger, white pepper, Shaoxing wine, sesame oil, salt and cornflour. Mix everything thoroughly to ensure the chicken is evenly coated, then let it marinate for at least 30 minutes.

To make the batter, mix the self-raising flour and cornflour in a separate bowl. Gradually add the water while whisking until the batter is smooth and free of lumps.

Fill a wok or large pot halfway full with vegetable oil and heat to 180°C (350°F) over medium–high heat. You can also test the oil with a wooden chopstick – if bubbles form around it when lowered in, the oil is hot enough. Once the oil is hot, add the marinated chicken to the batter, stirring to coat each piece evenly. Carefully lower the battered chicken pieces into the hot oil one by one, frying them in batches to avoid overcrowding the pot. Fry the chicken for 5–7 minutes per batch, or until golden brown and crispy. Remove the chicken with a slotted spoon and drain in a sieve or on paper towels. Set aside the oil for future use.

In the now-empty wok or pot, combine all the sauce ingredients and bring to a boil over medium heat, stirring continuously until the sauce thickens.

Once the sauce has thickened, add the fried chicken to the wok and toss until the chicken is evenly coated in the sauce. Top with sesame seeds and spring onions (if using) and serve immediately.

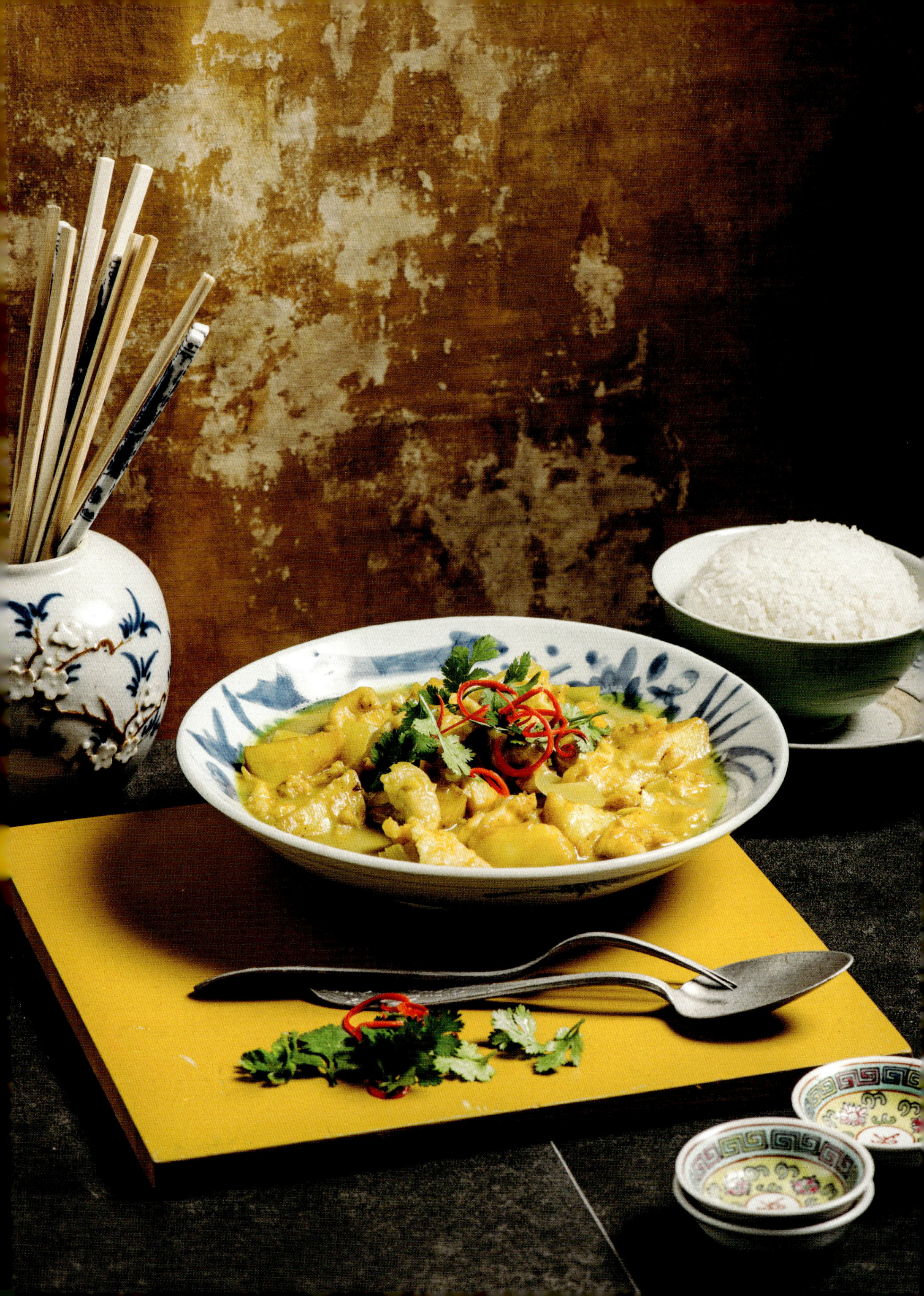

SERVES 3

CHINESE CHICKEN CURRY

WITH ITS RICHLY SPICED COCONUT GRAVY, CHINESE CHICKEN CURRY IS A POPULAR TAKEAWAY FAVOURITE. BUT YOU CAN EASILY TAKE COMFORT FOOD INTO YOUR OWN HANDS AND TRY IT OUT AT HOME.

STIR-FRY

vegetable oil, for flash-frying, plus 2 tablespoons extra

1 medium washed potato, cut into 3 cm (1¼ in) cubes

1 × quantity Velveted chicken (page 30)

½ small onion, cubed

4 garlic cloves, minced

240 ml (8 fl oz/1 cup) Chicken stock (page 32 or shop-bought)

2 tablespoons coconut milk

½ teaspoon chicken bouillon powder

¼ teaspoon salt

SPICE MIX

1½ teaspoons Madras curry powder (e.g. Clive of India)

1½ teaspoons Malaysian curry powder (e.g. Babas)

¼ teaspoon turmeric powder

Fill a wok or large pot one-third full with oil and bring to 190°C (375°F) over a medium–high heat. Once the oil is hot, add the potato and fry for 5 minutes, then remove with a slotted spoon and set aside. This step is optional, but it helps to keep the potato whole in the curry.

Add the velveted chicken to the wok and flash-fry for 1–2 minutes until the chicken is cooked through. Add the onion and fry for an additional 10 seconds. Carefully strain the chicken and onion from the oil and set aside on a plate lined with paper towels to drain. Set the leftover oil aside for future use.

In a small bowl, combine the curry powders and turmeric powder.

In the now-empty wok or pot, heat 2 tablespoons of vegetable oil over medium heat. Add the minced garlic and stir-fry for 1 minute until fragrant. Sprinkle the spice mix over the garlic and stir for another minute until the spices become aromatic. Pour in the chicken stock, coconut milk, chicken bouillon powder and salt, stirring everything together. Bring the mixture to a gentle boil.

Return the flash-fried chicken and vegetables to the wok or pot, stirring to combine them with the curry sauce. Lower the heat to a simmer and cook for an additional 5–7 minutes, or until the chicken is fully cooked and the sauce has thickened slightly.

Serve the Chinese chicken curry hot over steamed rice.

SERVES 4

PRISON CURRY

THIS IS MY TAKE ON A SIMPLE MALAYSIAN-STYLE CURRY. GROWING UP, MY DAD WOULD TELL ME IF I WAS NAUGHTY I'D HAVE TO GO TO PRISON AND EAT CURRY OFF A METAL TRAY. LITTLE DID HE KNOW THAT SOUNDED LIKE MY KIND OF LIFE. THIS DISH IS SPICED AND COMFORTING, PERFECT FOR A WARMING MEAL, AND MORE OF A TREAT THAN A PUNISHMENT.

FRIED POTATOES

vegetable oil, for deep-frying

3 potatoes, peeled and cut into 4 cm (1½ inch) chunks

CURRY

1 brown onion, chopped

2 red onions, chopped

8 garlic cloves, minced

1 tablespoon Malaysian curry powder (e.g. Babas)

2 tablespoons Madras curry powder (e.g. Clive of India)

3 teaspoons Tianjin or regular chilli powder

10–15 curry leaves

8 chicken drumsticks

500 ml (17 fl oz/2 cups) Chicken stock (page 32 or shop-bought)

1 tablespoon chicken bouillon powder

1 tablespoon light soy sauce

1½ teaspoons YumYum or MSG

1 teaspoon salt

240 ml (8 fl oz/1 cup) coconut cream

Fill a wok or large pot halfway full with vegetable oil and heat to 180°C (350°F) over medium–high heat. You can also test the oil with a wooden chopstick – if bubbles form around it when lowered in, the oil is hot enough. Fry the potatoes for 5–6 minutes, or until lightly golden. Once fried, carefully strain the potatoes from the oil and set them aside on a plate lined with paper towels to drain. Reserve 120 ml (4 fl oz/½ cup) of the oil and keep the remainder for future frying.

Pour the reserved oil into the now-empty wok. Add the chopped brown onion, red onions, minced garlic, curry powders, chilli powder and curry leaves. Cook the mixture on low heat for about 10 minutes, stirring constantly until the onions become soft and translucent and the spices are fragrant. Next, add the chicken drumsticks to the wok, frying them in the curry paste for about 5 minutes to ensure they are thoroughly coated with the spice mixture. Add the potatoes, then pour in the chicken stock, chicken bouillon powder, soy sauce, YumYum or MSG, and salt, and bring the mixture to a simmer. Cover the wok with a lid and cook on low heat for 1 hour, allowing the flavours to meld and the chicken to become tender.

Once the chicken is cooked through, add the coconut cream, bringing the curry to a gentle boil for 2–3 minutes, or until warmed. Serve the chicken curry hot with steamed rice.

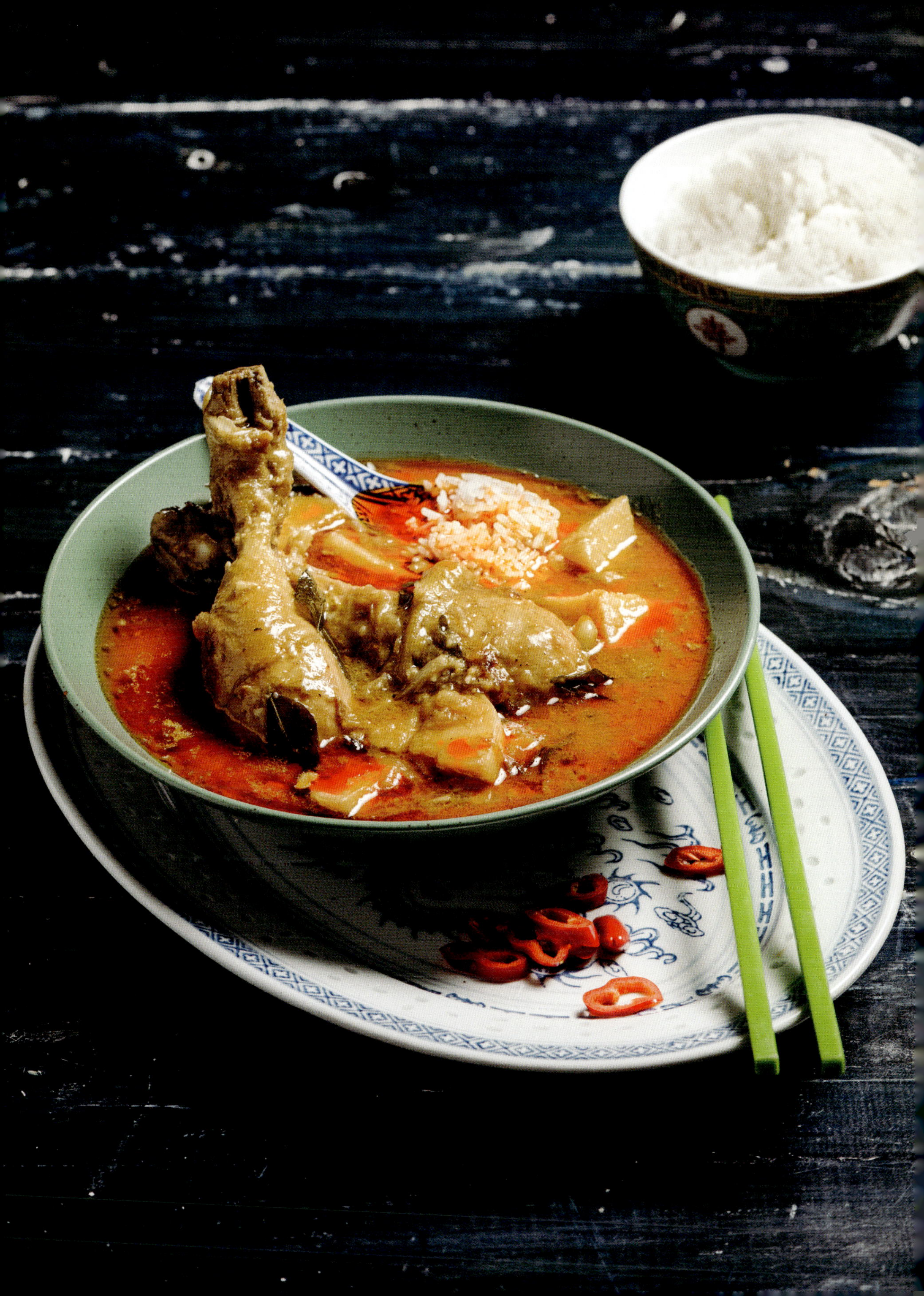

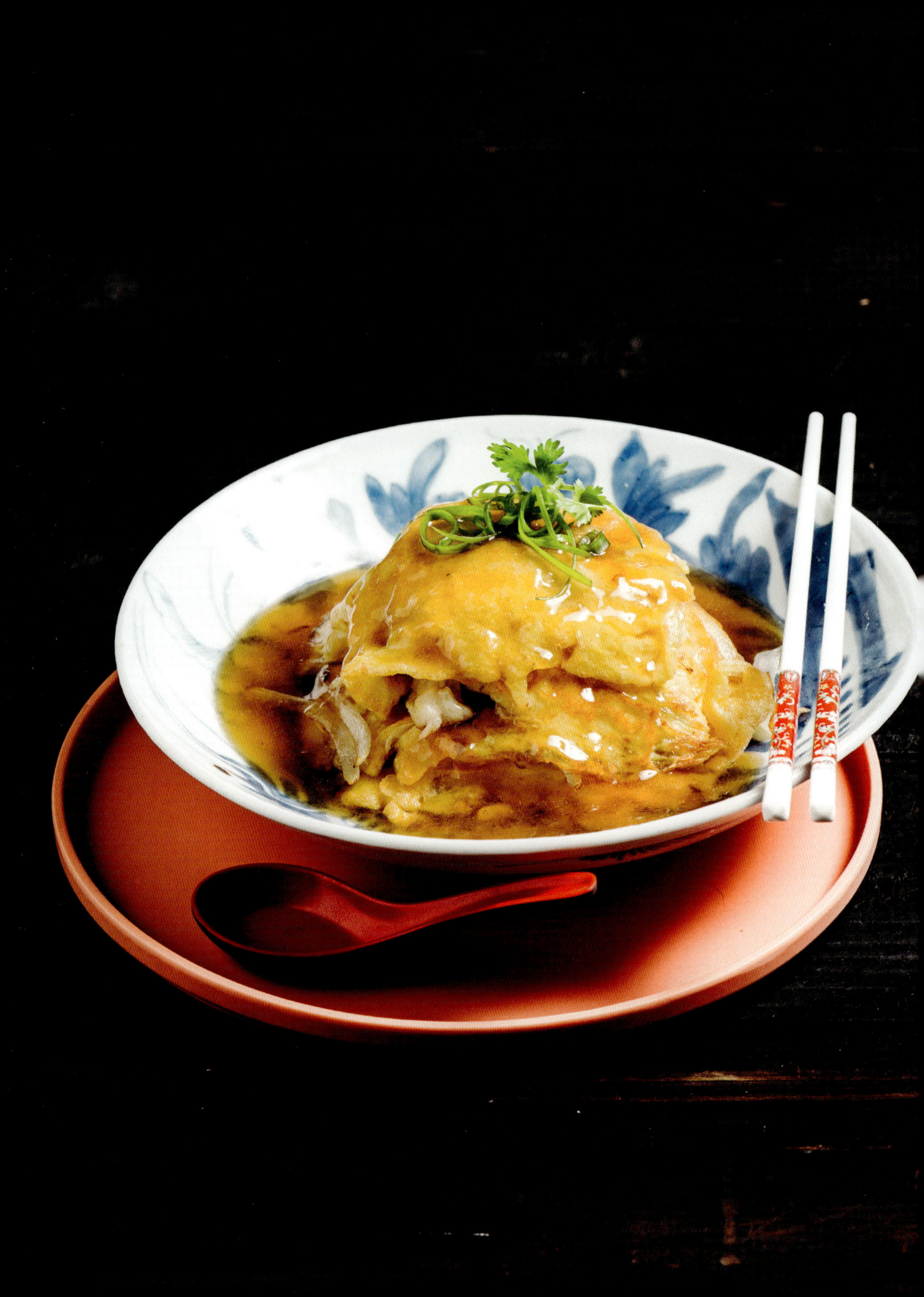

COMBINATION OMELETTE

SERVES 2

CHINESE COMBINATION OMELETTE IS A DISH PACKED WITH PRAWNS (SHRIMP), PORK AND VEGETABLES, ALL FOLDED INTO FLUFFY EGGS AND SERVED WITH A RICH BROWN GRAVY. THIS COMFORTING CLASSIC IS A MAINSTAY OF CHINESE CUISINE, OFFERING A DELICIOUS MIX OF FLAVOURS AND TEXTURES.

OMELETTE

5 prawns (shrimp), peeled and deveined

¼ teaspoon bicarbonate of soda (baking soda), plus ¼ teaspoon extra

50 g (1¾ oz) thinly sliced chicken breast

vegetable oil, for flash-frying

¼ small onion, thinly sliced

3 eggs

1 tablespoon potato starch

1 tablespoon water

1 spring onion (scallion), finely sliced, to serve

GRAVY

¼ teaspoon dark soy sauce

1 teaspoon sesame oil

1 teaspoon Shaoxing wine (Chinese cooking wine)

240 ml (8 fl oz/1 cup) Chicken stock (page 32 or shop-bought)

1 teaspoon vegetable oil

1 teaspoon oyster sauce

2 teaspoons potato starch

60 ml (2 fl oz/¼ cup) water

In a small bowl, combine the prawns with bicarbonate of soda. Mix to coat evenly, and set aside. Repeat the process in another bowl with the chicken. Let both marinate while you prepare the oil.

Fill a wok or large pot one-third full with oil and bring it to 190°C (375°F) over a medium–high heat. Once the oil is hot, fry the chicken and prawns until they are almost cooked through. Add the onion and stir-fry for another 30 seconds. Carefully strain the chicken, prawns and onion from the oil, placing them in a sieve or on a plate lined with paper towels to drain. Set aside the leftover oil for future use.

In a mixing bowl, whisk together the eggs, potato starch and water until the mixture is smooth and well combined. In the same wok or pan, heat 1 tablespoon of oil over medium heat. Pour in the egg mixture, spreading it evenly across the surface. Cook until the edges begin to set and the bottom becomes golden.

Evenly distribute the cooked chicken, prawns and onion mixture over the top of the omelette. Once the egg mixture is almost fully cooked but still slightly runny on top, gently flip the omelette and cook for another 1–2 minutes until fully set. Use a wok ladle or spatula to cut the omelette into three even pieces and set them aside on a serving plate.

In the now-empty wok or pan, prepare the gravy by combining the soy sauce, sesame oil, Shaoxing wine, chicken stock, vegetable oil and oyster sauce. Bring the mixture to a boil over medium heat.

Mix the potato starch and water to create a slurry, then slowly pour it into the sauce while stirring continuously. Cook until the gravy thickens slightly. Pour the gravy over the cooked omelette pieces and serve hot.

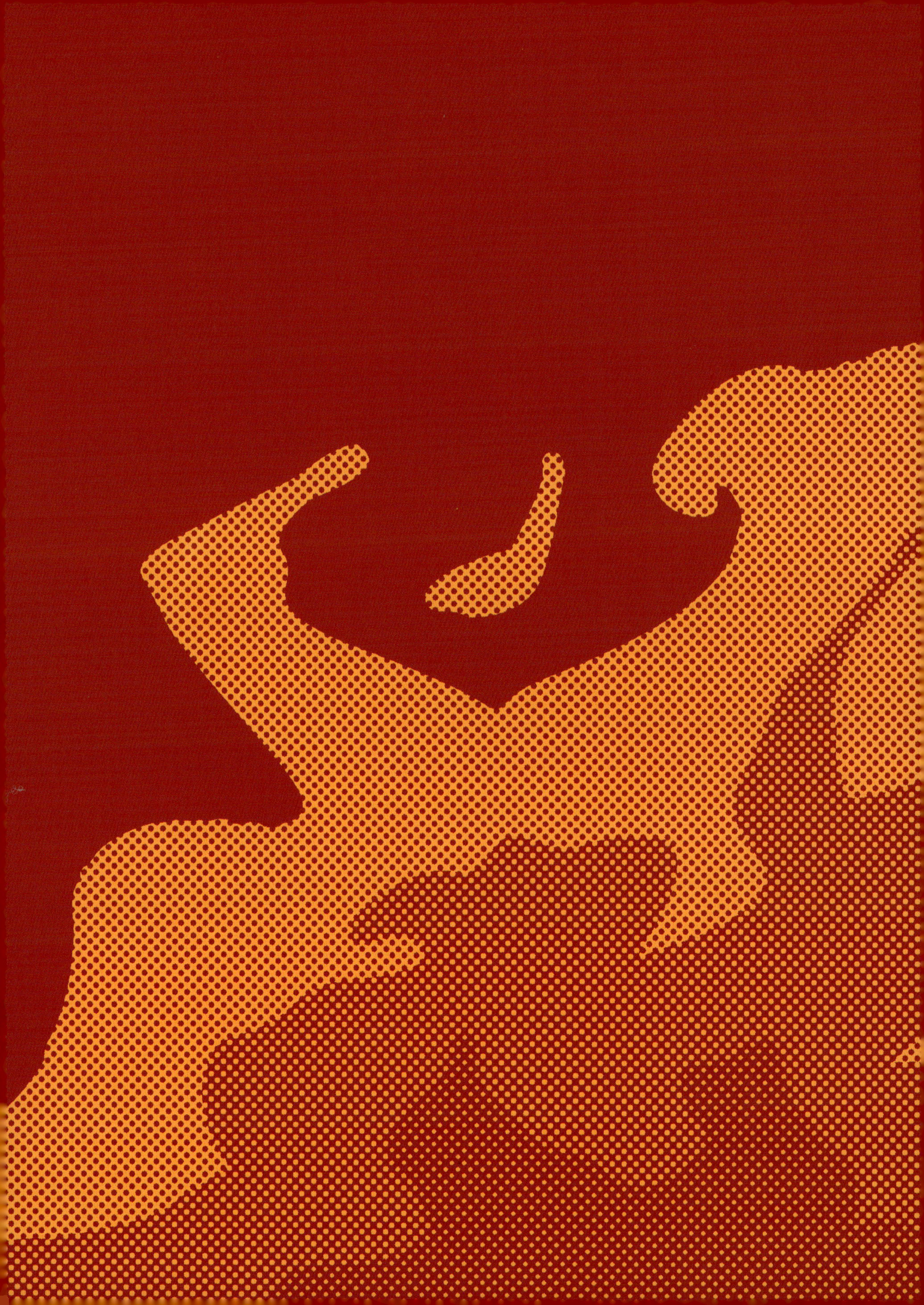

MEAT

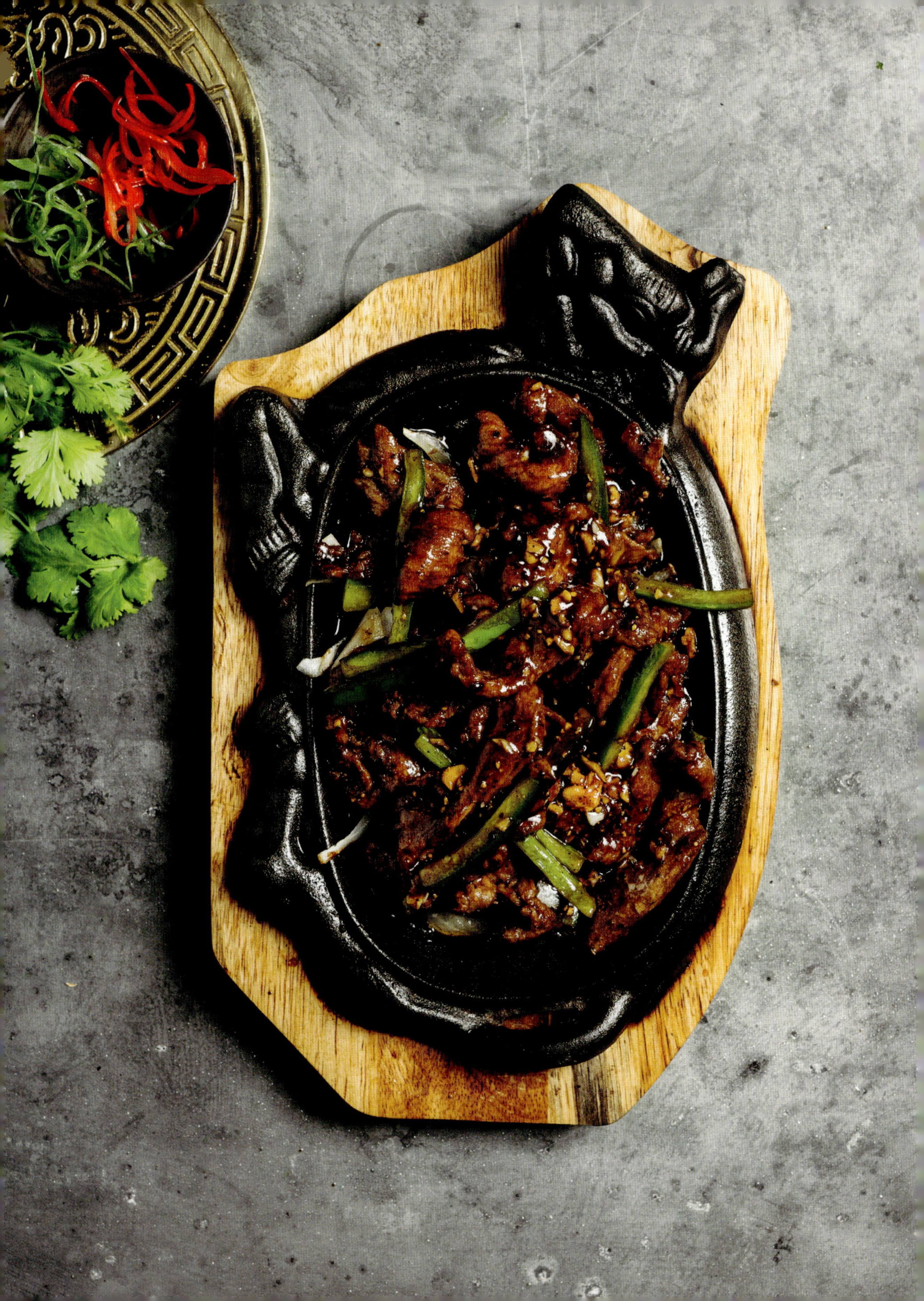

SERVES 2

PEPPER STEAK

THIS IS A CLASSIC STIR-FRY DISH OF TENDER STRIPS OF BEEF COOKED WITH VIBRANT CAPSICUMS (PEPPERS) AND ONIONS IN A SAVOURY SAUCE WITH PEPPERY ZING. SERVED SIZZLING ON A HOTPLATE, IT'S A CROWD-PLEASER IN CHINESE-AMERICAN CUISINE AND BEYOND.

BEEF AND VEGETABLES

vegetable oil, for flash-frying, plus 1 tablespoon extra

1 × quantity Velveted beef (page 30) or 250 g (9 oz) of your favourite cut of steak, thinly sliced

1 capsicum (bell pepper), chopped

SAUCE

6 garlic cloves, minced

1 teaspoon coarsely ground black pepper

120 ml (4 fl oz/½ cup) Chicken stock (page 32 or shop-bought)

1 teaspoon dark soy sauce

1 tablespoon oyster sauce

1 teaspoon potato starch

2 teaspoons water

1 tablespoon Shaoxing wine (Chinese cooking wine)

2 teaspoons sesame oil

SIZZLING PLATE

½ onion, thinly sliced

Fill a wok or large pot one-third full with oil and bring it to 190°C (375°F) over a medium–high heat. Once the oil is hot, carefully add the beef, flash-frying it for 1–2 minutes until just cooked through. Add the capsicum and cook for a further 10 seconds. Strain the beef and capsicum from the oil and set it aside on a plate lined with paper towels to drain. Reserve the leftover oil for future use.

After removing the beef, place a cast-iron sizzling plate on your wok burner, on top of a spare burner, or in an oven preheated to 220°C (430°F) to heat. You want the sizzling plate to be ready by the time the stir-fry is done.

To make the sauce, heat 1 tablespoon of oil in the now-empty wok over medium–high heat. Add the minced garlic, ginger and black pepper, stir-frying for an additional 30 seconds until fragrant.

Reduce the heat to medium–low and pour in the chicken stock, dark soy sauce and oyster sauce, stirring to combine. To thicken the sauce, make a slurry by mixing the potato starch and water, then slowly pour it into the sauce while stirring continuously. Allow the sauce to cook until it thickens slightly.

Increase the heat to high and return the flash-fried beef and capsicum to the wok, tossing it through the sauce until everything is evenly coated. Finish the dish by adding the Shaoxing wine and sesame oil, giving the beef a final toss to combine all the flavours.

By now, the sizzling plate should be hot. Carefully remove it from the heat and place it on a heatproof board. Arrange the thinly sliced raw onion evenly over the plate. Immediately pour the finished black pepper beef and sauce over the sizzling plate – it will sizzle as it comes into contact with the hot surface.

Serve immediately.

SERVES 3

RAINBOW BEEF

RAINBOW BEEF IS A CRISPY, FLAVOURFUL STIR-FRY WITH THIN SLICES OF BEEF COATED IN A SWEET AND TANGY SAUCE. IT'S A CROWD FAVOURITE FOR ITS BOLD FLAVOURS AND VIBRANT LOOK.

toasted sesame seeds, to garnish

BEEF

1 × quantity Velveted beef (page 31) or 250 g (9 oz) of your favourite cut of steak, thinly sliced

120 g (4½ oz/1 cup) cornflour (cornstarch)

vegetable oil, for deep-frying

SAUCE

160 ml (5½ fl oz/⅔ cup) sweet chilli sauce

half quantity of Sweet and sour sauce (page 31)

Coat the beef evenly with cornflour, making sure to shake off any excess.

Fill a wok or deep pan halfway full with oil and heat to 200°C (390°F) over medium–high heat (you can also test the oil with a wooden chopstick – if bubbles form around it, the oil is ready). Then, carefully fry the beef in batches until the pieces are golden and crispy, about 3–4 minutes per batch. Remove the beef with a slotted spoon and drain it in a sieve or on paper towels. Reserve the leftover oil for future deep-frying.

In the now-empty wok or pan, heat the sweet chilli sauce over medium heat. Add the sweet and sour sauce, stir to combine and heat through.

Once the sauce is ready, add the crispy fried beef to the wok, tossing it in the sauce until each piece is evenly coated. Transfer the rainbow beef to a serving plate and garnish with sesame seeds.

Serve hot.

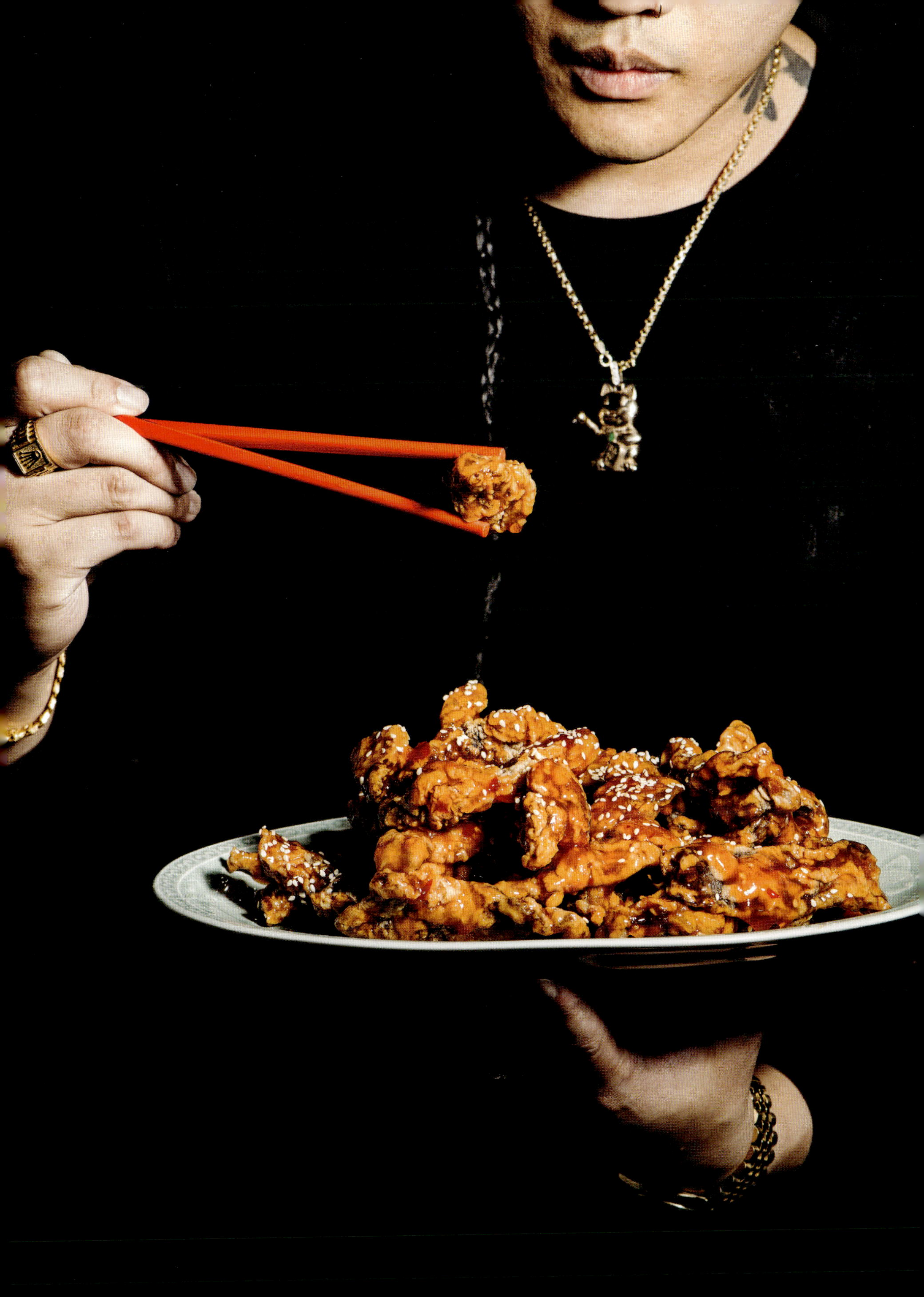

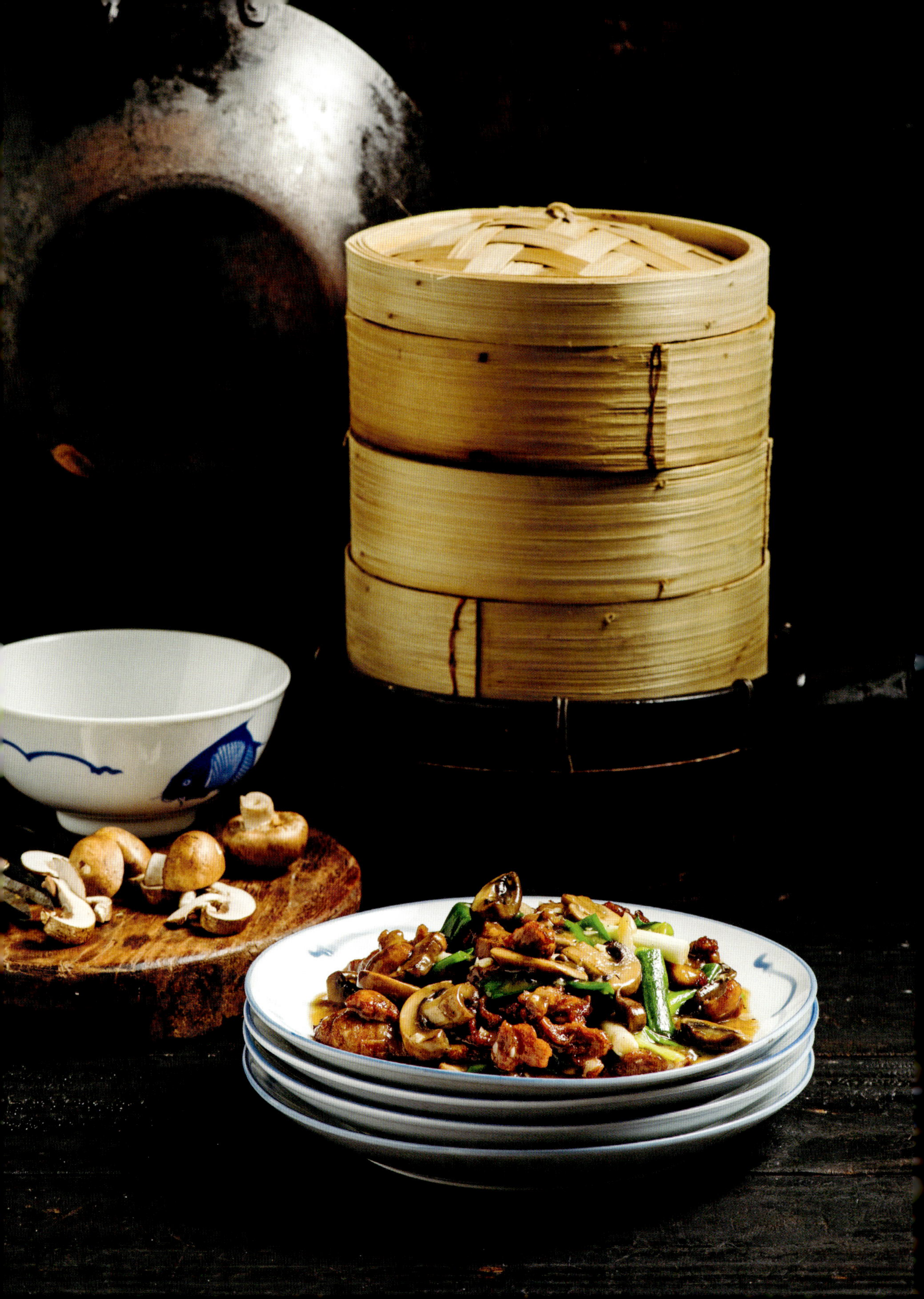

SERVES 2

BEEF AND MUSHROOM STIR-FRY

CHINESE-STYLE BEEF AND MUSHROOM STIR-FRY IS A QUICK, SAVOURY DISH FEATURING TENDER BEEF SLICES AND EARTHY MUSHROOMS TOSSED IN A FLAVOURFUL SAUCE. IT'S A SIMPLE AND SATISFYING DISH TO ADD TO YOUR WEEKNIGHT DINNER ROTATION.

BEEF AND VEGETABLES

vegetable oil, for flash-frying

1 × quantity Velveted beef (page 30), or 250 g (9 oz) of your favourite cut of steak, thinly sliced

8 Swiss brown mushrooms, thinly sliced

1 spring onion (scallion), cut into 3 cm (1¼ inch) stalks

SAUCE

2 teaspoons butter

1 teaspoon black pepper

2 tablespoons minced garlic

1 teaspoon chicken bouillon powder

½ teaspoon YumYum or MSG

1 teaspoon sugar

1 tablespoon oyster sauce

½ teaspoon dark soy sauce

240 ml (8 fl oz/1 cup) Chicken stock (page 32 or shop-bought)

2 teaspoons potato starch

1 tablespoon water

2 tablespoons Shaoxing wine (Chinese cooking wine)

1 teaspoon sesame oil

Fill a wok or large pot one-third full with oil and heat to 190°C (375°F) over a medium–high heat. Once the oil is hot, carefully add the velveted beef and flash-fry for 1–2 minutes until almost cooked through. In the last 30 seconds of cooking, add the thinly sliced mushrooms and spring onion stalks and continue frying until everything is just cooked, approximately 30 seconds. Strain the beef, mushrooms and spring onions from the oil and set them aside on a plate lined with paper towels to drain. Reserve the leftover oil for future use.

In the now-empty wok add the butter, black pepper, garlic, chicken bouillon powder, YumYum or MSG, sugar, oyster sauce, dark soy sauce and chicken stock, stirring to combine. Bring the mixture to a boil over medium heat, then reduce the heat and let it simmer for a few minutes.

In a small bowl, mix the potato starch and water to make a slurry. Once the sauce has thickened slightly, slowly add the slurry, stirring continuously to thicken the sauce further. Next, add the flash-fried beef, mushrooms and spring onions back into the wok, tossing to coat everything evenly in the sauce.

Finish the dish by adding the Shaoxing wine and sesame oil, giving the beef a final toss to combine all the flavours. Serve immediately.

MEAT

SERVES 2

BEEF AND BLACK BEAN

BEEF AND BLACK BEAN IS A CLASSIC CHINESE STIR-FRY DISH OF TENDER SLICES OF BEEF TOSSED WITH SAVOURY BLACK BEAN SAUCE AND CRISP VEGETABLES. DON'T BE FOOLED BY THE INGREDIENT LIST – IT'S QUICK TO PREP (AND FULL OF UMAMI FLAVOURS) AND MAKES A GREAT WEEKNIGHT DINNER.

STIR-FRY

vegetable oil, for flash-frying, plus 1 tablespoon extra

1 × quantity Velveted beef (page 30) or 250 g (9 oz) of your favourite cut of steak, thinly sliced

¼ onion, cubed

½ capsicum (bell pepper), thinly sliced

¼ broccoli, cut into small florets

½ carrot, thinly sliced

½ stalk celery, thinly sliced

6 slices of tinned bamboo shoots

BLACK BEAN PASTE

100 g (3½ oz) salted black beans, soaked in water overnight

2 tablespoons vegetable oil

3 tablespoons minced garlic

1 tablespoon minced ginger

3 tablespoons sugar

1 tablespoon chicken bouillon powder

1 teaspoon YumYum or MSG

1 tablespoon dark soy sauce

1 teaspoon white pepper

60 ml (2 fl oz/¼ cup) water

SAUCE

2 tablespoons Black bean paste, above

240 ml (8 fl oz/1 cup) Chicken stock (page 32 or shop-bought)

1 tablespoon oyster sauce

1 teaspoon dark soy sauce

2 teaspoons potato starch

1 tablespoon water

2 tablespoons Shaoxing wine (Chinese cooking wine)

1 teaspoon sesame oil

To start, drain the soaked salted black beans. Fill a wok or large pot one-third full with oil and bring to 190°C (375°F) over a medium–high heat. Once the oil is hot, carefully add the velveted beef and flash-fry for 1–2 minutes until just cooked through. Add the onion, capsicum, broccoli, carrot, celery and bamboo shoots to the wok. Continue cooking for 30 seconds, or until the vegetables begin to soften. Strain the beef and vegetables from the oil using a slotted spoon and set them aside on a plate lined with paper towels to drain. Reserve the leftover oil for future use.

To prepare the black bean paste, heat 2 tablespoons of oil in the wok over medium–high heat. Add the minced garlic and ginger, stir-frying for about 1 minute until fragrant. Lower the heat and add the remaining paste ingredients, except the water. Let the paste cook on low heat for 10 minutes, until the black beans soften and release their fragrance. Add the water and bring the mixture to a boil, cooking for an additional 2 minutes. Set aside 2 tablespoons of the paste for use in the stir-fry, and store the remainder in an airtight container in the fridge for up to 2 weeks.

In the now-empty wok, heat 1 tablespoon of vegetable oil over medium heat and add the black bean paste, stir-frying for 1 minute until fragrant. Return the flash-fried beef and vegetables to the wok and increase the heat to high. Add the chicken stock, oyster sauce and dark soy sauce, stirring well to combine.

In a small bowl, mix the potato starch and water to make a slurry. Slowly pour the slurry into the wok while stirring continuously to thicken the sauce. Cook for another 1–2 minutes until everything is heated through and the flavours are well combined.

Finish the dish by adding the Shaoxing wine and sesame oil. Serve immediately.

MEAT

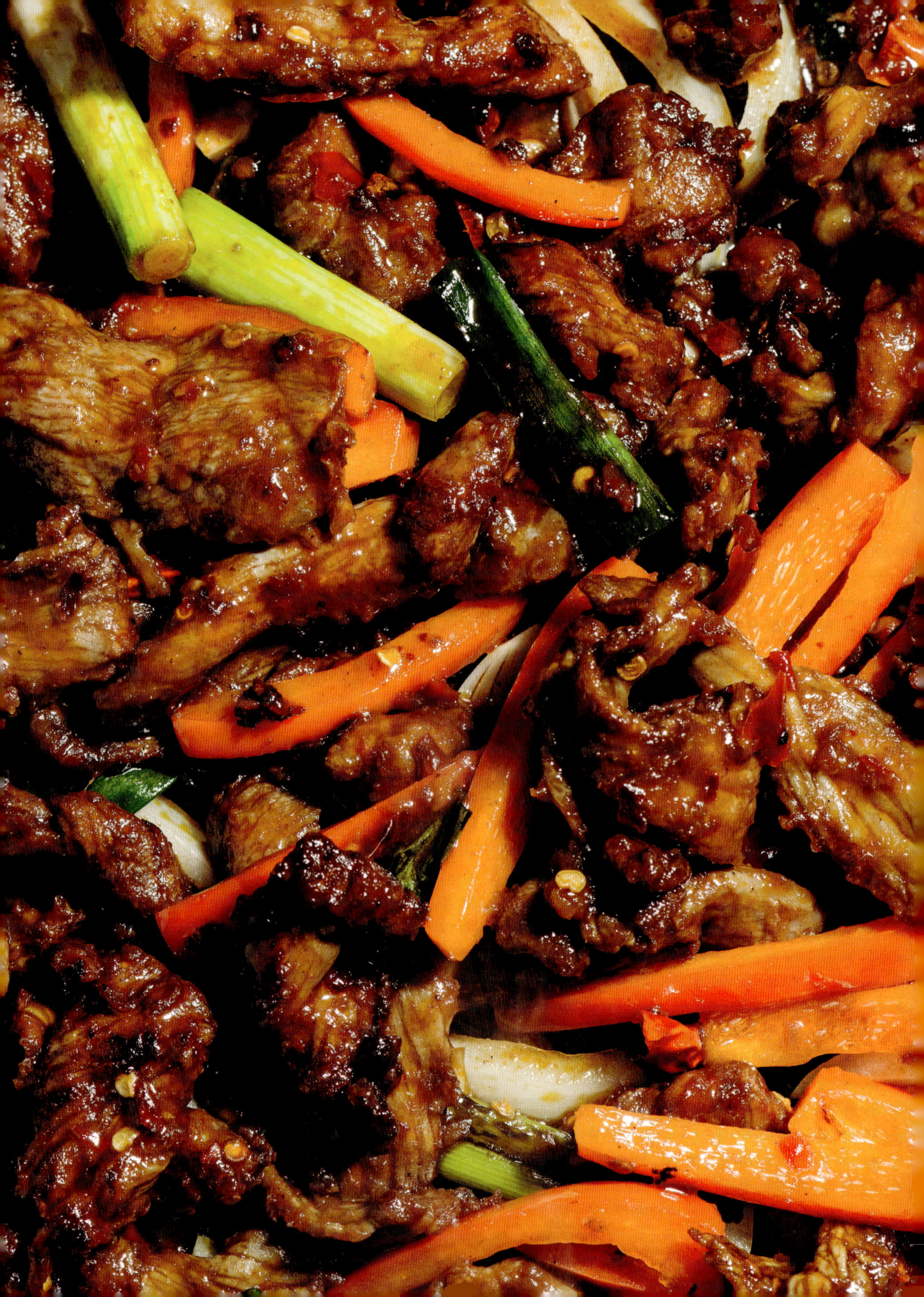

SERVES 2

SZECHUAN BEEF

SZECHUAN BEEF IS A SPICY, FLAVOURFUL STIR-FRY DISH THAT HAILS FROM CHINA'S SICHUAN PROVINCE, KNOWN FOR ITS BOLD USE OF CHILLI AND PEPPERCORNS. WITH TENDER SLICES OF BEEF COATED IN A TANGY, SPICY SAUCE, IT'S A GUARANTEED FAVOURITE FOR THOSE WHO LOVE A BIT OF HEAT IN THEIR MEALS.

STIR-FRY

vegetable oil, for flash-frying

1 × quantity Velveted beef (page 30), or 250 g (9 oz) of your favourite cut of steak, thinly sliced

¼ white onion, sliced

½ capsicum (bell pepper), thinly sliced

3 long dried chillies, cut into 1 cm (½ in) pieces

1 spring onion (scallion), cut into 4 cm (1½ in) batons

SAUCE

1 tablespoon vegetable oil

1 tablespoon minced garlic

2 teaspoons chilli oil (optional)

1 tablespoon doubanjiang (spicy bean paste)

½ teaspoon chilli powder

80 ml (2½ fl oz/⅓ cup) Chicken stock (page 32 or shop-bought)

1 teaspoon sugar

1 tablespoon oyster sauce

2 teaspoons tomato sauce (ketchup)

1 teaspoon YumYum or MSG

2 teaspoons potato starch

1 tablespoon water

Fill a wok or large pot one-third full with oil and heat to 190°C (375°F) over a medium–high heat. Once the oil is hot, carefully add the beef and flash-fry for 1–2 minutes until cooked through. Add the sliced onion, capsicum, long dried chillies and spring onion to the wok with the beef. Fry for about 10 seconds until the vegetables begin to soften.

Carefully strain the beef and vegetables from the oil and set them aside on a plate lined with paper towels to drain. Reserve the leftover oil for future use.

To make the sauce, heat 1 tablespoon of oil in the now-empty wok or frying pan, over medium heat. Add the minced garlic and stir-fry for 30 seconds until fragrant. Lower the heat and add chilli oil (if using), doubanjiang, chilli powder, chicken stock, sugar, oyster sauce, tomato sauce and YumYum or MSG. Increase the heat to medium and stir constantly until everything is well combined.

In a small bowl, mix the potato starch and water to make a slurry. Slowly pour the slurry into the wok, stirring continuously to thicken the sauce. Cook for another 1–2 minutes until the sauce thickens and the flavours meld together.

Add the flash-fried beef and vegetables back into the wok, tossing to ensure the beef and vegetables are well coated with the sauce. Cook for an additional 1–2 minutes until everything is heated through.

Transfer the Szechuan beef to a serving plate and serve hot.

SERVES 2

BEEF WITH OYSTER SAUCE

BEEF WITH OYSTER SAUCE IS A CLASSIC CHINESE STIR-FRY THAT BRINGS TOGETHER TENDER SLICES OF BEEF AND A RICH, SAVOURY SAUCE. IT'S THE KIND OF COMFORT FOOD YOU CAN MAKE IN A HURRY, ANY NIGHT OF THE WEEK.

STIR-FRY

3 tablespoons vegetable oil

1 × quantity Velveted beef (page 30) or 250 g (9 oz) of your favourite cut of steak, thinly sliced

½ onion, cut into 2 cm (¾ in) cubes

1 spring onion (scallion), cut into 7 cm (3 in) batons

SAUCE

120 ml (4 fl oz/½ cup) Chicken stock (page 32 or shop-bought)

1 heaped tablespoon oyster sauce

½ teaspoon dark soy sauce

1 teaspoon YumYum or MSG

2 teaspoons potato starch

1 tablespoon water

2 tablespoons Shaoxing wine (Chinese cooking wine)

1 teaspoon sesame oil

Heat the vegetable oil in a wok or large skillet over medium–high heat. Once the oil is hot, add the velveted beef and stir-fry for about 1 minute. Then, add the thinly sliced onion and continue stir-frying for 2–3 minutes until the beef is fully cooked and the onion starts to soften.

Next, add the spring onion pieces and toss everything together to combine. Pour in the chicken stock, oyster sauce, dark soy sauce and YumYum or MSG, stirring well to ensure all the ingredients are evenly coated.

In a small bowl, mix the potato starch and water to make a slurry. Slowly pour this mixture into the wok while stirring constantly, allowing the sauce to thicken slightly.

Finish the dish by adding the Shaoxing wine and sesame oil, giving the beef a final toss to combine all the flavours.

Serve immediately.

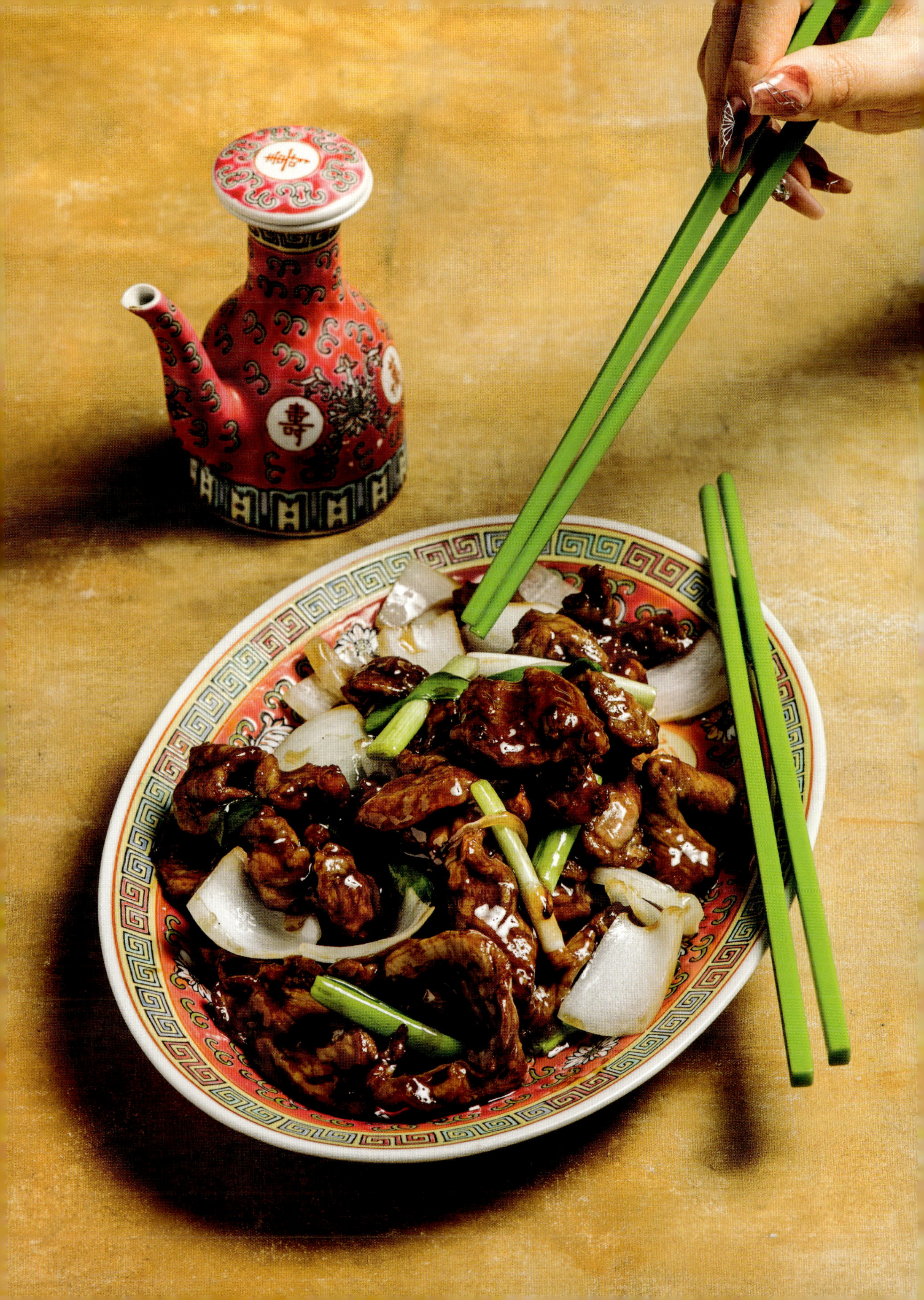

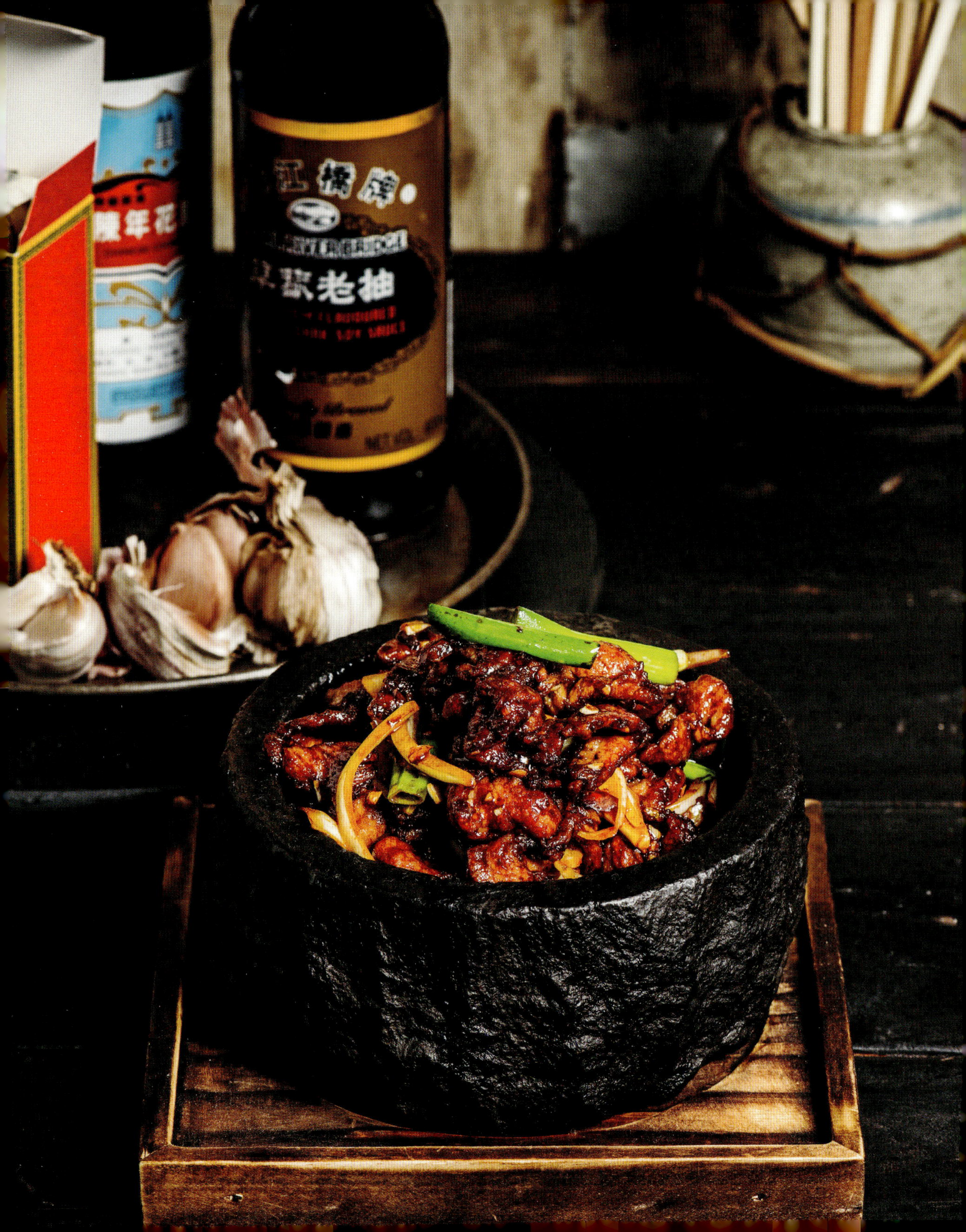
老抽

SERVES 2

MONGOLIAN LAMB

THERE'S TENDER, AND THEN THERE'S MONGOLIAN LAMB TENDER. THE SECRET TO THIS CHINESE-RESTAURANT FAVOURITE IS ALL IN THE VELVETING, BUT DON'T WORRY — WE'VE SET YOU UP WITH THE SIGNATURE SAUCE TOO.

STIR-FRY

vegetable oil, for flash-frying

250 g (9 oz) lamb shoulder, thinly sliced and velveted (see beef method on page 30)

1 spring onion (scallion), cut into 4 cm (1½ in) batons

½ brown onion, thinly sliced

SAUCE

1 tablespoon hoisin sauce

1 tablespoon doubanjiang

2 teaspoons sesame paste

2 teaspoons black bean chilli sauce

2 teaspoons finely chopped garlic

½ teaspoon YumYum or MSG

½ teaspoon sugar

2 tablespoons water

¼ teaspoon dark soy sauce

1 tablespoon Shaoxing wine (Chinese cooking wine), plus a little extra to finish

Fill a wok or large pot one-third full with oil and heat to 190°C (375°F) over a medium–high heat. Once the oil is hot, carefully add the velveted lamb and flash-fry for 2–3 minutes until just cooked through. Strain the lamb from the oil and set it aside on a plate lined with paper towels to drain. Leave about 1 tablespoon of oil in the wok, and reserve the rest for future use.

After removing the lamb, place a cast-iron sizzling plate on your wok burner, on top of a spare burner or in an oven preheated to 220°C (430°F) to heat. You want the sizzling plate to be ready by the time the stir-fry is done.

Return your wok to the heat, and add the sauce ingredients. Stir until the sauce is well combined and bubbling.

Add the flash-fried lamb and spring onion pieces to the wok. Toss everything together until the lamb is evenly coated with the sauce and heated through. Finish the dish by adding another splash of Shaoxing wine, giving the lamb a final toss to combine all the flavours.

By now, the sizzling plate should be hot. Carefully remove it from the heat and place it on a heatproof board. Scatter an even layer of thinly sliced onion onto the sizzling hot plate, then immediately spoon the Mongolian lamb and sauce over the top. It should sizzle as it makes contact with the hot plate. Serve immediately.

SERVES 4

AIR-FRYER CRISPY PORK BELLY

THIS EASY RECIPE FOR AIR-FRYER ROAST PORK BELLY GIVES YOU PERFECTLY CRISPY SKIN AND JUICY, TENDER MEAT WITH MINIMAL EFFORT. IT'S A SIMPLE, FUSS-FREE WAY TO ENJOY DELICIOUS ROAST PORK THAT'S JUST LIKE THE ONE AT ASIAN BBQ SHOPS.

1 kg (2 lb 3 oz) pork belly
¼ teaspoon YumYum or MSG
¼ teaspoon Chinese five-spice
½ teaspoon salt, for seasoning
¼ teaspoon sugar
1 teaspoon chicken bouillon powder
1 tablespoon Shaoxing wine (Chinese cooking wine)
2 teaspoons white vinegar
approx. 140 g (5 oz/½ cup) salt, for baking

Score the meat side of the pork belly with a sharp knife, making shallow cuts in a crisscross pattern and being careful not to cut down to the fat layer. On the meat side of the pork belly, scatter the YumYum or MSG, Chinese five-spice, salt, white sugar, chicken bouillon powder and Shaoxing wine. Rub the seasoning into the meat evenly.

Use a skewer or fork to poke several small holes in the skin – this will help release excess fat during cooking and create a crispier texture. Wrap the bottom of the pork belly in aluminium foil, forming a foil boat that covers the meat while leaving the skin exposed.

Pour the vinegar over the skin and rub it in thoroughly. Next, cover the skin with a layer of salt. Preheat your air fryer to 180°C (350°F) for a few minutes, then carefully place the pork belly into the basket.

Air-fry the pork belly for 30 minutes, allowing the salt crust to form and help render out excess fat. After 30 minutes, carefully remove the pork belly from the air fryer. The salt crust should have hardened on the skin.

Gently scrape off the salt crust using a spoon or brush, being careful not to tear the skin. Brush a thin layer of oil over the skin to encourage further crisping during the final cooking stage.

Return the pork belly to the air fryer basket, skin side up, and increase the temperature to 200°C (390°F). Air-fry the pork belly for an additional 30 minutes, until the skin turns golden brown and crispy.

Once fully cooked, remove the pork belly from the air fryer and let it rest for about 10 minutes before slicing. Slice the pork belly into thick pieces and serve hot with your favourite accompaniments.

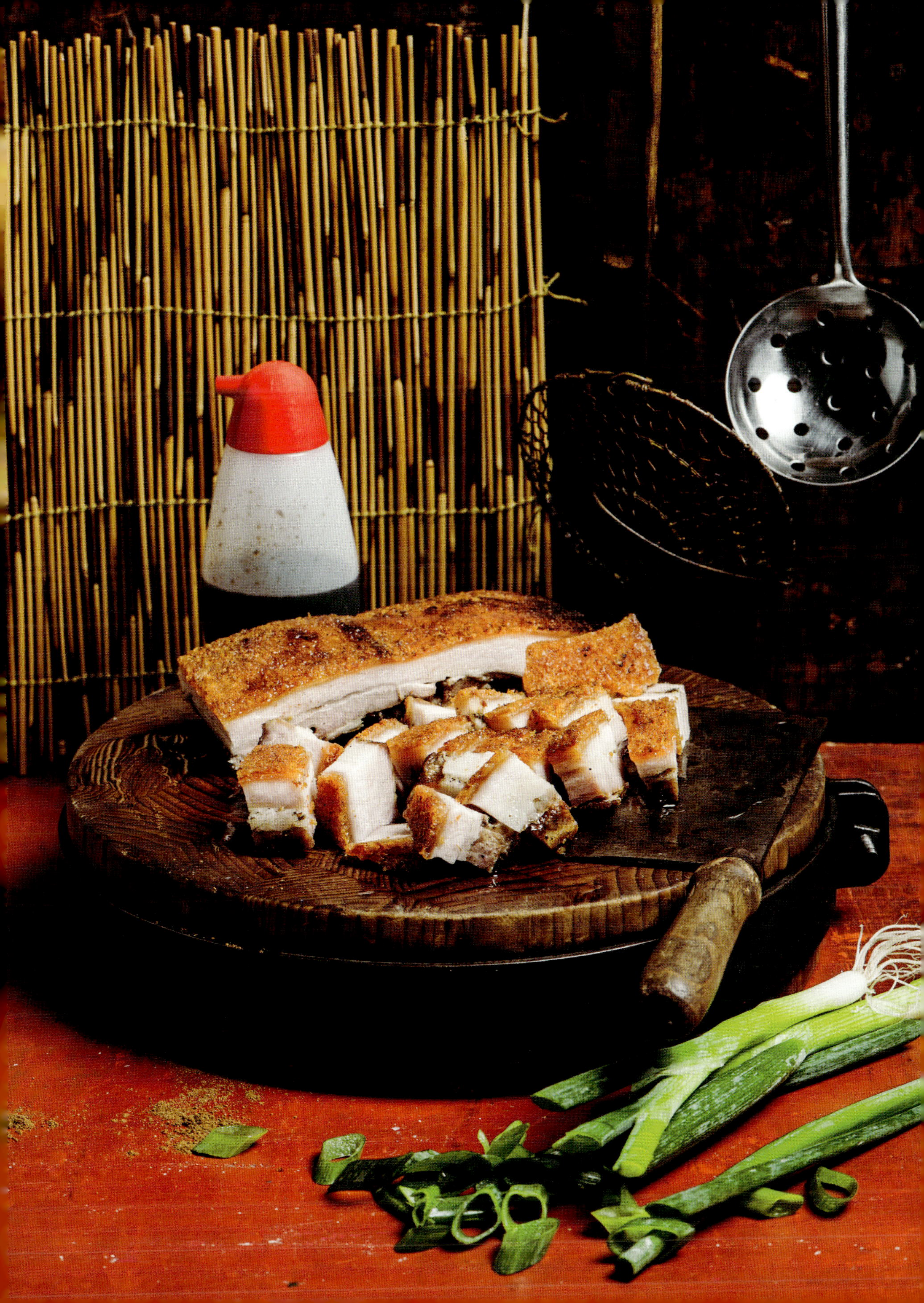

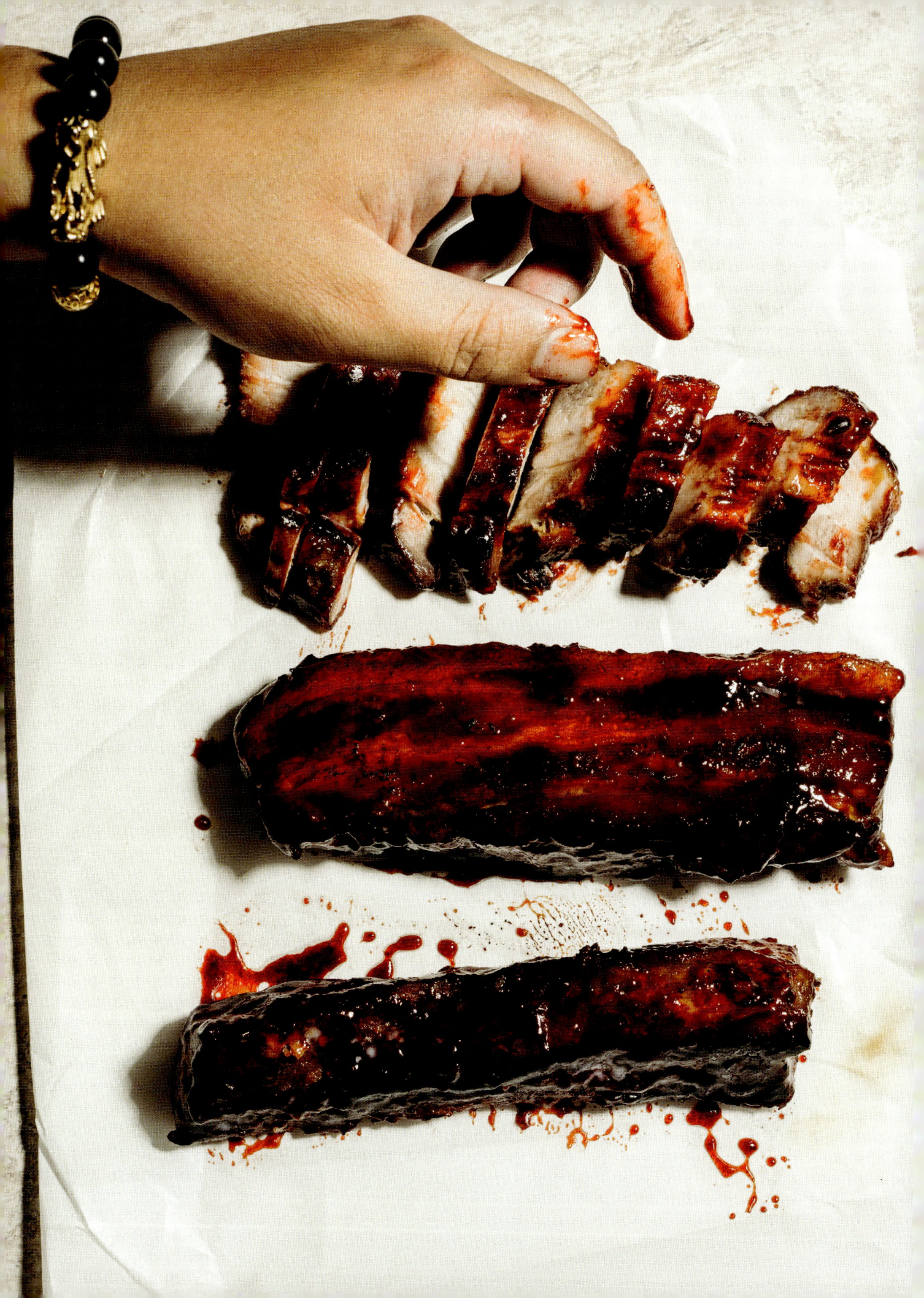

SERVES 3

EASY CHAR SIU PORK

THIS EASY STOVETOP CHAR SIU RECIPE GIVES YOU ALL THE SWEET, SAVOURY FLAVOURS OF TRADITIONAL CHINESE BARBECUE PORK, WITHOUT THE NEED FOR AN OVEN. USING A SIMPLE FRYING PAN, YOU CAN WHIP UP THE TENDER, CARAMELISED CHAR SIU OF YOUR DREAMS.

500 g (1 lb 2 oz) skin-on pork belly, cut into long strips (approx. 5 cm/2 in wide)

2 tablespoons maltose syrup

1 tablespoon hoisin sauce

1 teaspoon doubanjiang (spicy bean paste)

2 teaspoons dark soy sauce

2 tablespoons sugar

2 teaspoons light soy sauce

1 tablespoon oyster sauce

1 tablespoon honey

1 teaspoon YumYum or MSG

¼ teaspoon bicarbonate of soda (baking soda)

large pinch of Chinese five-spice

large pinch of white pepper

1 tablespoon mei gui lu jiu (Chinese rose cooking wine)

2–3 drops red food colouring

cucumber, sliced, to serve (optional)

Place the pork belly in a large bowl. Add all remaining ingredients, except the cucumber, to the bowl. Wearing food-safe gloves, thoroughly mix the sauces into the pork until it is evenly coated. Set the pork aside to marinate for at least 15 minutes.

Heat a large frying pan over low heat. Once heated, add the marinated pork to the pan and cook, turning occasionally, for about 20 minutes. Ensure the sauces absorb into the meat, creating a sticky coating, and that the pork is cooked through completely. Turn the pork regularly as it cooks to prevent the sauce from burning.

Once the pork is fully cooked, remove it from the pan and cut it into bite-sized pieces. Serve the char siu pork on a bed of warm steamed rice, accompanied by sliced cucumber for a fresh contrast, if desired.

MEAT

SERVES 2–3

SWEET AND SOUR PORK

SWEET AND SOUR PORK ORIGINATED IN GUANGDONG, CHINA, WHERE CANTONESE CHEFS COMBINED VINEGAR AND SUGAR TO CREATE A HARMONIOUS BALANCE OF TANGY AND SWEET FLAVOURS. TODAY, IT'S A CROWD FAVOURITE AND A CHINESE RESTAURANT STAPLE. THIS RECIPE HAS BEEN PASSED DOWN FROM MY FATHER AND WAS ALWAYS A FAVOURITE AT MY OLD RESTAURANT. NOW I AM FINALLY ABLE TO SHARE IT WITH YOU ALL.

BATTER

100 g (3½ oz/⅔ cup) self-raising flour
100 g (3½ oz/⅔ cup) cornflour (cornstarch)
200 ml (7 fl oz) water

SWEET AND SOUR PORK

200 g (7 oz) skinless pork shoulder (velveted using the Velveted beef method on page 30), cut into bite-sized pieces
vegetable oil, for deep-frying, plus 1 tablespoon extra
1 brown onion, cut into chunks
⅓ red capsicum (bell pepper), cut into chunks
⅓ green capsicum (bell pepper), cut into chunks
100 g (3½ oz) pineapple pieces (from approx. ½ tin)
1 × quantity Sweet and sour sauce (page 31)

TO SERVE

sesame seeds (optional)
spring onion (scallion), finely sliced, optional

In a large bowl, combine the self-raising flour and cornflour. Gradually whisk in the water until the batter becomes smooth. Add the pork shoulder pieces to the batter, stirring until they are fully coated.

Fill a wok or large pot halfway full with vegetable oil and heat to 180°C (350°F) over medium–high heat. You can also test the oil with a wooden chopstick – if bubbles form around it when lowered in, the oil is hot enough. Carefully add the pork pieces to the hot oil and fry for about 9 minutes, or until they are almost cooked through and golden brown. Then add the onion, red and green capsicum and pineapple pieces to the oil, frying for an additional 10 seconds.

Once done, carefully strain the pork and vegetables from the oil and place them on a plate lined with paper towels to drain. Reserve the leftover oil for future deep-frying.

In a clean wok, heat 1 tablespoon of oil over medium heat. Add the prepared sweet and sour sauce and bring it to a simmer. Once the sauce has thickened, add the fried pork and vegetables, tossing everything together until well coated.

Garnish with sesame seeds or spring onions if desired and serve immediately.

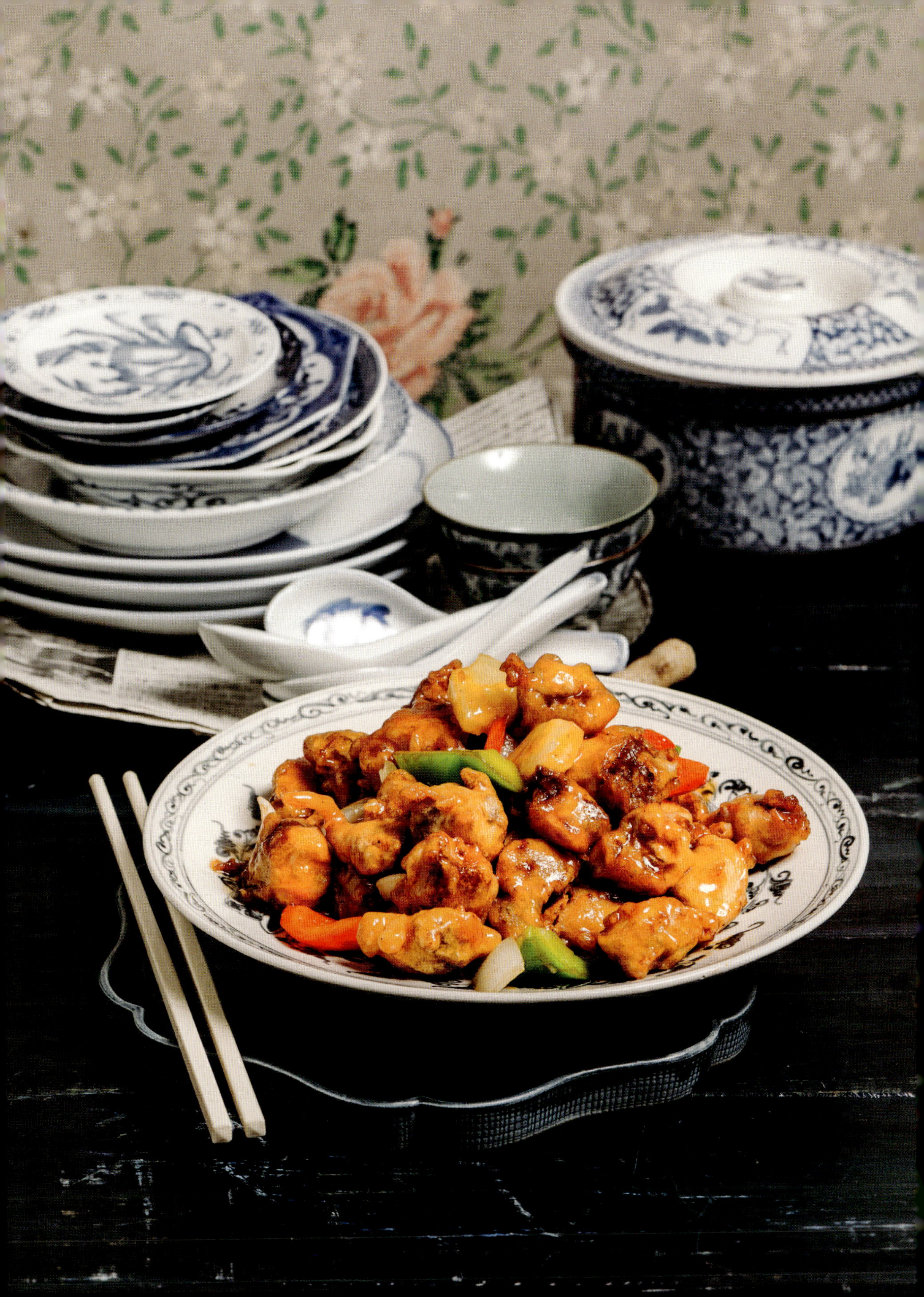

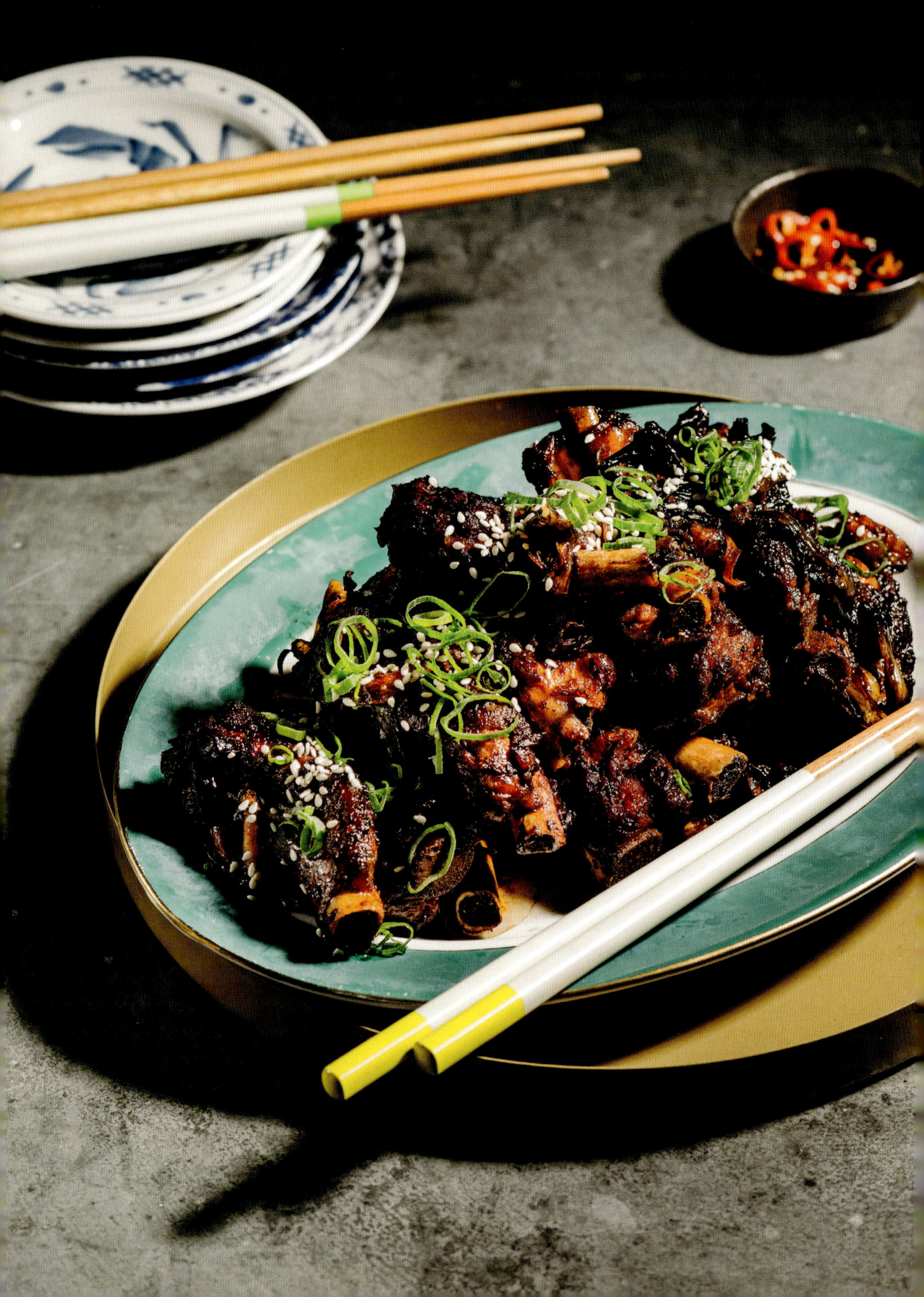

SERVES 4

SWEET AND SOUR RIBS

DURING MY TIME RUNNING A CHINESE RESTAURANT, SWEET AND SOUR RIBS WERE ALWAYS A CROWD FAVOURITE. THIS BELOVED DISH FEATURES TENDER PORK RIBS COATED IN A TANGY, STICKY SAUCE THAT PERFECTLY BALANCES RICH, SAVOURY FLAVOURS WITH A HINT OF SWEETNESS.

700 g (1 lb 9 oz) pork ribs
1 tablespoon vegetable oil
10 garlic cloves, peeled and smashed
3 slices of ginger
2 spring onions (scallions), cut into 7 cm (2¾ in) batons
5 tablespoons sugar (or 2 large lumps of rock sugar)
3 tablespoons Chinkiang vinegar (black vinegar), plus 1 tablespoon extra
1 tablespoon light soy sauce
1 teaspoon dark soy sauce
⅛ teaspoon salt

TO SERVE
sesame seeds, toasted
spring onions (scallions), finely chopped

Cut the pork ribs into bite-sized pieces and rinse them under cold water. Blanch the pork ribs in a pot of boiling water for 3–5 minutes to remove impurities. Drain and rinse the ribs under cold water, then pat them dry with paper towels.

Heat the oil in a wok or large pot over medium heat. Add the blanched pork ribs, smashed garlic, sliced ginger and spring onions to the pan. Sprinkle sugar (or rock sugar) over the ribs, then pour in the 3 tablespoons of Chinkiang vinegar, the light soy sauce, dark soy sauce and a pinch of salt. Stir everything to combine.

Add enough water to the pan to just cover the ribs. Bring the mixture to a boil, then reduce the heat to low. Cover the pan and braise the ribs for about 30 minutes, or until they are tender.

Uncover the pan and remove the ginger, garlic and spring onion pieces. Increase the heat to medium and add the extra 1 tablespoon of Chinkiang vinegar. Cook the sauce down, stirring occasionally, until it thickens and forms a glossy glaze that coats the ribs.

Once the ribs are nicely glazed, remove them from the pan and transter to a serving plate. Garnish with toasted sesame seeds and finely chopped spring onions. Serve the sweet and sour ribs hot.

SERVES 3

GUINNESS PORK

GUINNESS-BRAISED PORK IS A RICH AND SAVOURY DISH THAT COMBINES TENDER PORK WITH THE DEEP, MALTY FLAVOURS OF STOUT. THIS FUSION OF CHINESE COOKING TECHNIQUES AND THE BOLD TASTE OF THE ICONIC IRISH BEER CREATE A FLAVOURFUL, HEARTY MEAL THAT'S PERFECT FOR A COSY DINNER.

700 g (1 lb 9 oz) skin-on pork belly
2 slices of ginger
2 tablespoons vegetable oil
2 tablespoons rock sugar, or sugar
1 tablespoon light soy sauce
3 teaspoons dark soy sauce
1 tablespoon cooking caramel (karamel masakan)
440 ml (15 fl oz/1 large can) Guinness or stout
2 teaspoons potato starch
1 tablespoon water
spring onion (scallion), finely sliced, to garnish
coriander (cilantro) sprigs, to garnish

Use a blowtorch to singe off any hairs on the pork belly skin. If you don't have a blowtorch, you can carefully use the open flame on a gas stovetop. Once cleaned, cut the pork belly into 3 cm (1¼ in) thick pieces.

Place the pork into a large pot of cold water with the ginger and bring it to a boil. Blanch the pork belly for a couple of minutes to remove impurities and start the cooking process. Remove the pork from the pot, rinse it and set it aside. Discard the blanching water.

In a wok, heat the oil and sugar over low heat until the sugar starts to melt slightly. Add the pork belly pieces to the wok and raise the heat to medium. Cook the pork until it is lightly browned, stirring occasionally to ensure even browning.

Once browned, reduce the heat to low and add the light soy sauce, dark soy sauce and cooking caramel to the pot. Stir constantly to combine the ingredients and bring the mixture to a simmer, allowing the sauce to caramelise and stick to the meat.

Pour in the Guinness and cover the pot. Let the pork braise over medium heat for 30–45 minutes, until the pork becomes fork-tender. Stir the mixture every 5–10 minutes to prevent burning and add a little water if the sauce reduces too quickly.

When the pork is tender, uncover the pot and turn up the heat. Stir continuously to reduce the sauce until it forms a glistening coating on the pork.

Garnish with spring onion and coriander sprigs and serve the Guinness-braised pork belly hot.

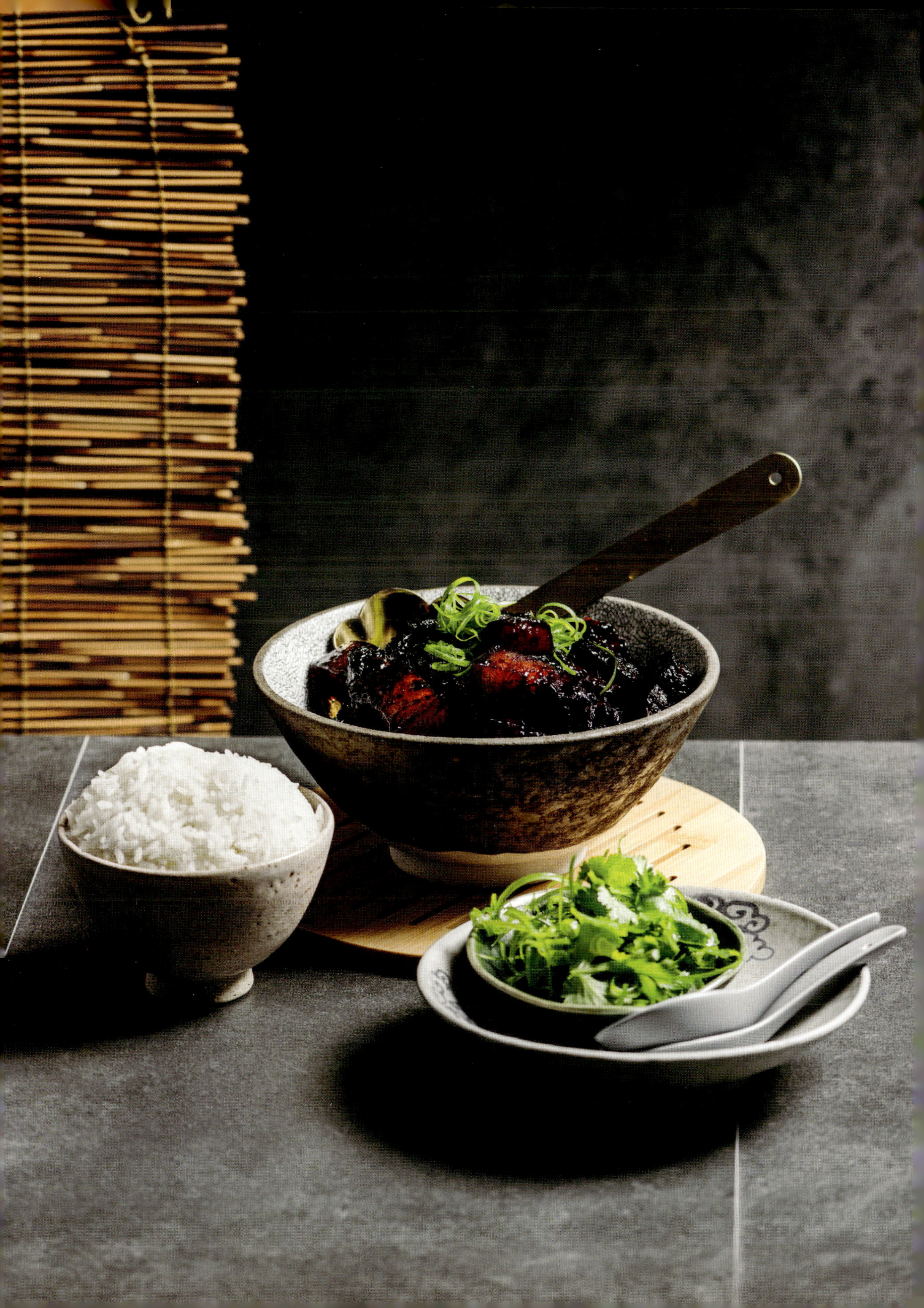

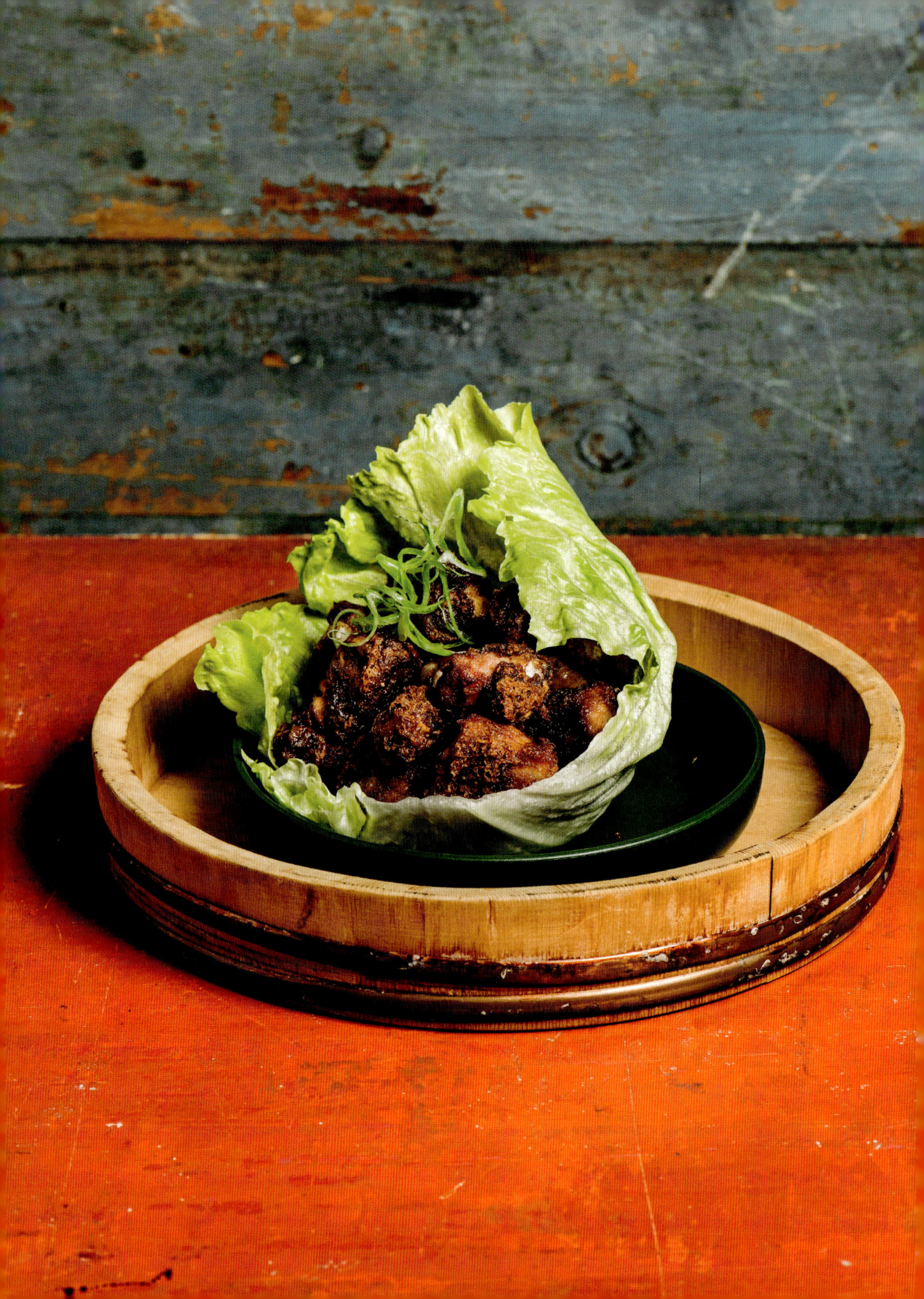

SERVES 3

NAM YU PORK RIBS

THESE TENDER PORK RIBS ARE MARINATED IN RED FERMENTED TOFU, INFUSING THEM WITH A RICH, UMAMI TASTE. THIS DISH IS DEEP-FRIED TO GOLDEN PERFECTION FOR A DELICIOUSLY CRISPY, SAVOURY DISH.

2 pieces jarred red fermented tofu, plus 2 tablespoons brine

½ teaspoon bicarbonate of soda (baking soda)

1½ teaspoons sugar

1 heaped tablespoon oyster sauce

1 tablespoon Shaoxing wine (Chinese cooking wine)

2 teaspoons cornflour (cornstarch), plus 60 g (2 oz/ ½ cup) extra

600 g (1 lb 5 oz) pork ribs, cut into separate pieces

vegetable oil, for deep-frying

small iceberg lettuce leaves (optional)

In a large bowl, mash the red fermented tofu and mix it with the brine, bicarbonate of soda, sugar, oyster sauce, Shaoxing wine and cornflour until well combined. Add the pork ribs to the marinade, ensuring each piece is evenly coated. Cover the bowl and let the pork marinate for at least 2 hours, or preferably overnight in the refrigerator, to allow the flavours to fully penetrate the meat.

When ready to cook, remove the marinated pork ribs from the refrigerator. In a separate bowl, coat each piece of pork with the extra cornflour, pressing lightly to ensure an even coating.

Fill a wok or large pot halfway full with vegetable oil and heat to 180°C (350°F) over medium–high heat. You can also test the oil with a wooden chopstick – if bubbles form around it when lowered in, the oil is hot enough. Carefully add the pork ribs in batches, making sure not to overcrowd the wok or fryer. Fry the ribs for 5–7 minutes, or until they are golden brown and crispy.

After frying the last batch, carefully strain the pork ribs from the oil and set them aside in a sieve or on a plate lined with paper towels to drain. Reserve the leftover oil for future deep-frying.

Spoon the deep-fried pork ribs into the prepared lettuce leaves. Serve immediately.

SERVES 4

SALT AND PEPPER PORK CHOPS

COATED IN A LIGHT, CRUNCHY BATTER AND TOSSED WITH A SIMPLE BLEND OF SALT, PEPPER AND AROMATIC SPICES, THESE CHOPS ARE A FLAVOUR-PACKED EXPERIENCE. WHETHER SERVED AS AN APPETISER OR A MAIN DISH, THEY'RE SURE TO PLEASE A CROWD.

PORK CHOPS

900 g (2 lb) pork chops, less than 1 cm (½ in) thick

1 tablespoon Shaoxing wine

1 tablespoon oyster sauce

2 teaspoons sugar

1 teaspoon white pepper

1 teaspoon light soy sauce

2 teaspoons sesame oil

125 g (4½ oz/1 cup) potato starch

vegetable oil, for deep-frying, plus 1 tablespoon extra

3 teaspoons Five-spice salt and pepper (page 33) or to taste

VEGETABLES

2 spring onions (scallions), chopped into batons

6 garlic cloves, thinly sliced

2 green or red chillies, thinly sliced

Cut each of the pork chops into three individual pieces and place in a large bowl. Add the Shaoxing wine, oyster sauce, sugar, white pepper, soy sauce and sesame oil to the chops, mixing well to ensure they are evenly coated. Cover the bowl and marinate for at least 1 hour, or preferably overnight, in the refrigerator to allow the flavours to penetrate.

Once marinated, coat each piece with potato starch, making sure to cover all sides evenly. Fill a wok or deep fryer half full with oil and heat to 180°C (350°F) over medium–high heat (you can also test the oil with a wooden chopstick – if bubbles form around it, the oil is ready). Once the oil is hot, carefully add the chop pieces in batches and fry them for 5–7 minutes, or until they are golden brown and crispy. Remove from the oil and place them in a sieve or on paper towels to drain. Set the leftover oil aside for future use.

In the now-empty wok or frying pan, heat 1 tablespoon of oil and stir-fry the chopped spring onions, thinly sliced garlic cloves and sliced chillies until fragrant and slightly crispy. Add the fried chops to the wok and toss them with the vegetables. Sprinkle the five-spice salt and pepper over the chops and mix everything together until the chops are well coated with the seasoning and vegetables. Adjust the seasoning to taste, if needed.

Serve immediately.

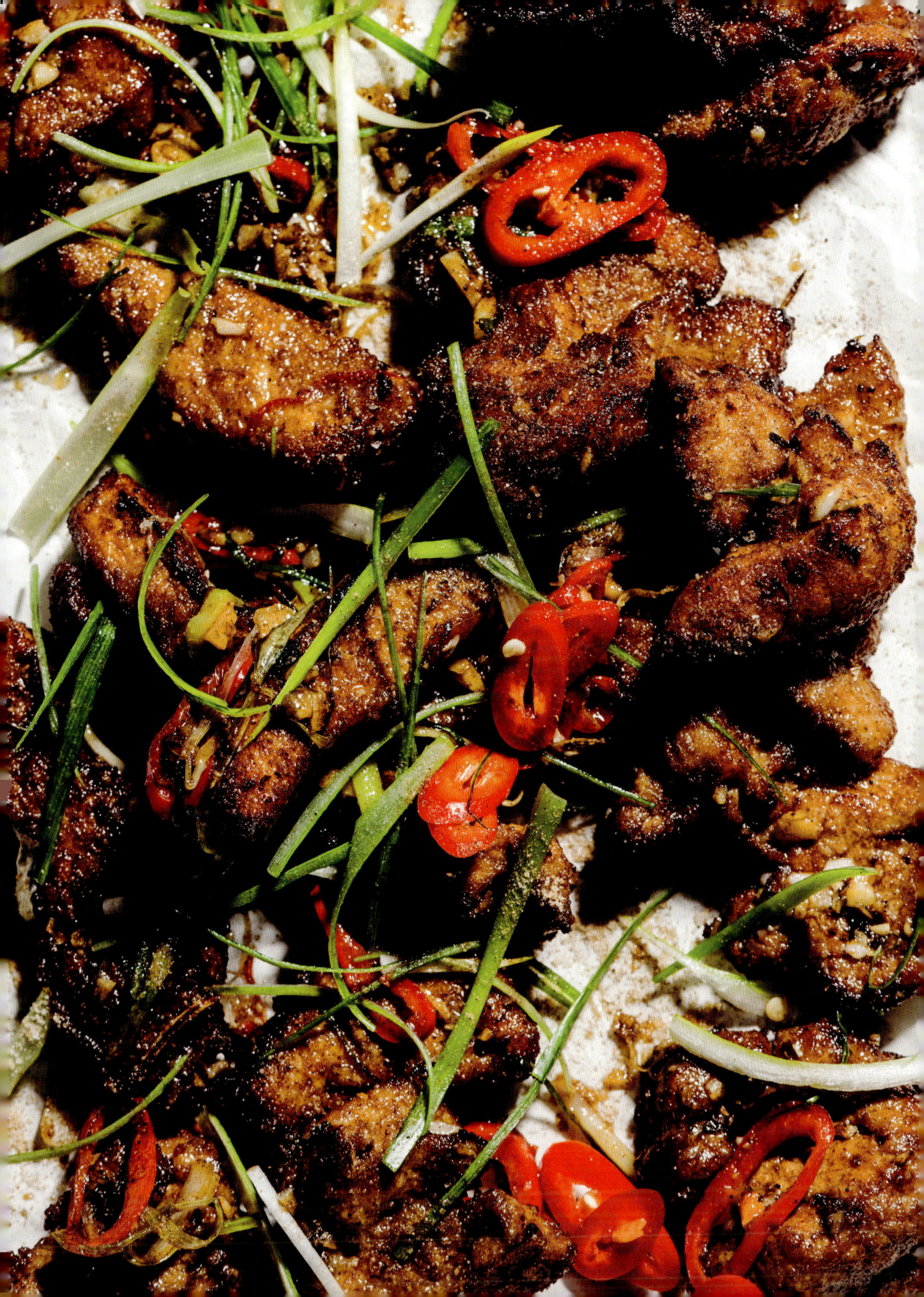

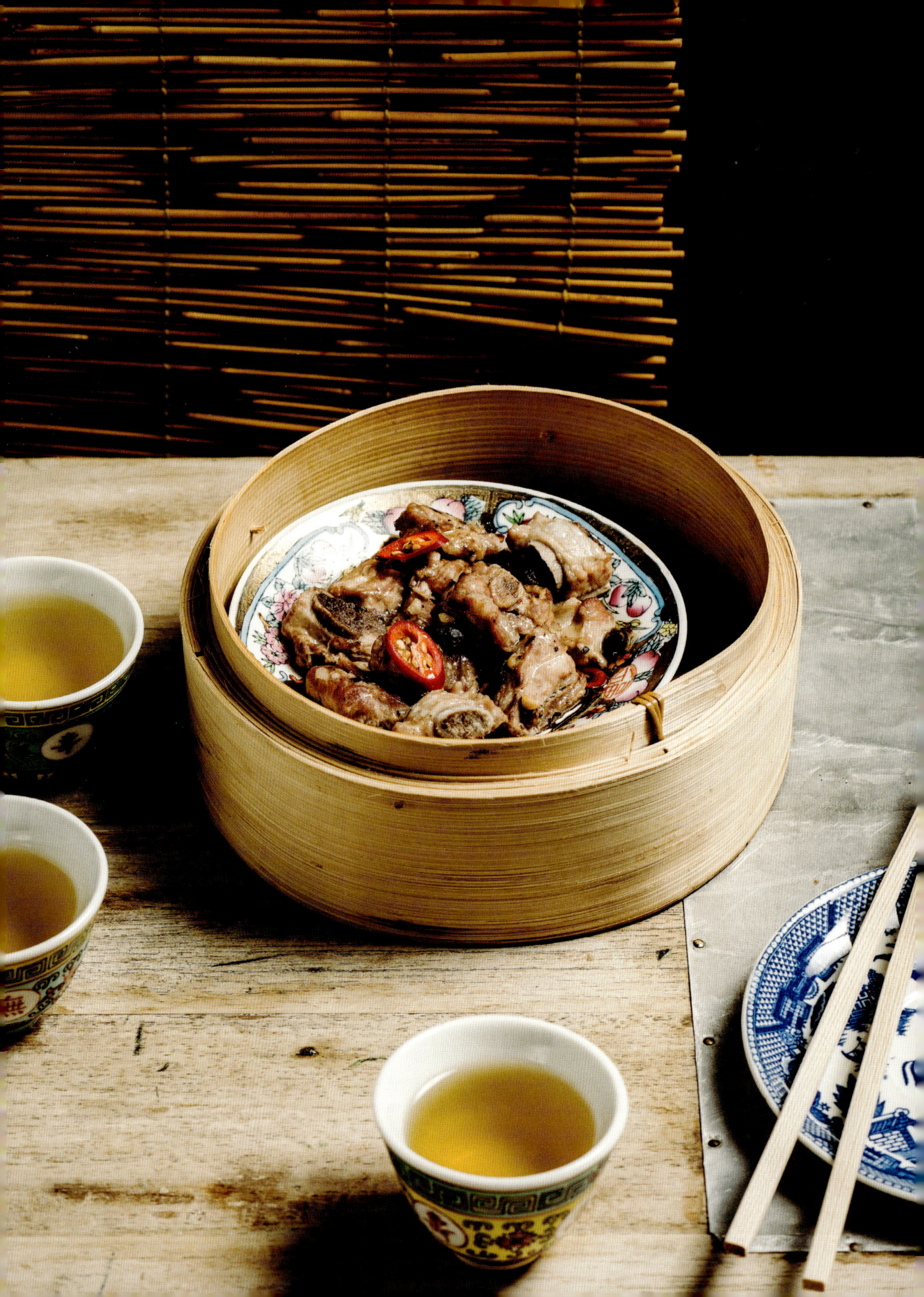

SERVES 3

YUM CHA STEAMED PORK RIBS

YUM CHA STEAMED PORK RIBS ARE A CLASSIC DIM SUM FAVOURITE, FEATURING TENDER PORK RIBS MARINATED IN SAVOURY SEASONINGS AND STEAMED TO PERFECTION. WITH THEIR DELICATE FLAVOUR AND JUICY TEXTURE, THESE RIBS ARE A MUST-HAVE AT ANY YUM CHA SPREAD.

PORK SPARE RIBS

680 g (1½ lb) pork spare ribs, cut into bite-sized pieces

1 heaped tablespoon fermented black beans (douchi), rinsed

2 garlic cloves, minced (about 1 tablespoon)

½ teaspoon oyster sauce

1 teaspoon Shaoxing wine (Chinese cooking wine), or dry sherry

½ teaspoon sesame oil

¼ teaspoon salt

2 teaspoons sugar

1 tablespoon water

2 teaspoons potato starch

1 tablespoon oil

TO SERVE

1 spring onion (scallion), finely chopped, optional

1 bird's eye chilli, finely sliced (optional)

Cut the pork spare ribs into bite-sized pieces and place them in a large bowl. In a small bowl, combine the fermented black beans, minced garlic, oyster sauce, Shaoxing wine, sesame oil, salt, sugar and water. Mix everything together well, then pour the marinade over the ribs, ensuring all the pieces are thoroughly coated. Cover the bowl and marinate the ribs for at least 1 hour, or preferably overnight in the refrigerator for deeper flavour.

Before steaming, add the potato starch to the marinated ribs and mix well to evenly coat them. Drizzle the ribs with a bit of oil for extra tenderness.

Set up a steamer over boiling water and arrange the marinated ribs in a single layer on a heatproof plate. Place the plate in the steamer and steam the ribs over high heat for about 20–25 minutes, or until they are tender and fully cooked through.

Once the ribs are ready, remove them from the steamer and garnish with finely chopped spring onion and chilli, if desired.

Serve the steamed pork spare ribs hot, either as part of a yum cha spread or as a main dish alongside steamed rice.

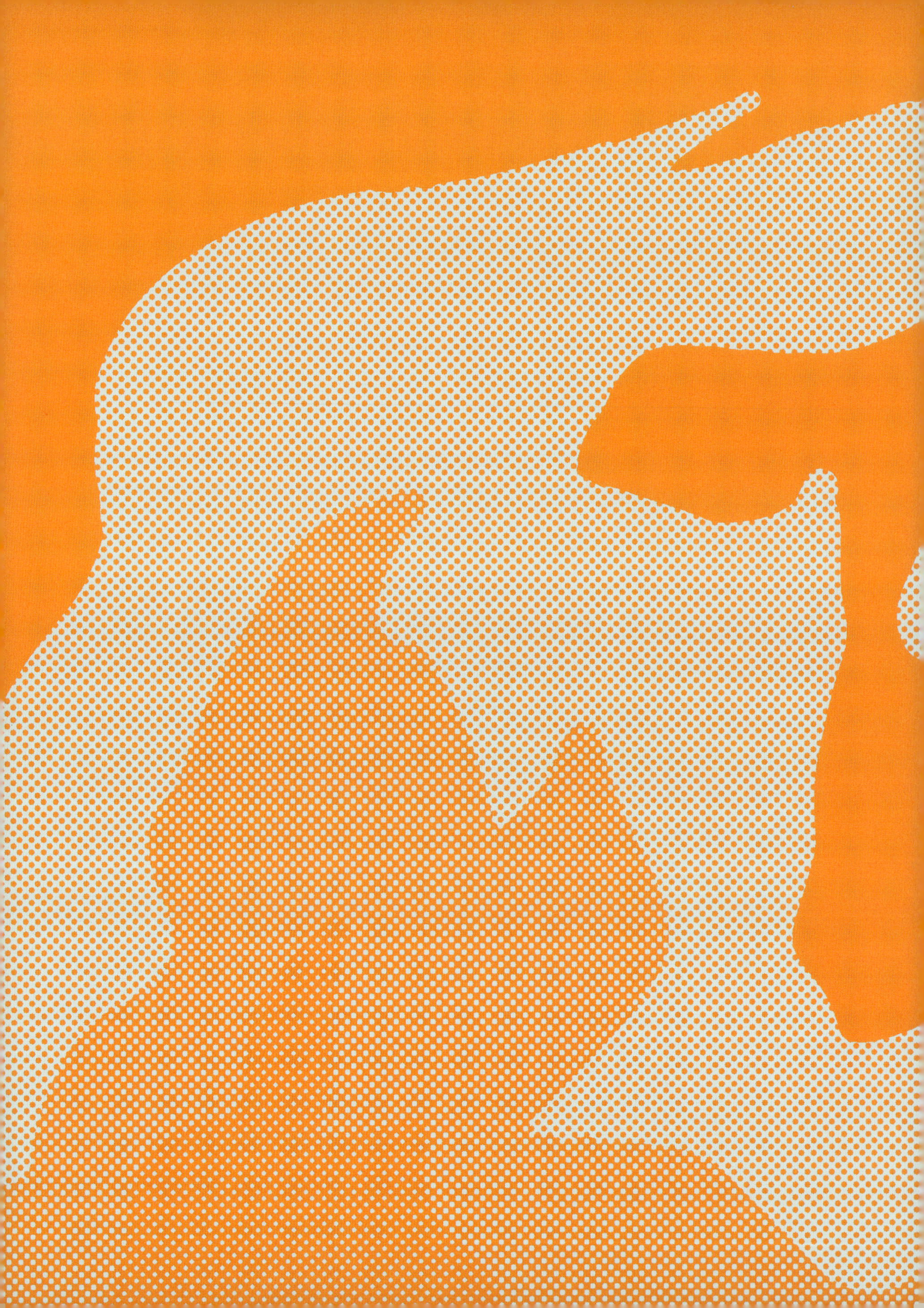

VEGETABLES

SERVES 2

SAMBAL KANGKONG

SAMBAL KANGKONG IS A SPICY AND FLAVOURFUL STIR-FRIED WATER SPINACH DISH THAT'S A STAPLE IN SOUTHEAST ASIAN CUISINE. TOSSED WITH A FRAGRANT SAMBAL SAUCE MADE FROM CHILLI, GARLIC AND SHRIMP PASTE, IT'S A QUICK AND DELICIOUS SIDE THAT PACKS A PUNCH OF HEAT AND UMAMI.

250 g (9 oz) kangkong (water spinach)

3 dried chillies

1 tablespoon dried prawns (shrimp)

½ teaspoon belacan (firm shrimp paste), crushed

2 bird's eye chillies, thinly sliced

3 shallots, diced

1 garlic clove, minced

2 tablespoons vegetable oil

½ teaspoon salt

¼ teaspoon sugar

Trim and discard the roots of the kangkong, then wash the leaves and stems thoroughly before draining. Cut the kangkong into 8 cm (3¼ in) lengths and lightly press the thick stems to break them for easier cooking.

Remove the stems from the dried chillies and soak them in warm water for about 30 minutes until softened, then drain and discard the soaking water. Soak the dried prawns in 1 tablespoon of room temperature water for about 15 minutes, then drain, reserving the soaking liquid for later use.

Toast the belacan in a wok or large frying pan until fragrant, then set it aside. Using a mortar and pestle or blender, grind the dried chillies, dried prawns, toasted belacan, bird's eye chillies, shallots and garlic into a smooth paste to create the sambal.

Heat a wok over high heat until very hot, then add the vegetable oil and stir-fry the sambal paste until it becomes fragrant. Season the sambal with salt and sugar, stirring well to combine. Taste and adjust the seasoning as needed.

Add the kangkong to the wok and stir-fry for about 30 seconds until it just begins to wilt. Taste again, adjusting seasoning if necessary. Once the kangkong is tender and well coated in the sambal, remove from heat and serve hot.

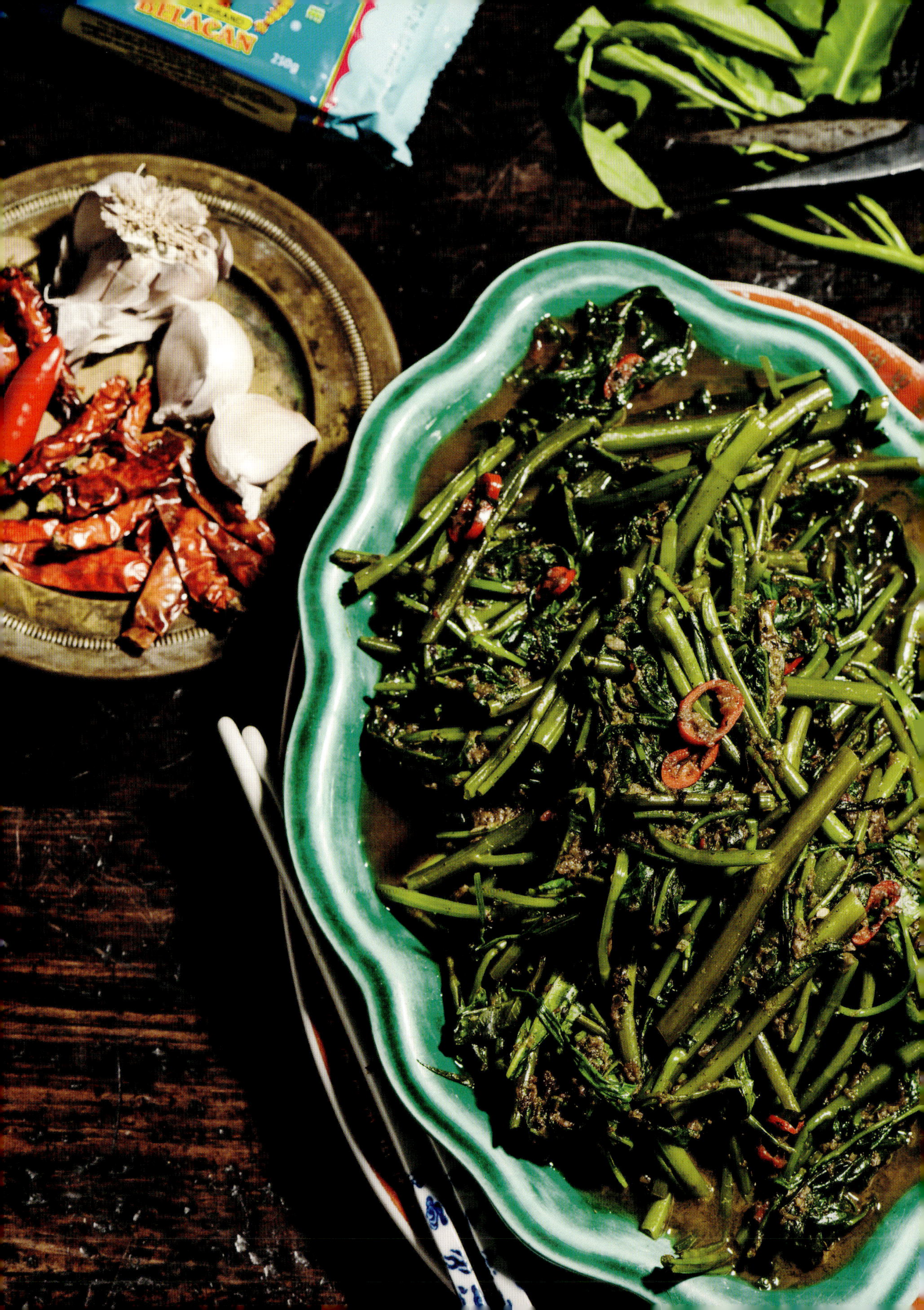
BELACAN
250g

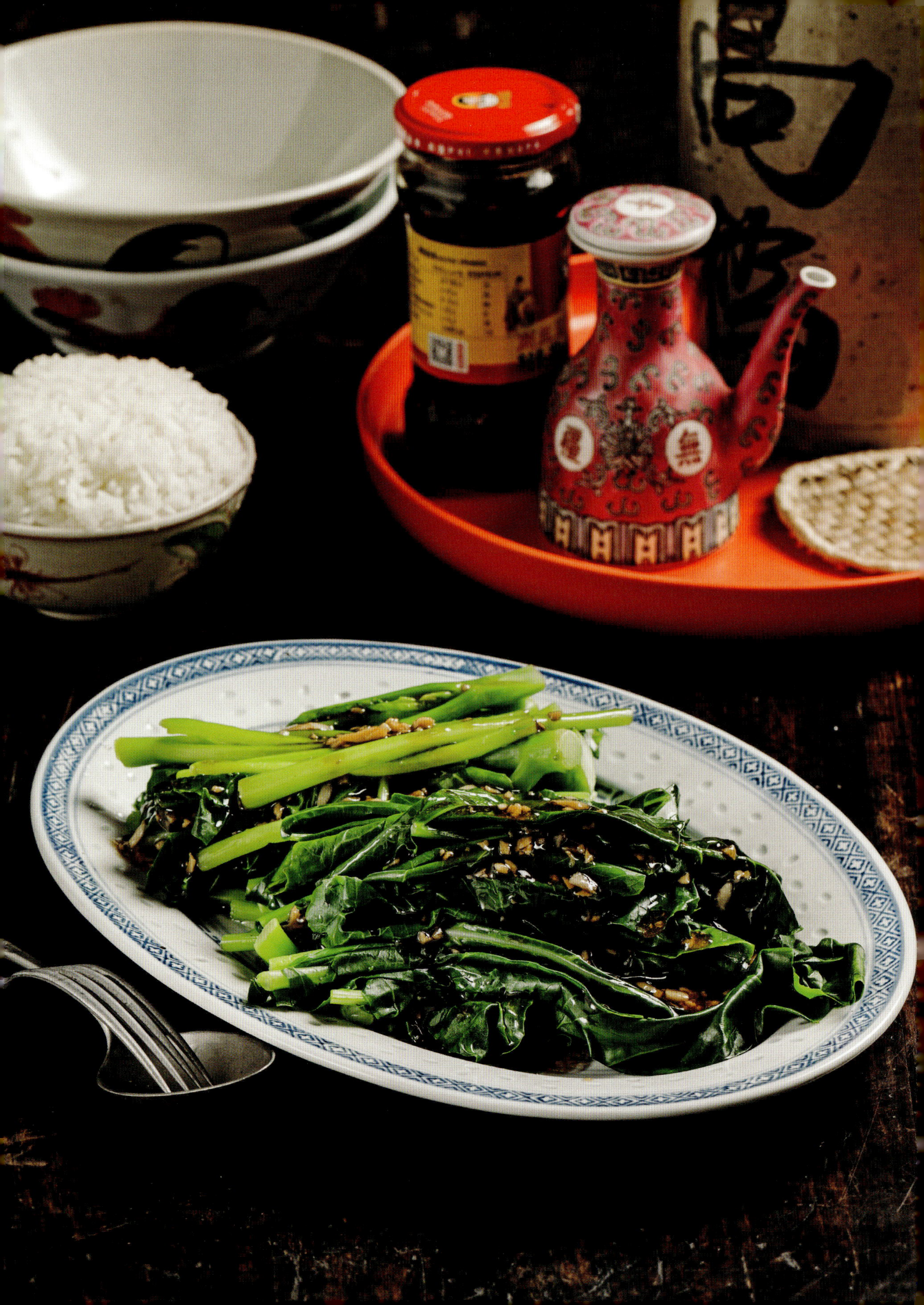

SERVES 2

OYSTER GAI LAN

OYSTER GAI LAN (CHINESE BROCCOLI) IS A SIMPLE AND DELICIOUS CANTONESE DISH OF CRISP CHINESE BROCCOLI DRIZZLED WITH A SAVOURY OYSTER SAUCE. IT'S A POPULAR SIDE DISH KNOWN FOR ITS BALANCE OF FRESH, CRUNCHY GREENS AND RICH UMAMI FLAVOURS, MAKING IT A GREAT COMPLEMENT TO ANY MEAL.

450 g (1 lb) gai lan (Chinese broccoli)

GARLIC-INFUSED OIL

2 tablespoons vegetable oil

6 garlic cloves, minced

SAUCE

2 tablespoons oyster sauce

1 teaspoon light soy sauce

1 teaspoon sugar

1 tablespoon Garlic-infused oil, above

1 tablespoon water

Trim the ends of the gai lan and separate the leaves from the stems, slicing the stems in half lengthways if they are thick. Wash the gai lan thoroughly and drain.

Heat the vegetable oil in a small pan over medium heat, then add the minced garlic. Stir-fry the garlic for about 30 seconds, until fragrant and lightly golden. Remove the oil and garlic from the heat and set aside.

In a small bowl, combine the oyster sauce, light soy sauce, sugar, garlic-infused oil and water, stirring until the sugar is fully dissolved.

Place the gai lan in a steamer over boiling water and steam for 4–5 minutes, or until the stems are tender and the leaves are wilted but still vibrant green.

Once steamed, arrange the gai lan on a serving plate and pour the sauce evenly over the top. Serve immediately.

SERVES 4

SWEET AND STICKY CHINESE EGGPLANT

WHAT HAPPENS WHEN YOU PAIR THE CRUNCHY-SMOOTH DELIGHT OF DEEP-FRIED EGGPLANT WITH A MOUTHWATERING SWEET AND SOUR STICKY SAUCE WITH JUST A HINT OF SPICE? YOU GET A DISH THAT BRINGS EVERYONE TO THE TABLE – AND THE CHOICE TO LET IT SING AS A MAIN OR A SIDE.

EGGPLANT

6 long Japanese eggplants (aubergines)

180 g (6½ oz/1½ cups) tapioca flour

180 g (6½ oz/1½ cups) cornflour (cornstarch)

120 ml (4 fl oz/½ cup) water

vegetable oil, for deep-frying

SAUCE

2 tablespoons vegetable oil

2.5 cm (1 in) piece ginger, finely cut into matchsticks

3 garlic cloves, finely cut into matchsticks

2 tablespoons doubanjiang (chilli bean paste)

2 teaspoons dried chilli flakes

2 teaspoons ground Sichuan peppercorns

400 g (14 oz/2 cups) sugar

80 ml (2½ fl oz/⅓ cup) light soy sauce

160 ml (5½ fl oz/⅔ cup) Chinese red vinegar

2 tablespoons Chinkiang vinegar (black vinegar)

85 g (3 oz/¼ cup) honey

TO SERVE

sesame seeds

1 long red chilli, thinly sliced (optional)

Wash and dry the eggplants, then cut them into thick batons or wedges. Set aside.

In a large bowl, combine 60 g (2 oz/½ cup) of the tapioca flour, 60 g (2 oz/½ cup) of the cornflour and the water to make a smooth wet batter.

In another bowl, combine the remaining tapioca flour and cornflour to make the dry batter.

Fill a deep fryer or large pot half full with oil and heat to 180°C (350°F). Dip the eggplant pieces into the wet batter, ensuring they are evenly coated, then dip them into the dry batter to coat. Carefully lower them into the hot oil in batches, frying for about 3–4 minutes per batch until golden and crispy. Use tongs to remove the eggplant pieces, and set them aside in a sieve or on a plate lined with paper towels to drain.

Once all the eggplant is fried, strain the oil and set it aside for future use.

In an empty wok or frying pan, heat 2 tablespoons of oil over medium heat. Add the chopped ginger and garlic, stir-frying until fragrant, about 30 seconds. Stir in the chilli bean paste, dried chilli flakes and ground Sichuan peppercorns, cooking for another minute to release the spices' aroma.

Add the sugar, light soy sauce, Chinese red vinegar, Chinkiang vinegar and honey to the wok. Stir to combine, bringing the sauce to a simmer. Let it simmer for 3–4 minutes until it thickens slightly.

Once the sauce has thickened, add the crispy eggplant pieces to the wok, tossing gently to ensure they're evenly coated in the sauce. Sprinkle sesame seeds over the eggplant and give it one final toss.

Transfer the sticky, crispy eggplant to a serving dish and garnish with thinly sliced red chilli, if desired.

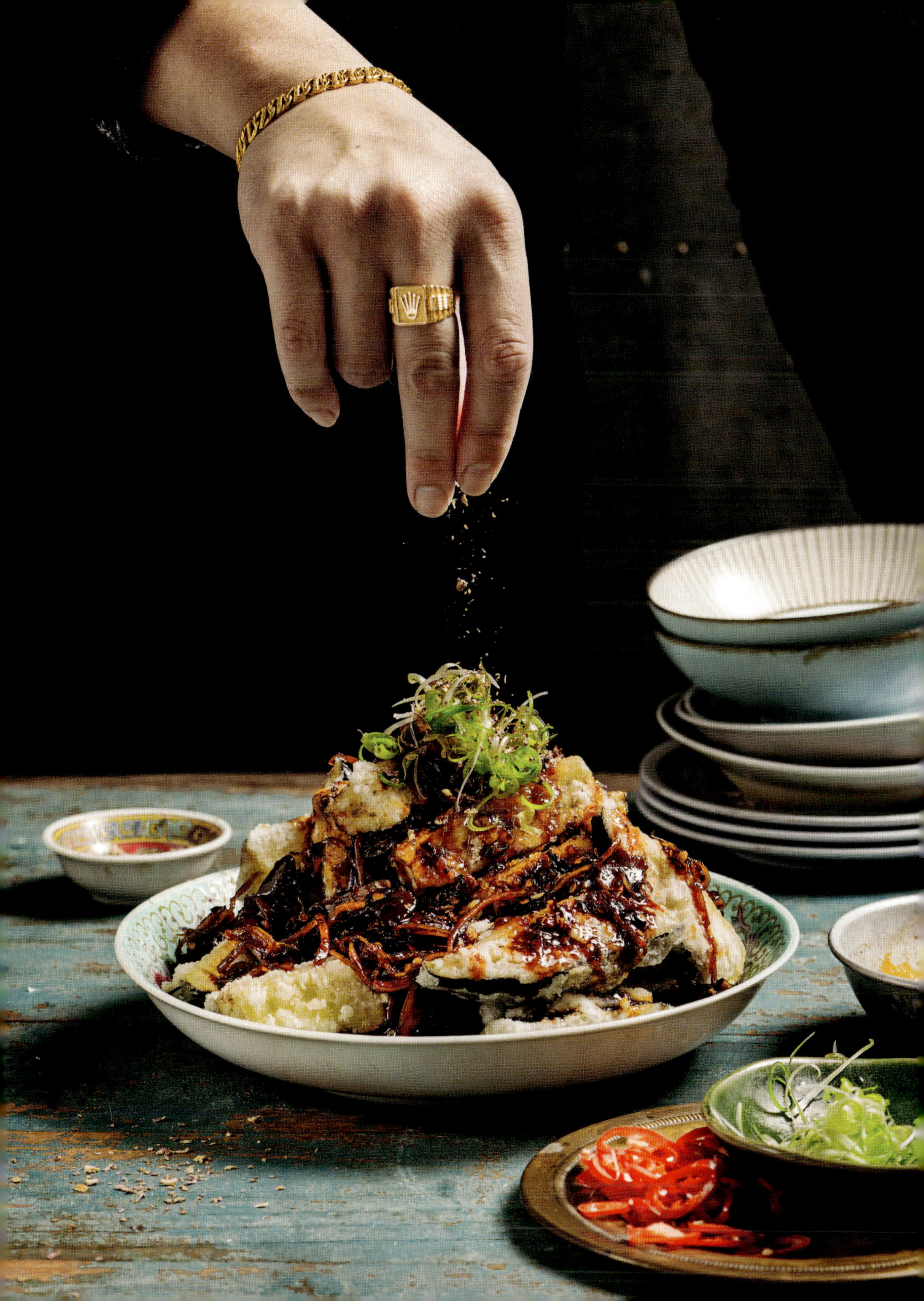

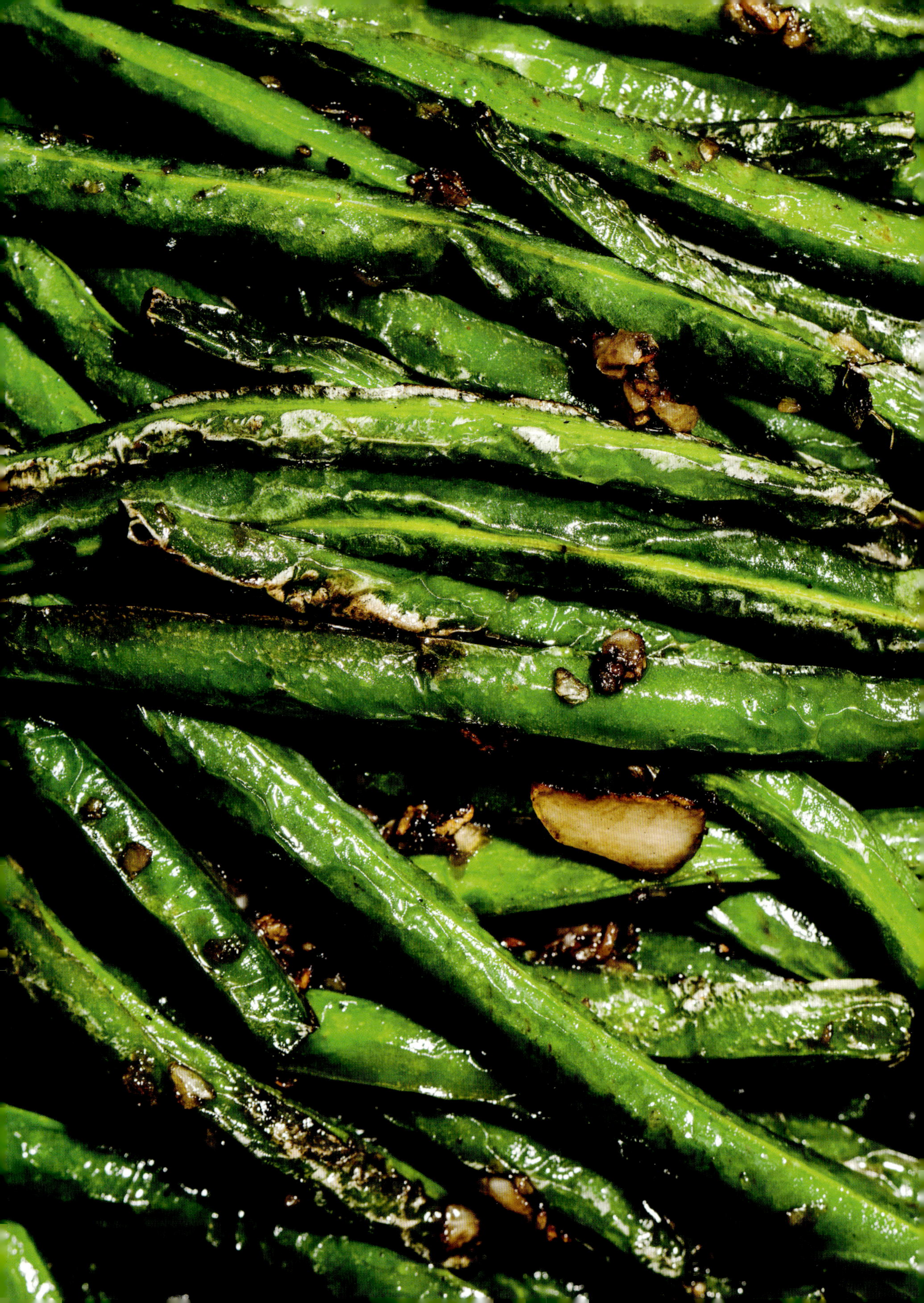

SERVES 2

GARLIC GREEN BEANS

THIS WAS ALWAYS ONE OF THE MOST REQUESTED VEGETABLE DISHES AT MY OLD RESTAURANT, AND FOR GOOD REASON. THIS ONE IS ALWAYS A CROWD PLEASER. TENDER GREEN BEANS QUICKLY STIR-FRIED WITH GARLIC – IT'S SIMPLE YET FLAVOURFUL, AND THE PERFECT ACCOMPANIMENT TO ANY DINNER SPREAD.

vegetable oil, for deep-frying, plus 1 tablespoon extra

450 g (1 lb) green beans, touch ends removed

10 garlic cloves, minced

1 tablespoon Shaoxing wine (Chinese cooking wine)

½ teaspoon YumYum or MSG

½ teaspoon salt

Fill a wok or large pot halfway full with vegetable oil and heat to 180°C (350°F) over medium–high heat. You can also test the oil with a wooden chopstick – if bubbles form around it, the oil is ready. Carefully add the green beans to the hot oil and fry for 2–3 minutes, or until they blister and turn slightly wrinkled. Once fried, strain the green beans from the oil and set them aside on a plate lined with paper towels to drain. Set the leftover oil aside for future use.

In the now-empty wok, heat 1 tablespoon of oil over medium heat. Add the minced garlic and stir-fry for about 30 seconds until fragrant and lightly golden.

Return the fried green beans to the wok and stir them with the garlic to combine. Pour in the Shaoxing wine and toss the beans well. Add the YumYum or MSG and salt, making sure to evenly coat the green beans.

Stir-fry for another 1–2 minutes to ensure the flavours are well combined and the green beans are heated through.

Transfer the green beans to a serving dish and enjoy your flavourful stir-fried Chinese green beans!

SERVES 2

CHINESE 'SEAWEED' (FRIED GAI LAN)

CHINESE 'SEAWEED', MADE FROM CRISPY FRIED GAI LAN (CHINESE BROCCOLI), IS A DELICIOUS SAVOURY TOPPING FOR RICE. THE LEAFY GREENS ARE DEEP-FRIED UNTIL LIGHT AND CRISPY, OFFERING A DELICIOUSLY SALTY AND CRUNCHY TEXTURE THAT'S ALMOST EXACTLY LIKE SEAWEED.

1 bunch gai lan (Chinese broccoli)
vegetable oil, for deep-frying
½ teaspoon sugar
½ teaspoon salt
¼ teaspoon YumYum or MSG
pinch of black pepper
1 tablespoon sesame seeds

Separate the Chinese broccoli leaves from the stems, setting the stems aside for another use. Thinly slice the leaves and set them aside.

Fill a wok or deep pan halfway full with oil and heat to 180°C (350°F) over medium–high heat (you can also test the oil with a wooden chopstick – if bubbles form around it, the oil is ready). Carefully add the sliced leaves and fry for 1–2 minutes until they become crispy, stirring gently to ensure even frying.

Use a sieve or slotted spoon to remove the crispy leaves from the oil and drain them on paper towels. Set the leftover oil aside for future use.

Place the crispy leaves in a bowl and sprinkle with sugar, salt, YumYum or MSG, black pepper and sesame seeds. Gently toss the leaves to evenly coat them with the seasoning.

Serve the crispy Chinese broccoli leaves as a tasty side dish or as a tasty topping to a humble bowl of rice.

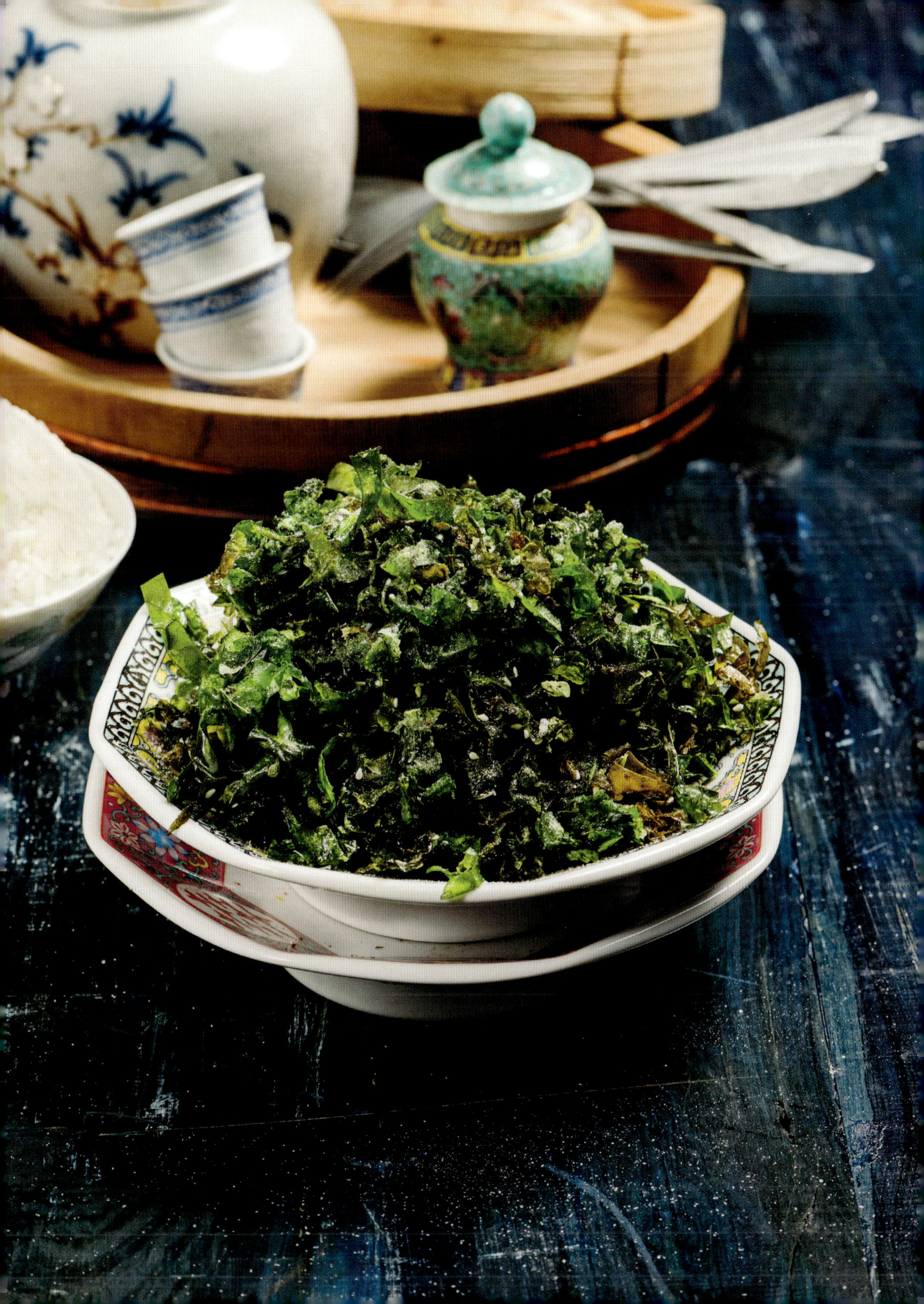

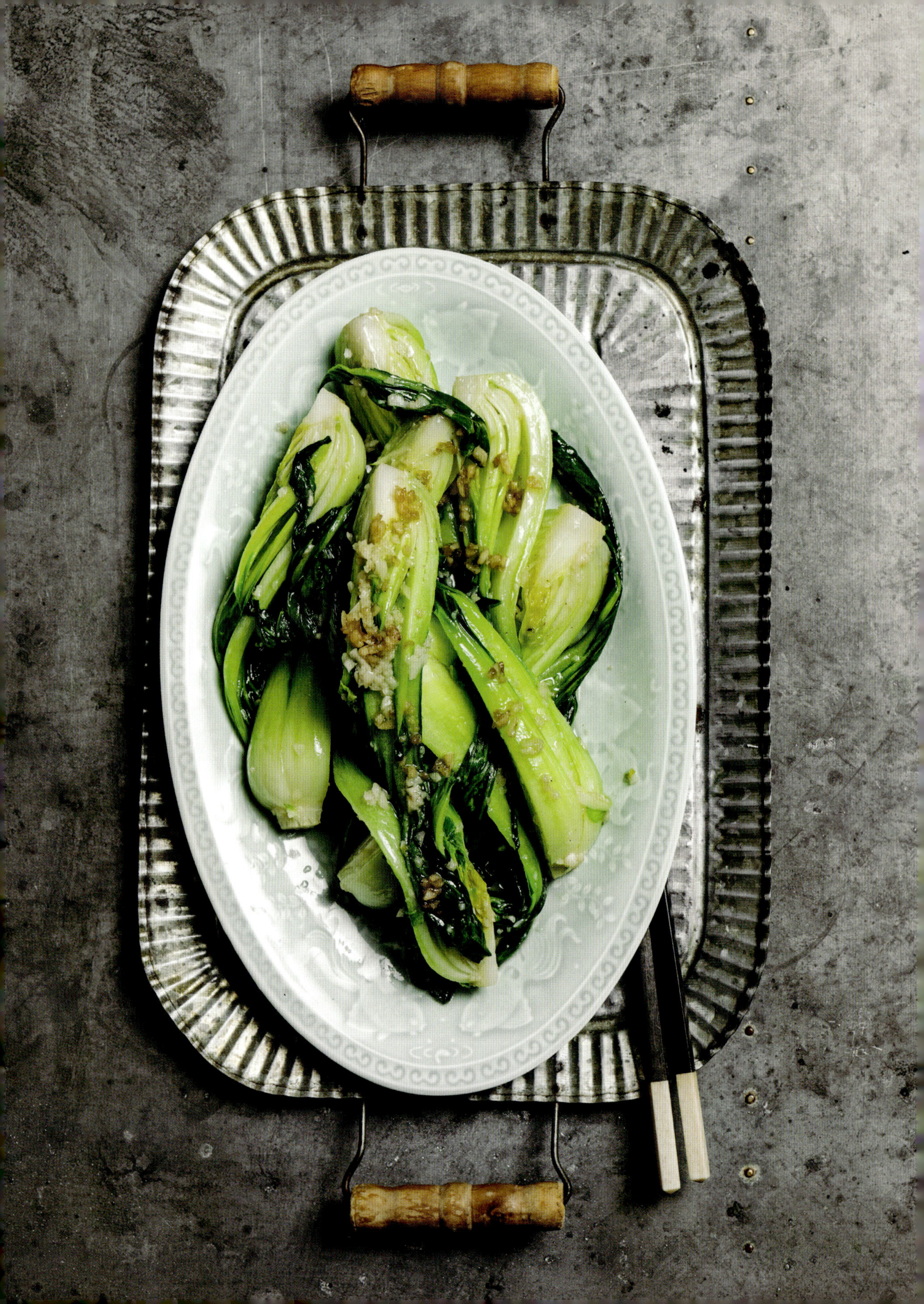

SERVES 2

GARLIC BOK CHOY

GARLIC BOK CHOY (PAK CHOY) IS A SIMPLE YET FLAVOURFUL DISH THAT HIGHLIGHTS THE NATURAL SWEETNESS AND CRUNCH OF BOK CHOY. STIR-FRIED WITH FRAGRANT GARLIC, THIS IS A QUICK-AND-EASY SIDE DISH WITH A FRESH AND SAVOURY BITE.

400 g (14 oz) bok choy (pak choy)
3 tablespoons vegetable oil
10 garlic cloves, minced
½ teaspoon salt
½ teaspoon sugar
¼ teaspoon YumYum or MSG

Cut the bok choy in half lengthways, or into quarters if it's large. Wash the bok choy thoroughly and drain well.

Heat the vegetable oil in a large wok or pan over medium heat. Add the minced garlic and stir-fry for about 30 seconds, until fragrant and lightly golden.

Add the bok choy to the wok, stirring to coat the leaves and stems in the garlic and oil. Sprinkle in the salt, sugar and YumYum or MSG and stir-fry for 2–3 minutes, until the bok choy is tender but still crisp and vibrant in colour.

Transfer the garlic bok choy to a serving plate and serve hot. Enjoy!

SERVES 2

SALTED EGG SWEET CORN

SALTED EGG CORN IS A DELICIOUSLY SAVOURY AND CRUNCHY SNACK THAT LEVELS UP SWEET CORN WITH THE RICH, UMAMI FLAVOUR OF SALTED EGG YOLK. THIS SUPER ADDICTIVE CORN IS QUICK TO PREPARE AND PERFECT AS AN APPETISER OR SIDE DISH.

vegetable oil, for deep-frying

400 g (14 oz/2 cups) sweet corn kernels

BATTER

60 g (2 oz/½ cup) cornflour (cornstarch)

120 g (4½ oz/1 cup) self-raising flour

375 ml (12½ fl oz/1½ cups) beer or soda water

SAUCE

2 tablespoons unsalted butter

10 curry leaves

2 long red chillies, thinly sliced

6 salted duck egg yolks, steamed and mashed (see recipe introduction on page 114)

In a large bowl, combine the cornflour and self-raising flour. Gradually whisk in the beer or soda water until the batter is smooth and free of lumps.

Fill a wok or large pot halfway full with vegetable oil and heat to 180°C (350°F) over medium–high heat. You can also test the oil with a wooden chopstick – if bubbles form around it, the oil is ready. Dip the sweet corn kernels into the batter, ensuring they are evenly coated. Carefully drop the battered corn kernels into the hot oil in small batches, frying until golden and crispy, about 2–3 minutes.

Once fried, strain the corn kernals from the oil and set them aside on a plate lined with paper towels to drain. Set the leftover oil aside for future use.

In a separate pan, melt the unsalted butter over medium heat. Add the curry leaves and sliced red chillies, stir-frying for about 30 seconds until fragrant. Then, add the mashed salted duck egg yolks to the pan, stirring continuously until the mixture becomes foamy and fragrant, about 2 minutes.

Toss the crispy corn kernels into the pan with the salted egg yolk sauce, ensuring the corn is evenly coated in the rich sauce.

Transfer the salted egg sweet corn to a serving dish and enjoy hot.

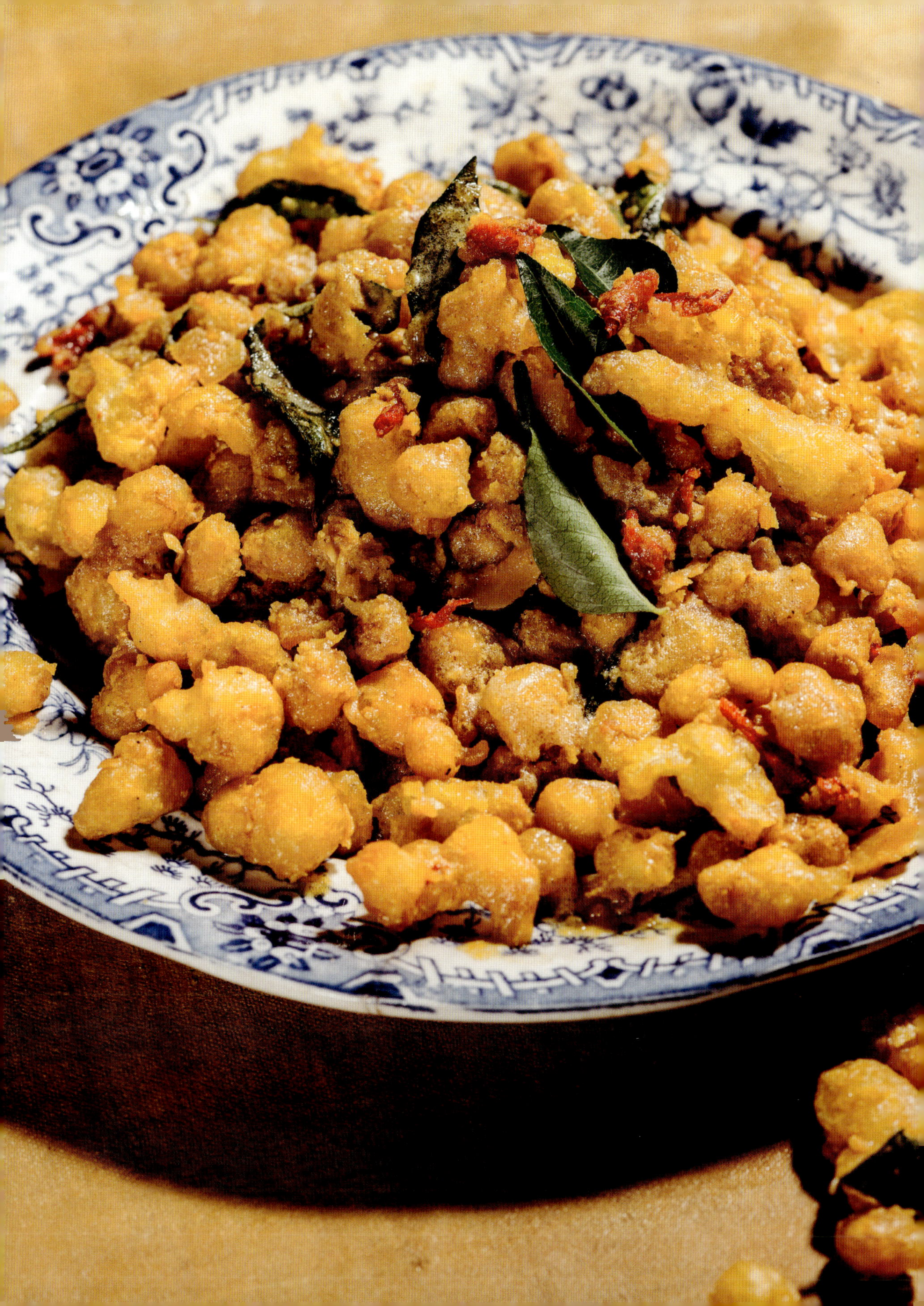

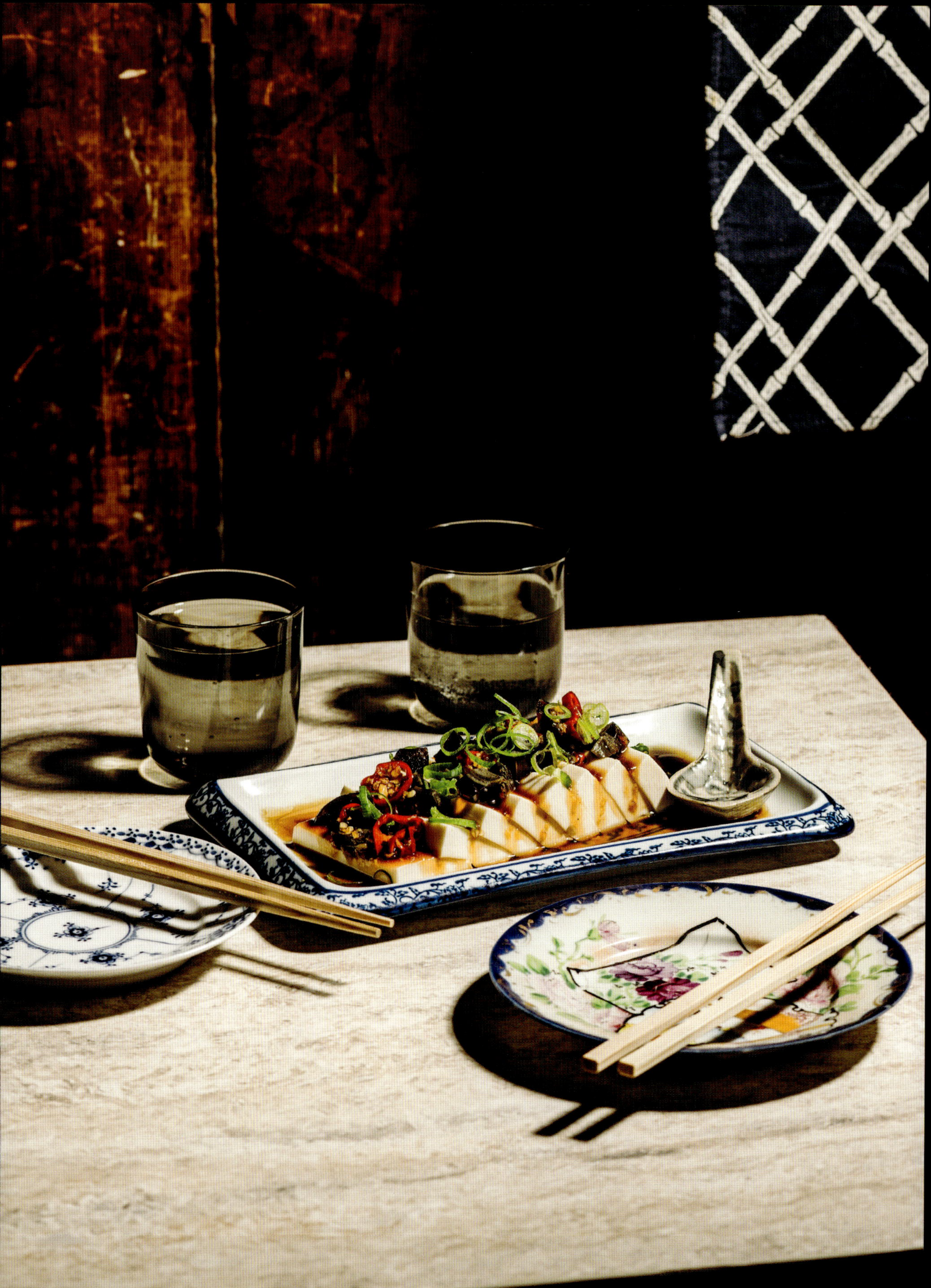

SERVES 2

CENTURY EGG AND TOFU

THOUSAND-YEAR EGG AND TOFU IS A CLASSIC CHINESE COLD DISH THAT COMBINES THE SILKY SMOOTH TEXTURE OF CHILLED TOFU WITH THE BOLD, SAVOURY FLAVOURS OF PRESERVED CENTURY EGGS. TOPPED WITH A LIGHT SOY SAUCE DRESSING, IT'S A SIMPLE YET FLAVOURFUL APPETISER THAT'S GREAT ON WARM DAYS.

300 g (10½ oz) block silken tofu
2 century eggs
4 garlic cloves, minced
2–3 red chillies, chopped (optional)
1½ teaspoons sugar
1 tablespoon Chinkiang vinegar (black vinegar)
2 tablespoons oyster sauce
1 heaped tablespoon light soy sauce
1 heaped tablespoon sesame oil
2 spring onions (scallions), thinly sliced, to garnish

Carefully remove the silken tofu from its packaging and drain any excess liquid. Gently place the tofu on a serving plate, ensuring it stays intact. Slice the century eggs into thin wedges and arrange them evenly on top of the tofu.

In a small bowl, mix together the minced garlic, chopped red chilli (if using), sugar, Chinkiang vinegar, oyster sauce, soy sauce and sesame oil. Stir the sauce until the sugar is fully dissolved.

Pour the sauce mixture evenly over the tofu and century eggs, allowing the flavours to soak in. Garnish with thinly sliced spring onions for a fresh touch.

Serve the century egg and silken tofu chilled for a refreshing, savoury dish.

VEGETABLES

SERVES 3

KUNG PAO CAULIFLOWER

KUNG PAO CAULIFLOWER IS A DELICIOUS PLANT-BASED TWIST ON THE CLASSIC KUNG PAO CHICKEN. THIS DISH FEATURES CRISPY CAULIFLOWER FLORETS TOSSED IN A SPICY, TANGY SAUCE WITH PEANUTS AND DRIED CHILLIES, OFFERING A FLAVOURFUL COMBINATION OF HEAT AND CRUNCH THAT'S PERFECT AS A SIDE OR MAIN DISH.

VEGETABLES

CAULIFLOWER

400 g (14 oz) cauliflower, cut into bite-sized florets

2 teaspoons vegetable bouillon powder

pinch of white pepper

1 tablespoon Shaoxing wine (Chinese cooking wine)

1 tablespoon sesame oil

¼ teaspoon salt

1 tablespoon cornflour (cornstarch)

BATTER

120 g (4½ oz/1 cup) self-raising flour

60 g (2 oz/½ cup) cornflour (cornstarch)

320 ml (11 fl oz) water

vegetable oil, for deep-frying

SAUCE

2 slices of ginger

12 garlic cloves, minced

6 dried chillies

2 teaspoons cooking caramel (karamel masakan)

2 teaspoons sugar

½ teaspoon dark soy sauce

½ teaspoon salt

1 tablespoon oyster sauce

½ teaspoon YumYum or MSG

1 teaspoon mushroom bouillon powder

1 tablespoon vegetable oil

2 teaspoons potato starch

60 ml (2 fl oz/¼ cup) water

2 teaspoons Shaoxing wine (Chinese cooking wine)

⅓ cup roasted peanuts

TO SERVE

sesame seeds

spring onions (scallions), thinly sliced

In a large bowl, toss the cauliflower florets with the vegetable bouillon powder, white pepper, Shaoxing wine, sesame oil, salt and cornflour, ensuring the cauliflower is evenly coated.

In a separate bowl, whisk together the self-raising flour and cornflour. Gradually add the water, whisking until the batter is smooth and free of lumps.

Fill a wok or large pot halfway full with oil and heat to 180°C (350°F) over medium–high heat (you can also test the oil with a wooden chopstick – if bubbles form around it, the oil is ready). Dip the marinated cauliflower florets into the batter, making sure they are well-coated. Carefully drop the battered cauliflower into the hot oil in batches, being careful not to overcrowd the pot. Fry for about 5–7 minutes per batch until the cauliflower is golden brown and crispy. Remove the cauliflower with a slotted spoon and drain on paper towels. Set the leftover oil aside for future use.

In a jug, combine the ginger, minced garlic, dried chillies, cooking caramel, sugar, dark soy sauce, salt, oyster sauce, YumYum or MSG and mushroom bouillon powder. Pour the mixture into a wok or saucepan and bring it to a boil over medium heat.

In a small bowl, mix the potato starch and water to make a slurry. Pour the slurry into the wok and stir until the sauce thickens. Once the sauce has reached the desired consistency, add the Shaoxing wine to the wok and stir for another 30 seconds.

Add the fried cauliflower and peanuts to the sauce and toss to coat evenly. Serve immediately with steamed rice or chow mein, garnished with sesame seeds and thinly sliced spring onions.

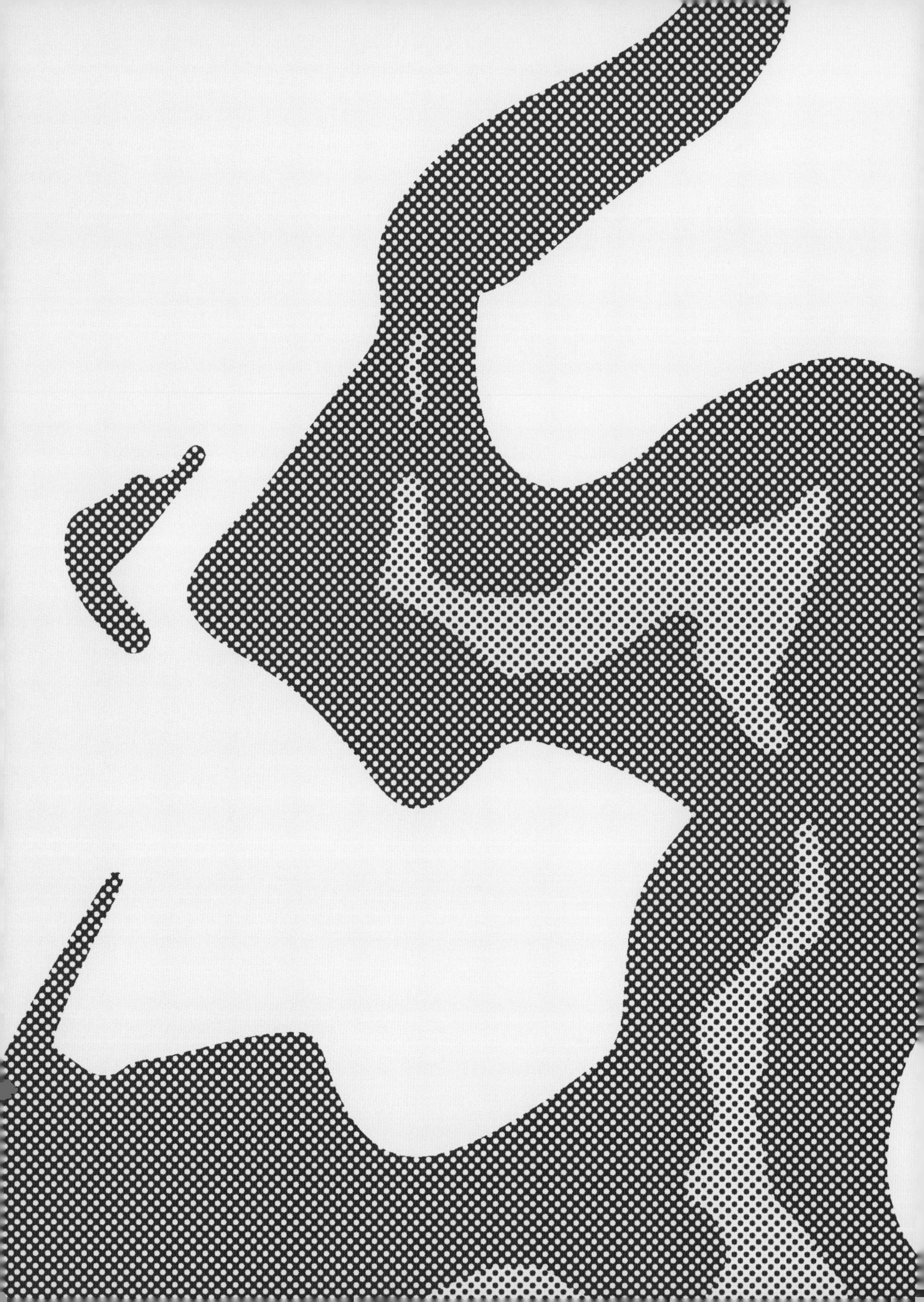

DESSERT

MAKES 12

MANGO PANCAKES

MANGO PANCAKES ARE A YUM CHA FAVOURITE! SOFT CREPES WRAPPED AROUND SWEET MANGO AND WHIPPED CREAM MAKE FOR A LIGHT AND REFRESHING TREAT. PERFECT FOR FINISHING OFF YOUR DIM SUM SPREAD OR JUST ENJOYING AS A SWEET SNACK.

PANCAKE

240 ml (8 fl oz) full-cream (whole) milk

50 g (1¾ oz/⅓ cup) plain flour

30 g (1 oz/¼ cup) cornflour (cornstarch)

2 tablespoons sugar

3 large eggs

15 g (½ oz/1 tablespoon) unsalted butter, melted

few drops of yellow food colouring

vegetable oil, for greasing

FILLING

600 ml (20½ fl oz/2½ cups) thickened (whipping) cream

150 g sugar (5½ oz/¾ cup)

1 teaspoon vanilla extract

3 large mangoes, peeled and cut into 3 cm (1¼ in) chunks

In a mixing bowl, whisk together the milk, flour, cornflour and sugar until the mixture is smooth. Once well-mixed, add the eggs and whisk again until everything is fully combined. Next, stir the melted butter into the batter. To give the batter a vibrant colour, add a few drops of yellow food colouring and mix until the colour is evenly distributed.

For a smoother consistency, strain the batter through a fine sieve to remove any lumps. Lightly grease a non-stick frying pan with vegetable oil and heat it over medium–low heat. Pour a small amount of batter into the pan, then tilt it to spread the batter thinly and evenly, forming a round pancake. Cook each pancake for about 1–2 minutes, or until the edges begin to lift. Remove the pancake from the pan and transfer it to a plate to cool. Repeat the process with the remaining batter.

In a separate bowl, whip the cream with the sugar and vanilla extract until stiff peaks form. To assemble the dessert, take one of the cooled pancakes and spread a generous layer of whipped cream in the centre. Place a few chunks of mango on top of the cream, then fold the pancake over the filling, tucking in the edges to form a neat parcel.

Repeat this process with the remaining pancakes and filling.

These mango pancakes are best served chilled, so be sure to refrigerate them for a few hours before serving.

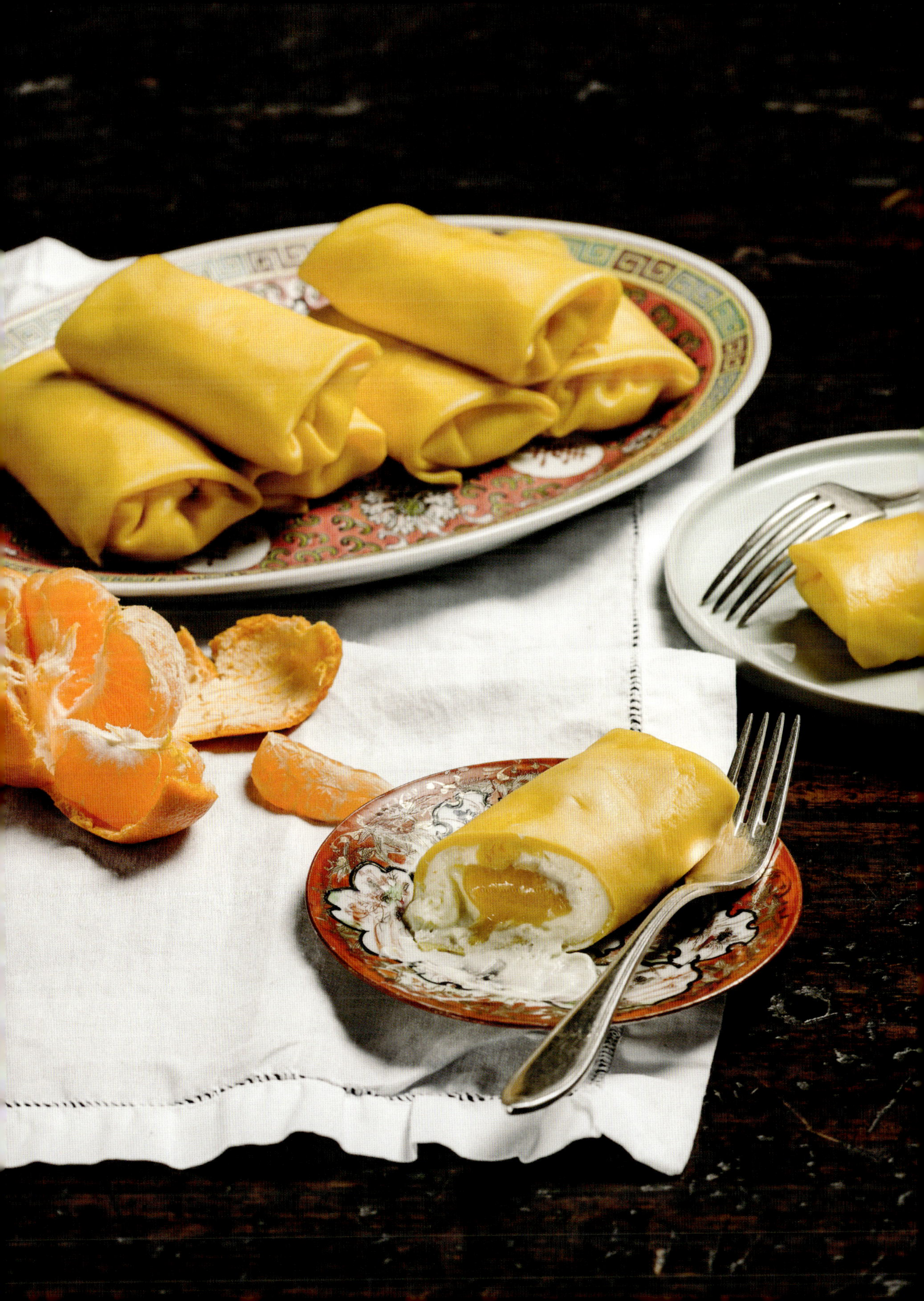

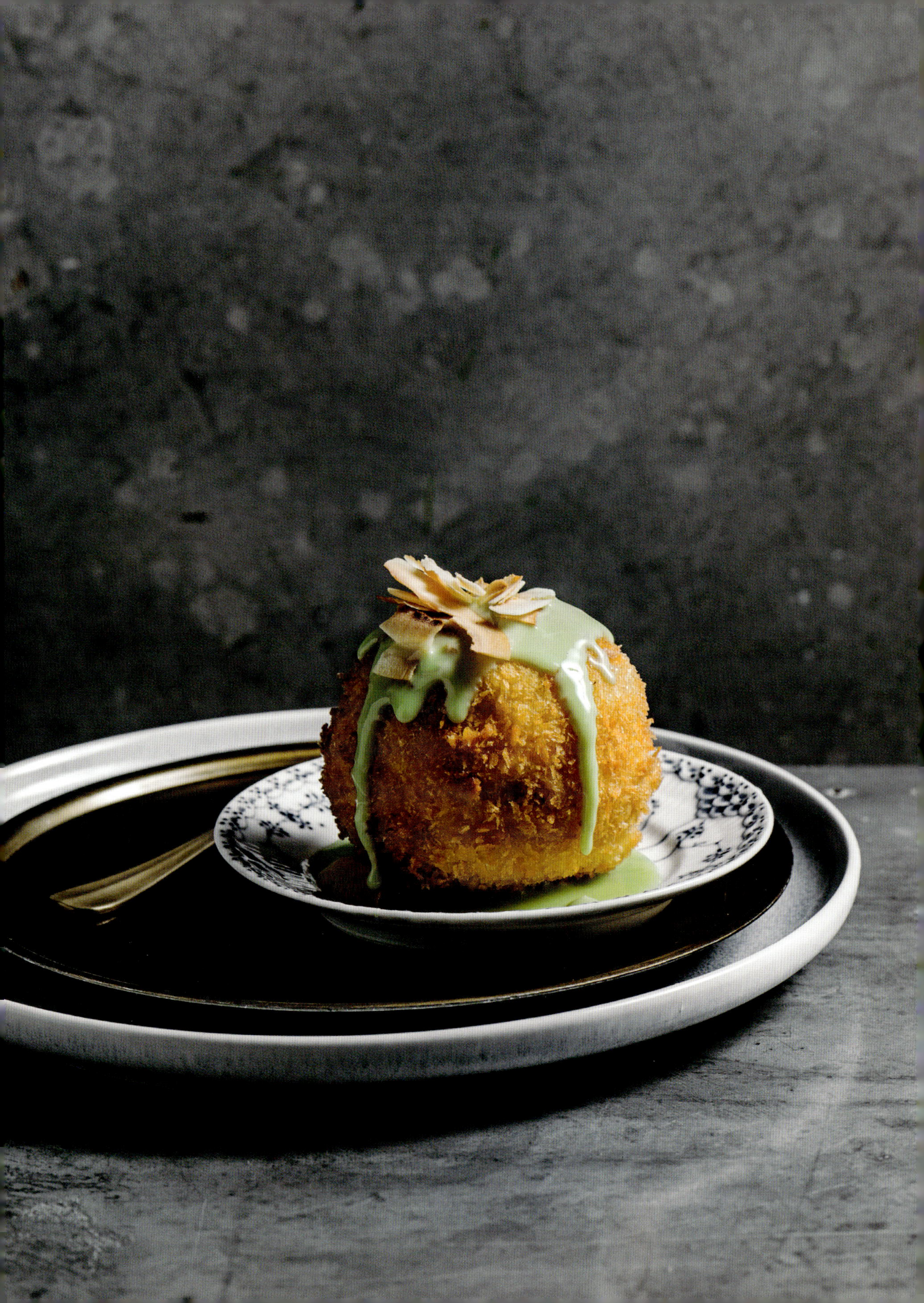

MAKES 4–5

PANDAN FRIED ICE CREAM

FRIED ICE CREAM WITH PANDAN SAUCE IS A DESSERT THAT BRINGS SOMETHING UNIQUE TO THE TABLE. THE CRISPY EXTERIOR CONTRASTS PERFECTLY WITH THE COLD, CREAMY ICE CREAM INSIDE, WHILE THE PANDAN SAUCE ADDS A SUBTLE SWEETNESS THAT ELEVATES THE WHOLE DISH.

FRIED ICE CREAM

700 g (1 lb 9 oz) ice cream of your choice
1 large egg, beaten
60 g (2 oz/1 cup) panko breadcrumbs
vegetable oil, for deep-frying

¼ cup coconut flakes, toasted, to serve

PANDAN SAUCE

125 ml (4 fl oz/½ cup) sweetened condensed milk
125 ml (4 fl oz/½ cup) thickened (whipping) cream
1 pandan leaf
1 drop pandan extract

To start, scoop the ice cream into balls about the size of a tennis ball. You should be able to make approximately 4–5 balls. Place the ice cream balls on a baking sheet lined with baking paper and freeze until firm – at least 4 hours, but preferably overnight.

While the ice cream is freezing, prepare the pandan sauce. In a small saucepan, combine the sweetened condensed milk and thickened cream. Add the pandan leaf to the mixture and heat over low heat, stirring constantly. Allow the flavours of the pandan leaf to infuse into the sauce, which should take about 5–7 minutes. Once the mixture is warm and fragrant, remove the saucepan from the heat and discard the pandan leaf. Stir in the pandan extract, ensuring the flavour and colour are evenly distributed. Let the pandan sauce cool slightly before serving. You can serve the sauce either warm or chilled, as desired.

As the ice cream continues to freeze, prepare two shallow bowls: one with the beaten egg and the other with the panko breadcrumbs. Once the ice cream balls are fully frozen, take one out of the freezer at a time. Coat the ball in the beaten egg, then roll it in the panko breadcrumbs, ensuring it's fully covered. For extra crunch and protection during frying, double-coat each ice cream ball by repeating the egg and panko coating process. Return the coated ice cream balls to the freezer for at least 1 hour to firm up again.

When you're ready to fry, fill a deep fryer or large pot halfway full with oil and heat to 180°C (350°F) over medium–high heat (for the pot option, you can also test the oil with a wooden chopstick – if bubbles form around it, the oil is ready). Fry the ice cream balls one at a time for about 20–30 seconds or until golden brown, turning them gently to ensure even frying on all sides. Remove the fried ice cream with a slotted spoon and drain excess oil on paper towels. Serve immediately with the pandan sauce and top with the toasted coconut flakes.

MAKES 4

MANGO PUDDING

MANGO PUDDING IS A CLASSIC ASIAN DESSERT THAT YOU'LL OFTEN FIND GRACING THE FINISH LINE OF A YUM CHA SESSION. IT'S LIGHT AND BALANCED, LETTING THE NATURAL SWEETNESS OF MANGO SHINE AND, WHEN PAIRED WITH THE EVAPORATED MILK, TAKES ME RIGHT BACK TO HONG KONG.

1 tablespoon gelatine powder

60 ml (2 fl oz/¼ cup) cold water

500 g (1 lb 2 oz) mango, peeled and pitted

2 tablespoons sugar, to taste

240 ml (8 fl oz/1 cup) evaporated milk

extra mango chunks and evaporated milk, to serve

In a small bowl, combine the gelatine powder and cold water, then set it aside to bloom.

Meanwhile, place the peeled and pitted mango in a blender and blend until the mixture is completely smooth.

Next, add the sugar and evaporated milk to the mango puree. Taste, and add more sugar as desired. Pulse the blender just until everything is combined. Once the gelatine has bloomed, melt it in the microwave in 10-second bursts, stirring between each burst until it is fully dissolved.

Carefully pour the dissolved gelatine into the blender and pulse the mixture until it becomes smooth and all the ingredients are well incorporated. Once the mixture is ready, pour it into your serving glasses. Gently tap the glasses on the countertop to remove any air bubbles.

Place the glasses in the refrigerator and allow the pudding to set for at least 2 hours. Before serving, top each pudding with a little extra evaporated milk and some fresh mango chunks.

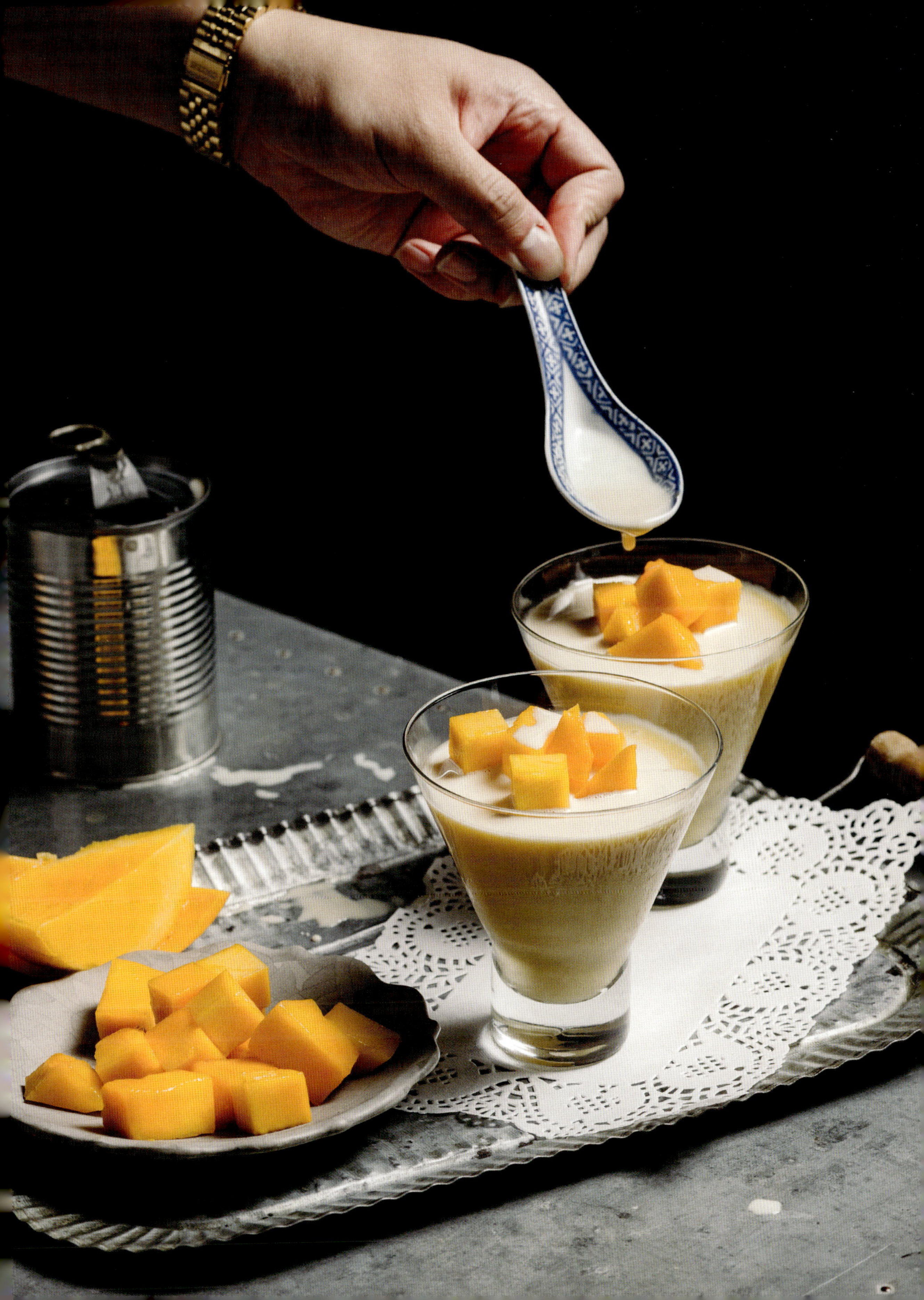

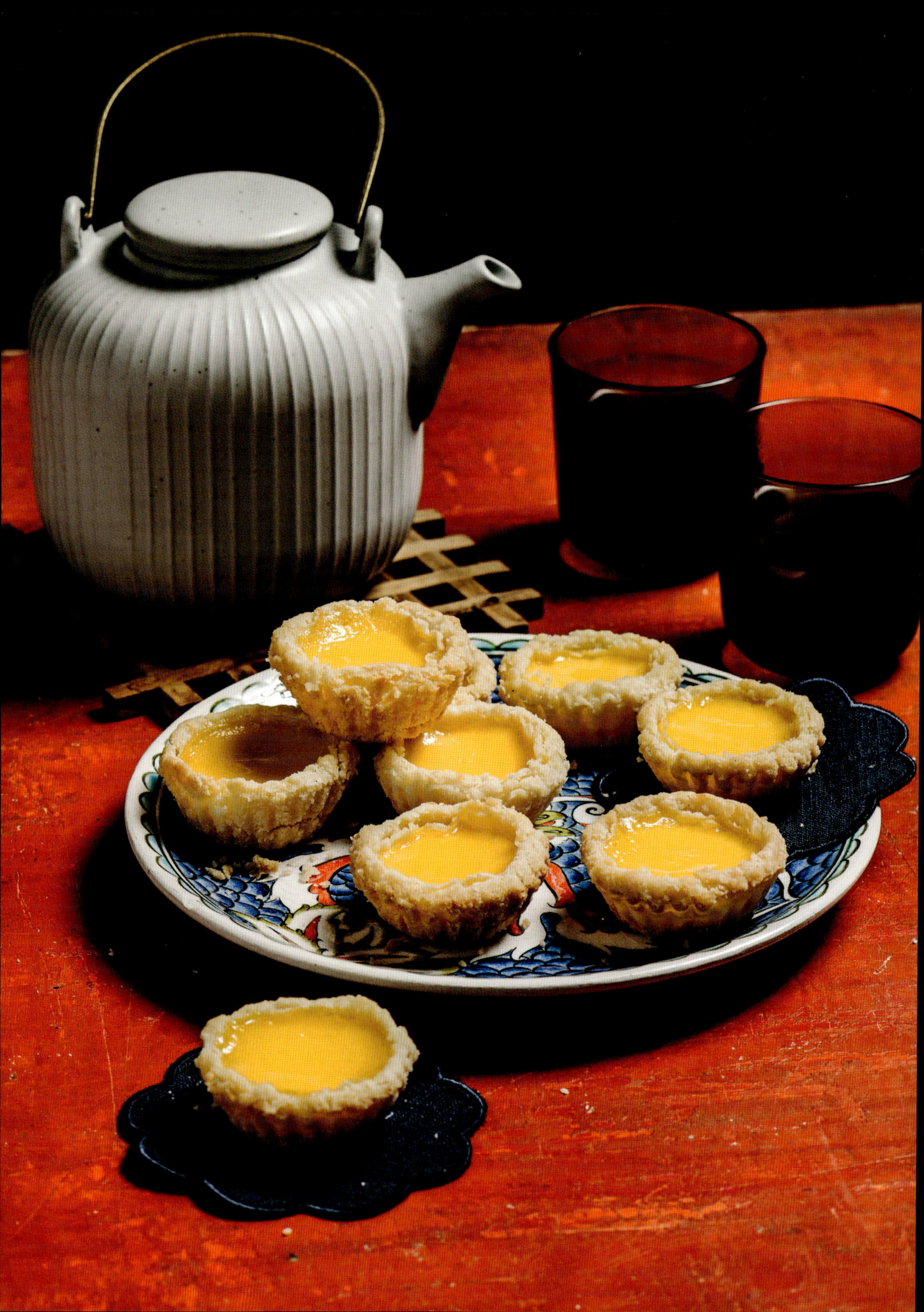

MAKES 12

HONG KONG EGG TART

IN HONG KONG THERE ARE TWO VERSIONS OF THE EGG TART, COOKIE CRUST AND FLAKY CRUST. THIS RECIPE IS A TAKE ON THE COOKIE CRUST EGG TART, WITH A SUPER BUTTERY, MELT-IN-YOUR-MOUTH PASTRY THAT PAIRS PERFECTLY WITH THE SILKY SMOOTH EGG CUSTARD.

PASTRY

210 g (7½ oz/1¾ cups) plain flour, plus extra for dusting

2 tablespoons icing (confectioners') sugar

120 g (4½ oz/½ cup) unsalted butter, chilled and cubed, plus extra for greasing

1 large egg yolk

CUSTARD

320 ml (11 fl oz/1⅓ cups) full-cream (whole) milk

130 g (4½ oz/⅔ cup) sugar

4 large eggs

1 teaspoon vanilla extract

In a large bowl, combine the flour, icing sugar and cubed unsalted butter. Using your fingertips, rub the butter into the flour mixture until it resembles the texture of sand. Add the egg yolk and mix gently until a shaggy dough begins to form. Transfer the dough onto a lightly floured surface and knead it gently until it comes together into a smooth ball. Wrap the dough in plastic wrap and chill in the refrigerator for about 30 minutes, or until firm.

Meanwhile, grease 12 egg tart moulds with butter and lightly dust them with flour. Once the dough is chilled, divide it into 12 equal portions, each weighing approximately 30 g (1 oz). Press the dough into each mould, allowing it to extend about 5 mm (¼ in) above the edge of the mould to form slightly taller tart shells. Place the tart shells in the refrigerator to chill for 1 hour, or until firm.

As the tart shells chill, prepare the custard. In a small saucepan, heat the milk and sugar over medium heat, stirring occasionally until the sugar has completely dissolved, about 5 minutes. In a separate heatproof bowl, whisk together the eggs and vanilla extract until smooth and well combined. Gradually pour the warm milk mixture into the egg mixture, whisking continuously to prevent the eggs from curdling. Once combined, strain the custard through a fine-mesh sieve to ensure a smooth texture. Set the custard aside while the tart shells finish chilling.

Preheat the oven to 160°C (320°F). Once the tart shells are firm, remove them from the refrigerator and fill each one to the top with the prepared egg custard. Bake the tarts for about 35 minutes, or until the custard is just set. To test the doneness, insert a toothpick into the centre of the custard. If it stands upright, the custard is set.

Allow the egg tarts to cool in the moulds for about 10 minutes before carefully unmoulding them (it's easier to do this when they're still warm). Serve the egg tarts either warm or at room temperature.

MAKES 12

SESAME BALLS

RED BEAN SESAME BALLS ARE A TIMELESS TREAT OFTEN FOUND AT DIM SUM. MADE WITH GLUTINOUS RICE FLOUR, THEY HAVE A MOCHI-LIKE CHEWY EXTERIOR STUDDED WITH A CRIPSY SESAME COATING. BUT THE TEXTURES DON'T STOP THERE — INSIDE, YOU'LL FIND A RICH AND SATISFYING SWEET ADZUKI (RED BEAN) PASTE. I DARE YOU TO STOP AT ONE.

RED BEAN PASTE

100 g (3½ oz) adzuki beans (red beans)

90 g (3 oz/½ cup) brown sugar

DOUGH

210 g (7½ oz/1¼ cup) glutinous rice flour

65 g (2¼ oz/⅓ cup) sugar

150 ml (5 fl oz) boiling water

1 tablespoon vegetable oil

ASSEMBLY

95 g (3¼ oz/⅔ cup) white and black sesame seeds

250 ml (8/½ fl oz/1 cup) water

vegetable oil, for frying

Fill a medium saucepan with water and add the adzuki beans. Bring to a boil and simmer for 1 to 1.5 hours, or until you can easily mash the beans between your fingers. Drain the beans and return them to the saucepan. Add the brown sugar and heat over medium–high heat, stirring constantly until the sugar has melted. Continue to cook for 10–15 minutes, stirring, until the mixture thickens to a paste that can form a small mound. Remove from the heat and chill in the fridge until firm. Once chilled, divide the red bean paste into 12 balls and keep them in the fridge until you're ready to assemble them.

In a heatproof bowl, combine the glutinous rice flour and sugar. Add the boiling water and mix until a shaggy dough forms, then knead with your hands.

Add the vegetable oil and continue to knead until the dough is smooth. Adjust the consistency by adding more flour or more water if needed; the dough should be soft but not sticky, similar to the texture of an earlobe. Cover the dough with plastic wrap and let it rest for 30 minutes.

Uncover the rested dough and divide it into 12 balls. Flatten a portion of dough between your palms and place a ball of red bean paste in the centre. Pull the sides of the dough over to enclose the filling and roll it between your palms to form a smooth ball. Place it on a baking tray lined with baking paper. Repeat with the remaining dough and filling.

Place the sesame seeds in a small bowl and the water in another. Submerge each ball in the water, then roll it in the sesame seeds. Roll the sesame seed-coated ball between your palms to secure the seeds, then repeat with the remaining balls.

Fill a heavy-bottomed pot halfway full with oil and heat to 150°C (300°F) over medium–high heat (you can also test the oil with a wooden chopstick – if bubbles form around it, the oil is ready). Add 4–5 sesame balls at a time and fry, stirring occasionally, for about 5 minutes.

Increase the heat to 180°C (350°F) and cook for an additional 2–3 minutes, or until the sesame balls are golden brown. Remove from the oil and drain on a wire rack or paper towels. Repeat with the remaining sesame balls. Eat when warm for the best texture, or keep in an airtight container at room temperature for up to 2 days.

MAKES 8
GUAVA-BUTTER PINEAPPLE BUN

GUAVA-BUTTER PINEAPPLE BUNS ARE A FRESH TWIST ON THE BELOVED HONG KONG PASTRY. THE SOFT, PILLOWY BUN IS TOPPED WITH THE SIGNATURE SWEET, CRUMBLY CRUST, BUT WITH A SURPRISE INSIDE – RICH GUAVA BUTTER. LIKE THE ORIGINAL, OUR TROPICAL TAKE IS DELICIOUS FOR BREAKFAST OR AN AFTERNOON SNACK ALIKE.

BREAD DOUGH

300 g (10½ oz/2 cups) strong (bread) flour
50 g (1¾ oz/¼ cup) sugar
pinch of salt
15 g (½ oz/2 tablespoons) milk powder
1 teaspoon instant yeast
200 ml (7 fl oz) full-cream (whole) milk, lukewarm
2 tablespoons unsalted butter, room temperature

GUAVA BUTTER

250 g (9 oz/1 cup) unsalted butter, softened
125 g (4½ oz/½ cup) guava marmalade or jam

TOPPING

20 g (¾ oz) milk powder
120 g (4½ oz/1 cup) plain (all-purpose) flour
½ teaspoon baking powder
¼ teaspoon bicarbonate of soda (baking soda)
100 g (3½ oz/½ cup) sugar
30 g (1 oz/2 tablespoons) unsalted butter
20 ml (¾ fl oz) full-cream (whole) milk
1 large egg yolk, plus 1 more egg yolk, beaten
½ teaspoon vanilla extract

Combine the strong flour, sugar, salt, milk powder and instant yeast in the bowl of a stand mixer fitted with a dough hook, or in a large mixing bowl if working by hand. Add the lukewarm milk and stir until a rough dough ball begins to form. Once combined, add the unsalted butter and continue kneading the dough for 10–15 minutes with the mixer, or about 20 minutes by hand, until the dough is smooth and elastic.

Shape the dough into a ball and place it in a large greased bowl. Cover the bowl with plastic wrap and allow the dough to proof in a warm spot for 1 to 1.5 hours, or until it has doubled in size.

While the dough is proofing, prepare the guava butter. In a bowl, combine the softened butter with the guava marmalade, mixing until smooth. Spread the guava butter onto a sheet of baking paper, rolling it into a cylinder. Use the flat surface of your bench to form the butter into a rectangular shape, then place it in the fridge to firm up.

Once the dough has doubled in size, remove it from the bowl and punch out any air bubbles. Divide the dough into 8 equal portions and roll each portion into a ball. Place the dough balls on a large baking tray lined with baking paper, then cover them with plastic wrap. Let the dough balls proof in a warm spot for another 30–60 minutes, or until they are nearly doubled in size.

Preheat the oven to 180°C (350°F). In the meantime, prepare the topping. In a bowl, whisk together the milk powder, plain flour, baking powder, bicarbonate of soda and sugar. Add the unsalted butter, milk, egg yolk and vanilla extract, mixing until a dough forms. If the dough seems too dry, add a bit more milk. Once mixed, divide the topping dough into 8 equal portions and roll each into a ball.

Using a rolling pin, flatten each topping ball into a circle and place it on top of a proofed bun. Brush the tops of the buns with beaten egg yolk to give them a golden finish when baked.

Bake the buns in the preheated oven for about 15 minutes, or until the tops are golden brown. Remove the buns from the oven and transfer them to a cooling rack, allowing them to cool for at least 10 minutes before serving.

To serve, slice each bun horizontally with a serrated knife, making sure not to cut all the way through. Place two thick slice of the chilled guava butter inside each bun and enjoy.

DESSERT

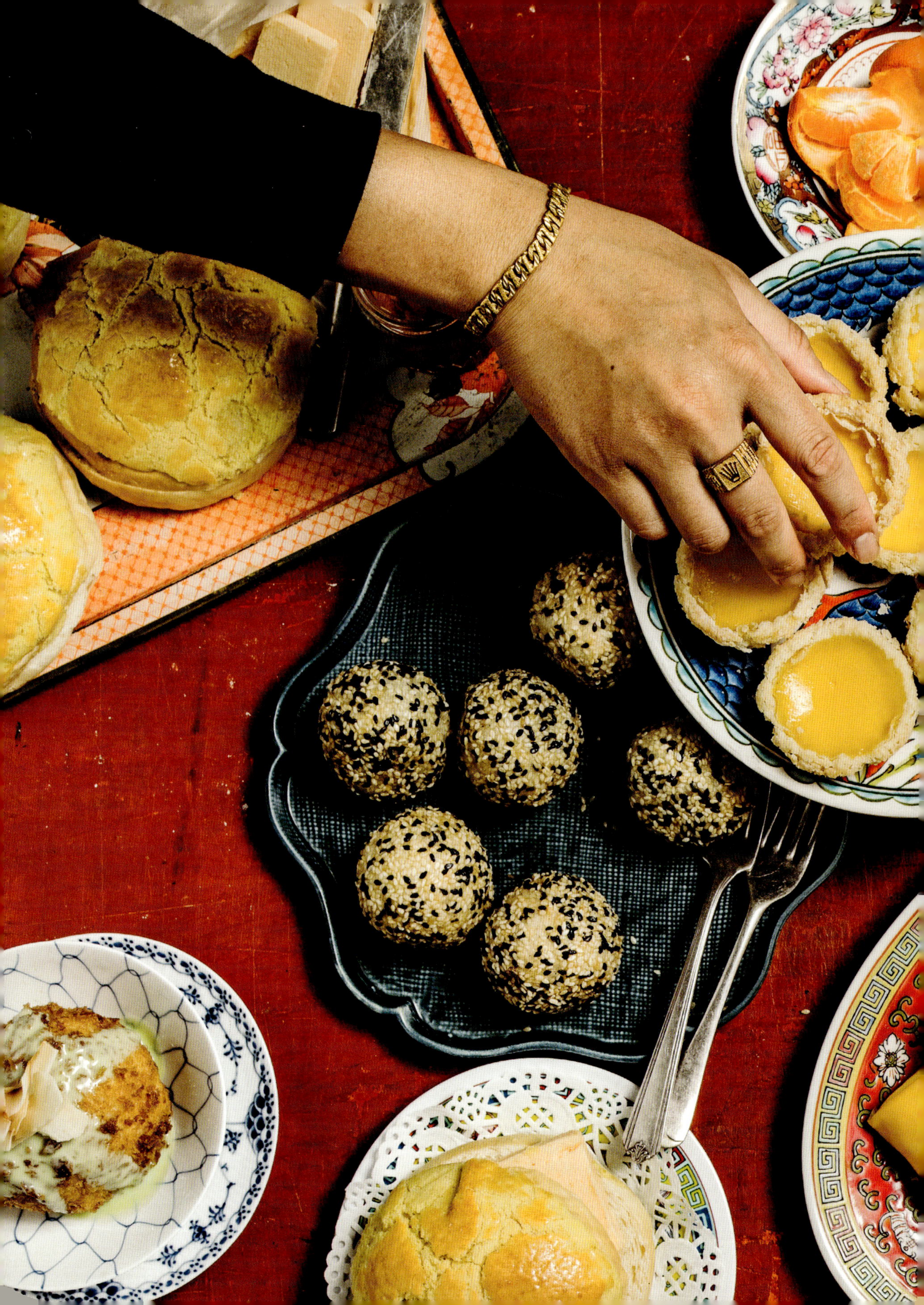

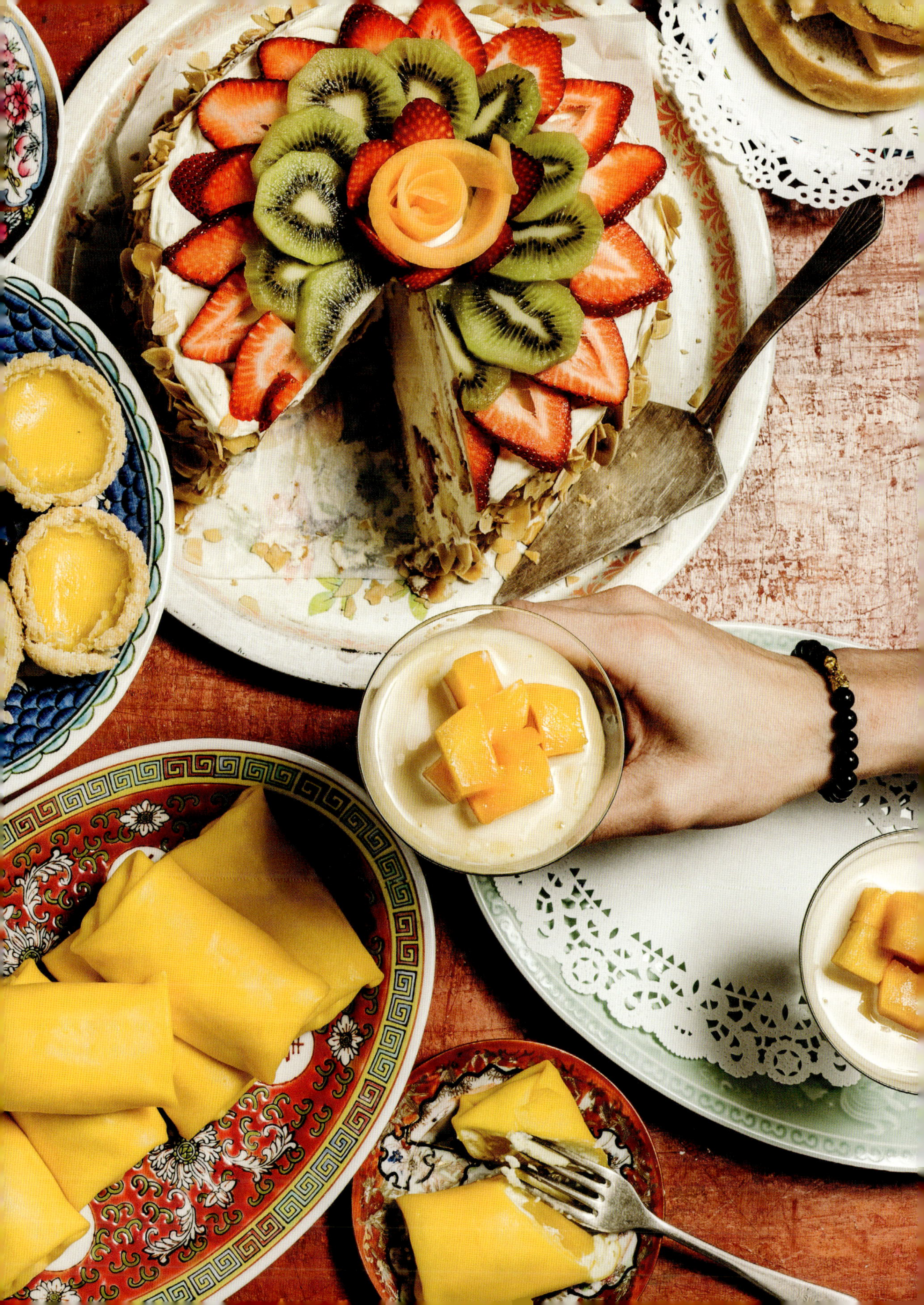

SERVES 2

HONG KONG FRENCH TOAST WITH SALTED EGG 'LAVA'

WITH ITS CRISPY, GOLDEN EXTERIOR AND SOFT, BUTTERY CENTRE, HONG KONG FRENCH TOAST IS A CAFE FAVOURITE. YOU'LL USUALLY FIND IT DEEP-FRIED TO PERFECTION AND STUFFED WITH PEANUT BUTTER — BUT MY VERSION TAKES IT UP ANOTHER NOTCH WITH A DECADENT SALTED EGG LAVA.

LAVA FILLING

2 salted duck egg yolks, steamed (see recipe introduction on page 114)

50 g (1¾ oz/¼ cup) unsalted butter, softened

25 g (1 oz/¼ cup) icing (confectioners') sugar

1 heaped tablespoon custard powder

15 g (½ oz/2 tablespoons) milk powder

2 tablespoons evaporated milk

FRENCH TOAST

8 slices of white bread

85 g (3 oz/⅓ cup) creamy peanut butter

2 large eggs

2 tablespoons full-cream (whole) milk

240 ml (8 fl oz/1 cup) vegetable oil

30 g (1 oz/2 tablespoons) butter, cut into 2 cubes

2 tablespoons sweetened condensed milk, to serve

Mash the steamed salted egg yolks with a fork until the egg yolk is smooth. Add the butter, icing sugar, custard powder, milk powder and evaporated milk and mix until smooth. Cover the mixture with plastic wrap and chill for 20 minutes. Once firm, remove it from the fridge and roll into 4 balls, flattening each slightly.

To assemble one toast stack, spread peanut butter on three slices of bread, leaving one slice plain. Place a salted egg yolk disc on two of the peanut butter-spread slices. Stack these two peanut butter and egg yolk slices, topping-side up, then add the slice with peanut butter only. Finally, place the plain slice of bread on top to complete your stack.

Repeat the same process with the remaining 4 bread slices and egg yolk discs to form a second stack. Using a serrated knife, carefully trim the crusts off each bread stack.

In a shallow bowl, whisk together the eggs and milk until well combined.

Pour the vegetable oil into a wok or large pot and bring to 180°C (350°F) over medium–high heat. Dip each bread stack into the egg mixture so it's well-coated all over and the egg has soaked into the bread.

Once the oil is ready, carefully add one coated bread stack to the hot oil and fry for about 3 minutes, or until the underside is golden brown. Flip the toast and fry for another 2 minutes, or until both sides are golden brown and crispy. Remove the toast from the oil and drain on a wire rack or paper towels. Repeat the process with the remaining bread stack.

Once the toast is drained, place it on a serving plate and top each piece with a cube of butter. Drizzle with sweetened condensed milk and serve immediately.

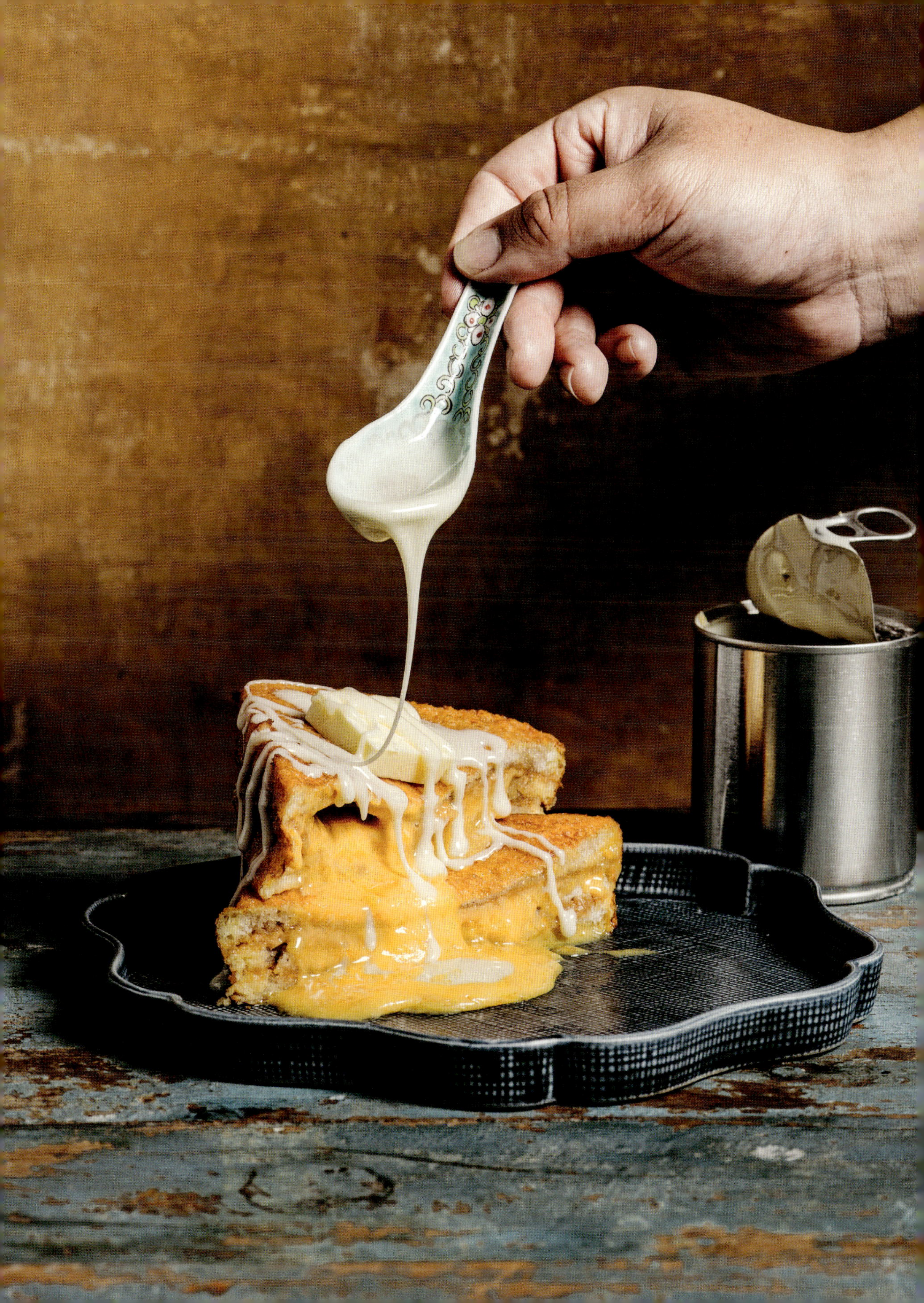

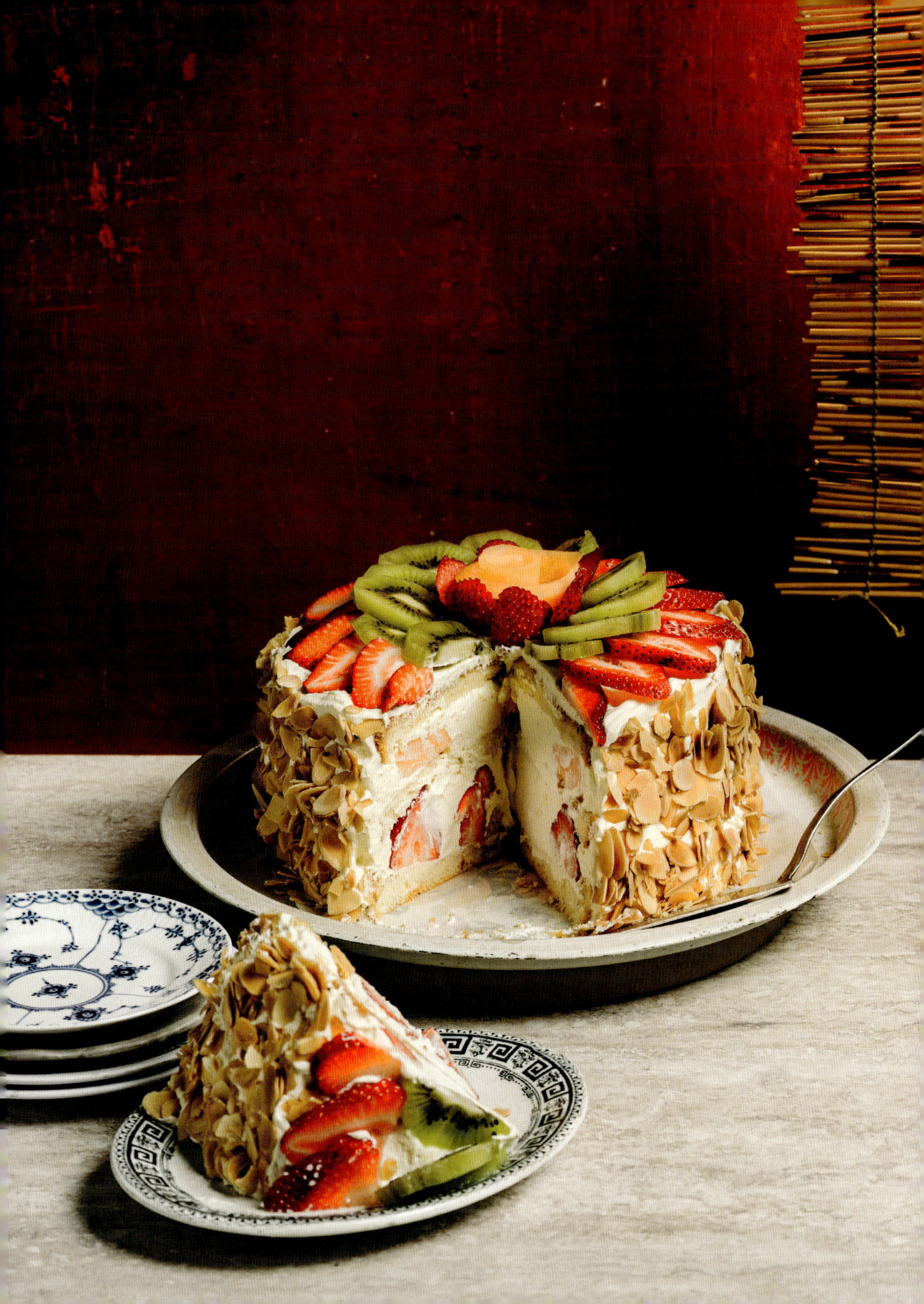

MAKES A 20 CM (8 IN) CAKE

ASIAN FRUIT CAKE

ASIAN-STYLE FRUIT CAKE IS A STAPLE AT ANY TRADITIONAL BAKERY, KNOWN FOR ITS LIGHT, AIRY SPONGE AND FRESH FRUIT LAYERS. TOPPED WITH WHIPPED CREAM AND COLOURFUL FRUIT, THIS CAKE IS A GO-TO FOR BIRTHDAYS AND CELEBRATIONS IN MANY ASIAN FAMILIES.

CAKE

4 large eggs, separated

60 ml (2 fl oz/¼ cup) full-cream (whole) milk

3 tablespoons vegetable oil

60 g (2 oz/½ cup) plain (all-purpose) flour

60 g (2 oz/½ cup) cornflour (cornstarch)

90 g (3 oz/½ cup) caster sugar

SIMPLE SYRUP

65 g (2¼ oz/⅓ cup) sugar

80 ml (2½ fl oz/⅓ cup) water

WHIPPED CREAM

600 ml (20½ fl oz/2½ cups) thickened (whipping) cream

100 g (3½ oz/½ cup) caster sugar

1 teaspoon vanilla extract

ASSEMBLY

90 g (3 oz/1 cup) flaked almonds, toasted

250 g (9 oz) strawberries

2 kiwi fruit

½ rockmelon (cantaloupe) or honeydew

Preheat the oven to 140°C (285°F) fan-forced (or 150°C/300°F convection) and line the bottom of a 20 cm (8 in) cake tin with baking paper. In a medium bowl, whisk together the egg yolks, milk and vegetable oil. Sift the plain flour and cornflour into the yolk mixture and stir until well combined.

In a separate bowl, use an electric whisk or a stand mixer to whip the egg whites and sugar until stiff peaks form. Gently fold one-third of the meringue into the egg yolk mixture until smooth. Then, carefully fold this lightened egg yolk mixture into the remaining meringue until just combined.

Pour the batter into the prepared cake tin, and place the tin into a water bath (a baking tray half-filled with boiling water) and bake for about 70 minutes. Once baked, remove the cake from the oven and let it cool completely. Onced cooled, run a knife around the edges of the cake tin and invert the pan to release the cake. Wrap the cooled cake in plastic wrap and refrigerate until you're ready to assemble.

To make the simple syrup, combine the sugar and water in a small bowl, then microwave for about 30 seconds or until the sugar melts. Set aside to cool.

For the whipped cream, use an electric whisk to beat the cream while gradually adding the sugar. Continue whisking until stiff peaks form, then mix in the vanilla extract.

To assemble the cake, slice it into three even layers. Place the first layer on a serving plate and brush it with the cooled simple syrup. Spread a layer of whipped cream over the top, followed by a layer of sliced fruit, then cover it with another layer of whipped cream. Repeat this process with the remaining cake layers.

Place the final layer of cake on top and apply a thin crumb coat of whipped cream to seal in any crumbs. Cover the entire cake with the remaining whipped cream, top with the remaining fruit, then press the sliced almonds around the edge to finish.

PANDAN CHIFFON CAKE

MAKES A 20 CM (8 IN) CAKE

PANDAN CHIFFON CAKE IS A LIGHT, AIRY DESSERT THAT'S SUPER POPULAR IN SOUTHEAST ASIA, ESPECIALLY IN PLACES LIKE MALAYSIA, SINGAPORE AND INDONESIA. WITH ITS BRIGHT GREEN COLOUR AND DELICATE PANDAN FLAVOUR, IF YOU LOVE A LIGHT TREAT, THIS ONE IS SOFTER THAN ANY CLOUD

240 ml (8 fl oz) coconut milk

10 pandan leaves, roughly chopped

6 large egg yolks

3 tablespoons caster (superfine) sugar, plus 90 g (3 oz/⅓ cup) extra

80 ml (2½ fl oz/⅓ cup) vegetable oil

150 g (5½ oz/1½ cups) cake flour

2 teaspoons baking powder

6 large egg whites

Preheat the oven to 170°C (340°F) and have on hand an ungreased 20 cm (8 in) chiffon cake tin with a removable base. It's important not to grease the tin, as the cake needs to cling to the sides to rise properly.

In a blender, combine the coconut milk and pandan leaves, blending until smooth. Strain the mixture through a fine-mesh sieve to extract 135 ml (4½ fl oz) of pandan milk, using the back of a spoon to press the pulp and extract as much liquid as possible. If needed, add a little extra coconut milk to reach the required amount.

In a medium bowl, whisk together the egg yolks, 3 tablespoons of sugar, vegetable oil and pandan milk until well combined. Sift in the cake flour and baking powder, then whisk until smooth. Set this mixture aside.

In the bowl of a stand mixer fitted with a whisk attachment, whisk the egg whites on medium–high speed for about 2 minutes, or until foamy. Gradually add the extra sugar, then continue whisking for 5 minutes, or until stiff, glossy peaks form.

Gently fold one third of the meringue into the egg yolk mixture until fully incorporated. Then, carefully fold this mixture into the remaining meringue, just until combined to avoid deflating the batter.

Slowly pour the batter into the cake tin and bake for about 45 minutes, or until a skewer inserted into the centre comes out clean. Once baked, remove the cake from the oven and invert the tin onto a wire rack, letting the cake cool inside completely for about 1 hour.

Once cooled, run a thin knife around the edges and base of the cake to release it from the tin. For optimal fluffiness, the cake is best enjoyed on the day it's baked. Store any leftovers in an airtight container at room temperature for up to 3 days.

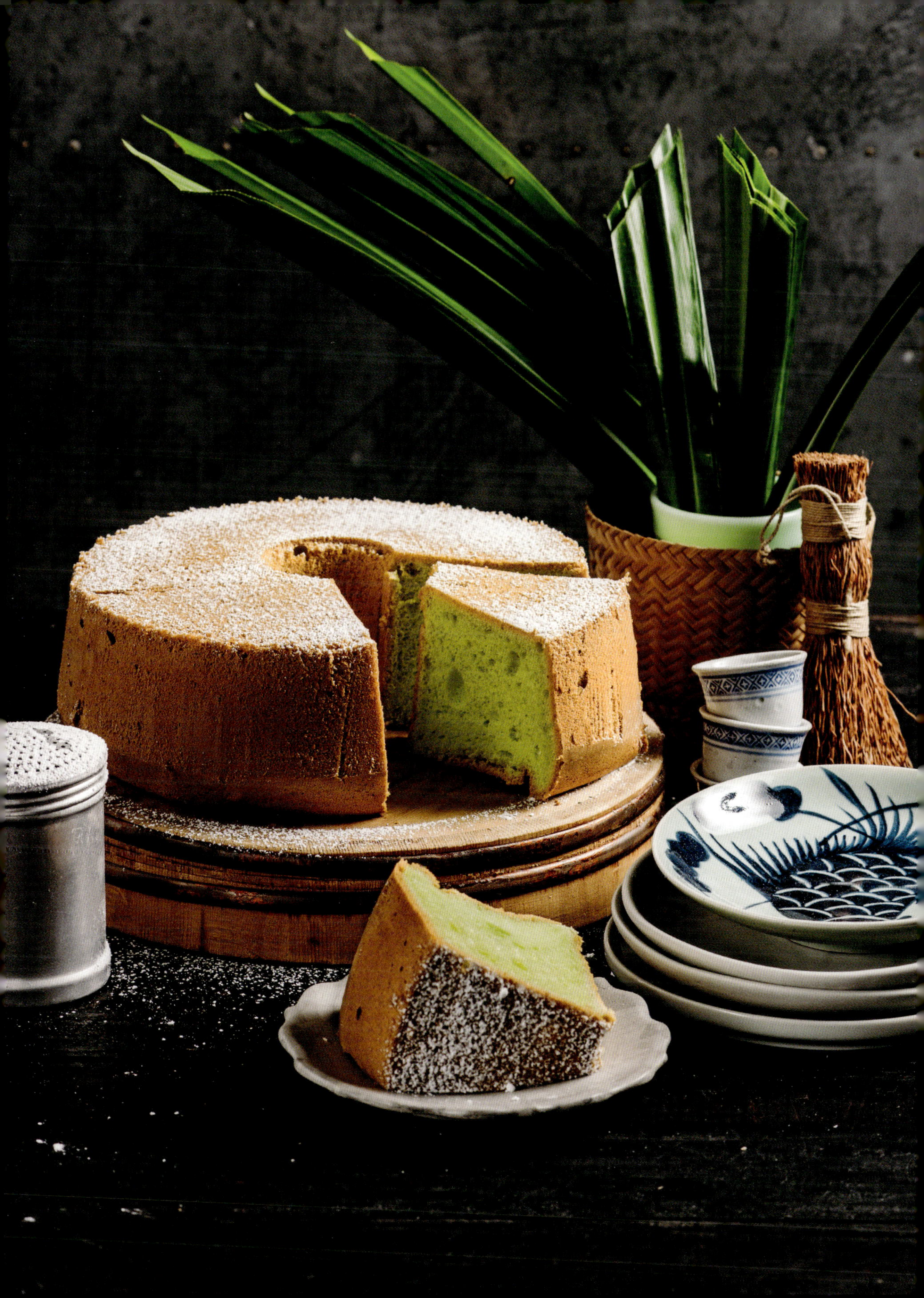

ABOUT THE AUTHOR

Vincent Yeow Lim (aka DimSimLim) is a chef, restaurant owner and content creator with a following of over 4 million and over 1 billion views across his social media platforms.

With more than twenty years of experience in the kitchen, he believes he can share with his audience the most authentic and well-kept secrets in the Asian restaurant industry, while showcasing wok cooking to the world in a new and entertaining style. He has made numerous appearances on Australian TV – as a special guest on *Masterchef Australia*, but also on *Snackmasters, The Cook Up, The Morning Show,* Channel 10, Channel 7 and SBS. In February 2004 he launched an umami seasoning 'YumYum' that sold 45,000 units nationally in less than 3 months. But his proudest achievement to date is opening his own 200-seat restaurant at the age of twenty-two after his father passed away and realising his true passion for wok cooking.

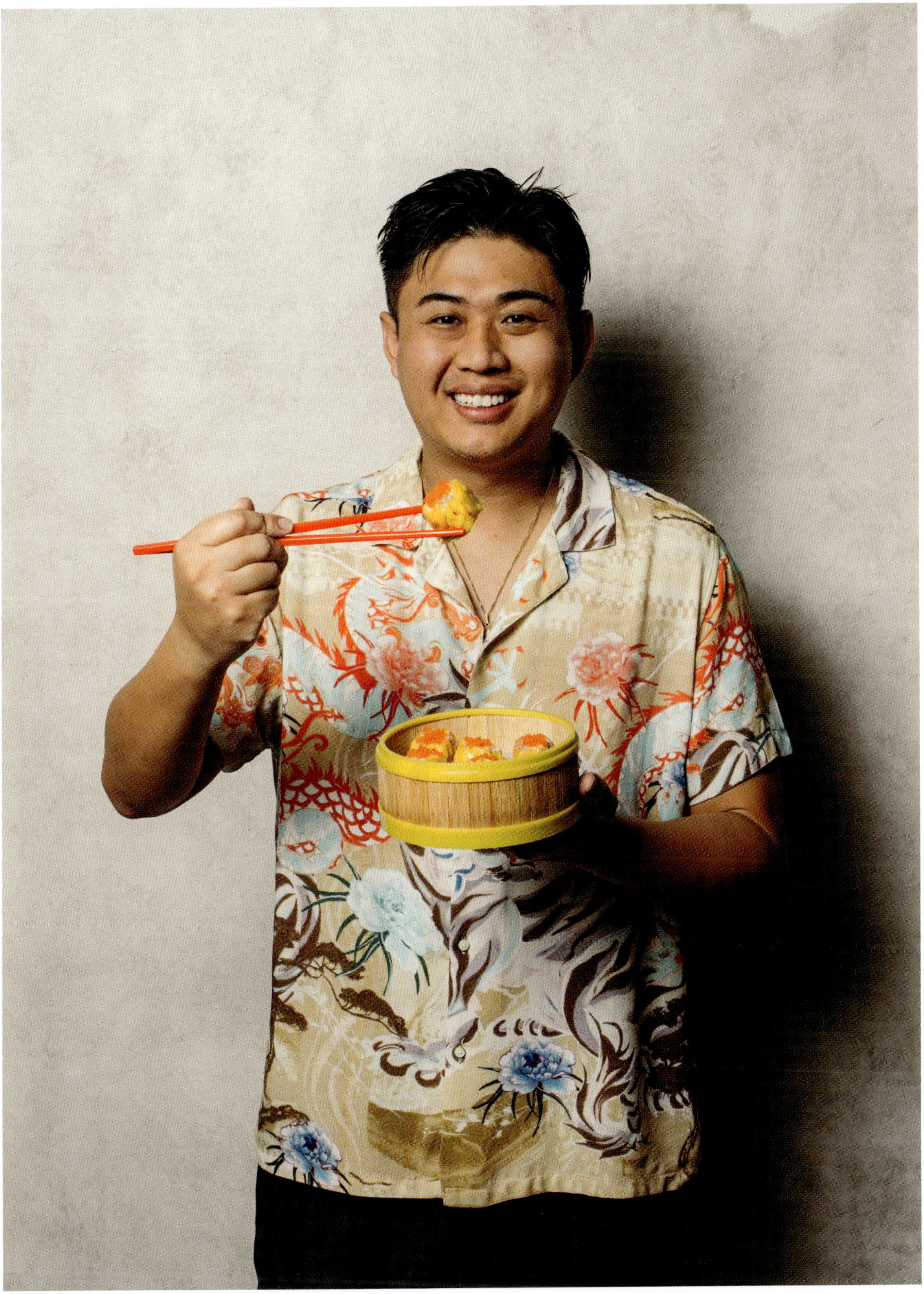

INDEX

A
abalone
  Truffled chicken and abalone xiao long bao 44
ABC soup 62
Air-fryer crispy pork belly 176
Asian fruit cake 231

B
Bak kut teh 65
beef
  Beef and black bean 168
  Beef and mushroom stir-fry 167
  Beef with oyster sauce 172
  Braised beef noodle soup 72
  Pepper steak 163
  Rainbow beef 164
  Szechuan beef 171
  Velveted beef 30
black bean
  Beef and black bean 168
  Black bean paste 169
bok choy
  Braised beef noodle soup 72
  Garlic bok choy 205
bread
  Guava-butter pineapple bun 24
  Hong Kong French toast with salted egg 'lava' 228
  Prawn toasts 37
Braised beef noodle soup 72

C
Candied walnuts 129
cake
  Asian fruit cake 231
  Pandan chiffon cake 232
cauliflower
  Kung pao cauliflower 210
Century egg and pork rib congee 98
Century egg and tofu 209

Char kway teow 80
Char siu bao 53
chicken
  ABC soup 62
  Chicken and sweet corn soup 66
  Chicken rice 146–7
  Chicken stock 32
  Chinese chicken curry 155
  Combination omelette 159
  Emergency Hainanese chicken 146–7
  gel 45
  General Tao chicken 152–3
  Honey chicken 138
  Kung pao chicken 134
  Lemon chicken 142
  Orange chicken 136
  Prison curry 156
  San choy bao 54
  Shandong chicken 145
  Sizzling garlic chicken 141
  Special fried rice 94
  Taiwanese fried chicken 151
  Truffled chicken and abalone xiao long bao 44
  Velveted chicken 30
chilli
  Chilli sauce 146
  Emergency Hainanese chicken 146–7
  Sambal kangkong 194
  Singapore chilli crab 116
  Typhoon shelter scallops 125
  Chinese chicken curry 155
  Chinese 'seaweed' (Fried gai lan) 202
  Combination omelette 159
crab
  Singapore chilli crab 116
curry
  Chinese chicken curry 155
  Curry wonton noodle 76
  Prison curry 156
Custard 221

D
dessert
  Asian fruit cake 231
  Guava-butter pineapple bun 224
  Hong Kong egg tart 221
  Hong Kong French toast with salted egg 'lava' 228
  Mango pancakes 214
  Mango pudding 218
  Pandan chiffon cake 232
  Pandan fried ice cream 217
  Sesame balls 222
Dim sims 58
Din tai fung fried rice 93
dumpling
  Dim sims 58
  Har gow 50
  Pork and prawn siu mai 43
  Truffled chicken and abalone xiao long bao 44
  wrappers 45, 51

E
Easy char siu pork 179
egg
  Century egg and pork rib congee 98
  Century egg and tofu 209
  Combination omelette 159
  Hong Kong egg tart 221
  Hong Kong French toast with salted egg 'lava' 228
  Salted egg sweet corn 206
  Salted egg yolk lobster 114
eggplant
  Sweet and sticky Chinese eggplant 198
Emergency Hainanese chicken 146–7
equipment 20–3

F
fish
  Steamed ginger-shallot coral trout 108
  Toro toro 107
five-spice
  Five-space salt and pepper 33
Flying lobster noodles 110–11

G
gai lan
  Chinese 'seaweed' (Fried gai lan) 202
  Oyster gai lan 197

236

garlic
  Garlic bok choy 205
  Garlic green beans 201
  General Tao chicken 152–3
ginger
  Ginger scallion oil 33
  Steamed ginger-shallot coral trout 108
Guava-butter pineapple bun 224
Guinness pork 184

H
Har gow 50
Hokkein mee 83
Honey chicken 138
Honey prawns 118
Honey walnut shrimp 129
Hong Kong egg tart 221
Hong Kong French toast with salted egg 'lava' 228
Hot and sour soup 68

I
ice cream, Pandan fried 217

K
Kon loh mee 79
Kung pao cauliflower 210
Kung pao chicken 134

L
lamb
  Mongolian lamb 175
lemon
  Lemon chicken 142
  Lemon sauce 143
lobster
  Flying lobster noodles 110–11
  Salted egg yolk lobster 114
Lo mai gai 97

M
mango
  Mango pancakes 214
  Mango pudding 218
Mongolian lamb 175
MSG 13–4

mushroom
  Beef and mushroom stir-fry 167

N
Nam yu pork ribs 187
noodle
  Braised beef noodle soup 72
  Char kway teow 80
  Curry wonton noodle 76
  Flying lobster noodles 110–11
  Hokkein mee 83
  Kon loh mee 79
  'Panda Express' chow mein 84
  Prawn cheung fun 49
  Sizzling yee mein 87
  Steamed scallops with vermicelli 104
  Wat dan hor 90
  see also vermicelli

O
oil
  Ginger scallion oil 33
orange
  Orange chicken 136
  Orange sauce 137
oyster
  Oyster gai lan 197
  XO butter steamed oysters 130

P
pancakes, Mango 214
'Panda Express' chow mein 84
pandan
  Pandan chiffon cake 232
  Pandan fried ice cream 217
  Pandan sauce 217
paste
  Black bean paste 169
  Red bean paste 222
  Rempah (Spice paste) 117
  Prawn paste 37
Pastry 221
Pepper steak 163
pipis
  XO pipis 103
prawn
  Char kway teow 80
  Combination omelette 159

Curry wonton noodle 76
Din tai fung fried rice 93
Har gow 50
Honey prawns 118
Honey walnut shrimp 129
Hokkein mee 83
Kon loh mee 79
paste 37
Pork and prawn siu mai 43
Pork and prawn wontons 40
Prawn cheung fun 49
Prawn toasts 37
Prawn wontons 39
Sizzling garlic prawns 121
Sizzling yee mein 87
Slippery shrimp 126
Velveted prawns 31
Wat dan hor 90
pork
ABC soup 62
  Air-fryer crispy pork belly 176
  Bak kut teh 65
  Century egg and pork rib congee 98
  Char kway teow 80
  Char siu bao 53
  Curry wonton noodle 76
  Dim sims 58
  Easy char siu pork 179
  Guinness pork 184
  Hokkein mee 83
  Hot and sour soup 68
  Kon loh mee 79
  Lo mai gai 97
  Nam yu pork ribs 187
  Pork and prawn siu mai 43
  Pork and prawn wontons 40
  Pork lard 32
  Pork rib soup 70
  Pork spring rolls 57
  Salt and pepper pork chops 188
  Sizzling yee mein 87
  Special fried rice 94
  Sweet and sour pork 180
  Sweet and sour ribs 183
  Wat dan hor 90
  Yum cha steamed pork ribs 191
Prison curry 156

R

Rainbow beef 164
Red bean paste 222
rice
  Century egg and pork rib congee 98
  Chicken rice 146–7
  Din tai fung fried rice 93
  Emergency Hainanese chicken 146–7
  Lo mai gai 97
  Special fried rice 94

S

Salt and pepper pork chops 188
Salt and pepper squid 122
Salted egg sweet corn 206
Salted egg yolk lobster 114
Sambal kangkong 194
San choy bao 54
sauce
  Chilli sauce 146
  Lemon sauce 143
  Orange sauce 137
  Pandan sauce 217
  sweet and sour sauce 31
sausage
  Char kway teow 80
  Lo mai gai 97
scallion
  Ginger scallion oil 33
  Steamed ginger-shallot coral trout 108
scallop
  Steamed scallops with vermicelli 104
  Typhoon shelter scallops 125
seafood
  Char kway teow 80
  Combination omelette 159
  Curry wonton noodle 76
  Flying lobster noodles 110–11
  Din tai fung fried rice 93
  Har gow 50
  Honey prawns 118
  Honey walnut shrimp 129
  Hokkein mee 83
  Kon loh mee 79
  Pork and prawn siu mai 43
  Pork and prawn wontons 40
  Prawn cheung fun 49
  Prawn paste 37
  Prawn toasts 37
  Prawn wontons 39
  Salt and pepper squid 122
  Salted egg yolk lobster 114
  Singapore chilli crab 116
  Sizzling garlic prawns 121
  Sizzling yee mein 87
  Slippery shrimp 126
  Typhoon shelter scallops 125
  Velveted prawns 31
  Wat dan hor 90
  XO butter steamed oysters 130
  XO pipis 103
  see also crab, lobster, prawn, scallop, squid
seasoning
  Five-space salt and pepper 33
sesame
  Sesame balls 222
Singapore chilli crab 116
Sizzling garlic chicken 141
Sizzling garlic prawns 121
Sizzling yee mein 87
Slippery shrimp 126
Shandong chicken 145
soup
  ABC soup 62
  Bak kut teh 65
  Braised beef noodle soup 72
  Chicken and sweet corn soup 66
  Curry wonton noodle 76
  Hot and sour soup 68
  Pork rib soup 70
  Soy dressing 146–7
  Special fried rice 94
spinach
  Sambal kangkong 194
spring rolls, Pork 57
squid
  Salt and pepper squid 122
  Steamed ginger-shallot coral trout 108
  Steamed scallops with vermicelli 104
  Sweet and sour pork 180
  Sweet and sour ribs 183
  sweet and sour sauce 31
  Sweet and sticky Chinese eggplant 198
sweet corn
  Chicken and sweet corn soup 66
  Salted egg sweet corn 206
stock
  Chicken stock 32
Szechuan beef 171

T

Taiwanese fried chicken 151
tofu
  Bak kut teh 65
  Century egg and tofu 209
  Hot and sour soup 68
  Nam yu pork ribs 187
Toro toro 107
Truffled chicken and abalone xiao long bao 44
Typhoon shelter scallops 125

U

umami 12–3

V

Velveted beef 30
Velveted chicken 30
Velveted prawns 31
vermicelli
  Steamed scallops with vermicelli 104

W

walnut
  Candied walnuts 129
  Honey walnut shrimp 129
Wat dan hor 90
wok 16, 18–19
  seasoning 19
  storing 19
  wok hei 18
wonton
  Curry wonton noodle 76
  Pork and prawn wontons 40
  Prawn wontons 39

X

XO butter steamed oysters 130
XO pipis 103

Y

Yum cha steamed pork ribs 191
YumYum 12, 15

Published in 2025 by Hardie Grant Books,
an imprint of Hardie Grant Publishing

Hardie Grant Books (Melbourne)
Wurundjeri Country
Level 11, 36 Wellington Street
Collingwood, Victoria 3066

Hardie Grant North America
2912 Telegraph Ave
Berkeley, California 94705

hardiegrant.com/books

Hardie Grant acknowledges the Traditional Owners of the Country on which we work, the Wurundjeri People of the Kulin Nation and the Gadigal People of the Eora Nation, and recognises their continuing connection to the land, waters and culture. We pay our respects to their Elders past and present.

All rights reserved. No part of this publication may be reproduced, stored in a retrieval system or transmitted in any form by any means, electronic, mechanical, photocopying, recording or otherwise, without the prior written permission of the publishers and copyright holders.

The moral rights of the author have been asserted.

Copyright text © Vincent Lim 2025
Copyright photography © Alana Dimou 2025
Copyright design © Hardie Grant Publishing 2025

This book uses US 240 ml (8 fl oz) cup measurements and 15 ml tablespoons (equivalent to 3 teaspoons).

Cooks outside the US should be scant with cup measurements as metric cups are 250 ml (8½ fl oz). Meanwhile, Australian cooks should be scant with their tablespoon measurements, as local tablespoons are 20 ml (equivalent to 4 teaspoons).

Oven temperatures in this book are for conventional ovens. If using a fan-forced oven, reduce the temperature by 20°C (35°F) or vice versa.

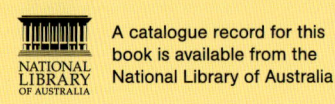

A catalogue record for this book is available from the National Library of Australia

The Wolf of Wok Street
ISBN 978 1 76145 171 3
ISBN 978 1 76145 172 0 (ebook)

10 9 8 7 6 5 4 3 2 1

Publisher: Simon Davis
Head of Editorial: Jasmin Chua
Project Editor: Ana Jacobsen
Editor: Ruby Goss
Creative Director: Kristin Thomas
Designer: George Saad
Photographer: Alana Dimou
Stylist: Lucy Tweed
Photo chef: Jimmy Callaway
Head of Production: Todd Rechner
Production Controller: Jessica Harvie

Colour reproduction by Splitting Image Colour Studio.

Printed in China by Leo Paper Products LTD.

MIX
Paper | Supporting responsible forestry
FSC® C020056

The paper this book is printed on is from FSC®-certified forests and other sources. FSC® promotes environmentally responsible, socially beneficial and economically viable management of the world's forests.